# Classical Thermodynamics
## of Non-Electrolyte Solutions

# Classical Thermodynamics
# of Non-Electrolyte Solutions

by

## H. C. VAN NESS

PROFESSOR OF CHEMICAL ENGINEERING
RENSSELAER POLYTECHNIC INSTITUTE
TROY, NEW YORK

## PERGAMON PRESS

OXFORD · LONDON · NEW YORK · PARIS

1964

PERGAMON PRESS LTD.
Headington Hill Hall, Oxford
4 & 5 Fitzroy Square, London W. 1

PERGAMON PRESS INC.
122 East 55th Street, New York 22, N.Y.

GAUTHIER-VILLARS ED.
55 Quai des Grands-Augustins, Paris 6ᵉ

PERGAMON PRESS G.m.b.H.
Kaiserstrasse 75, Frankfurt am Main


Distributed in the Western Hemisphere by
THE MACMILLAN COMPANY · NEW YORK
pursuant to a special arrangement with
**Pergamon Press Incorporated**

Library of Congress Catalog Card No. 63-17230

*Made in Great Britain*

# CONTENTS

# PREFACE

THE purpose of this monograph is to treat systematically and in depth that portion of classical thermodynamics which has to do with the properties of vapor and liquid solutions of non-electrolytes. This area has perhaps been too much neglected during the past several decades, with interest diverted to the developments of statistical thermodynamics, statistical mechanics, and molecular theory. However, such considerations are in no sense substitutes for classical thermodynamics, but are rather adjuncts through which one hopes to obtain added and perhaps more fundamental information.

The profound work of J. Willard Gibbs and the later contributions by G. N. Lewis and others put the classical thermodynamics of solutions on a firm base. Subsequent development has added to the structure, but it is even now by no means complete.

It should be remarked at the outset that this monograph is written from the viewpoint of an engineer. The ultimate aim of application to engineering problems has therefore had a vital influence on the content. To the engineer, thermodynamics has two faces. First is its application to the solution of practical problems from data at hand, and second is the calculation of the requisite data from experimental measurements. We shall be concerned here only with the latter. Many excellent texts are already available to point the way to the solution of engineering problems once the necessary data are available. But the general methods of developing such data from experimental measurements are not so well documented.

It is assumed that the reader is already well versed in the basic principles of classical thermodynamics. Nevertheless, an initial chapter on basic principles has been included for review purposes and as a summary. While disclaiming here any intention of writing a general textbook on advanced thermodynamics, I would not wish to deny the appropriateness of this material in advanced courses. This monograph has in fact been prepared from my notes for one term of a two-term course in thermodynamics for advanced students in chemical engineering.

This work is in no sense a record of the historical development of the thermodynamics of solutions, nor is it a compilation of pertinent material from the literature. It merely represents my own efforts to develop the known theory through concise derivation of the most general equations applicable to fluid systems. A knowledge of this material is usually assumed on the part of the reader by authors of works on statistical thermodynamics and molecular theory. Yet a convenient source from which to study it in depth is not available. It is with the hope of satisfying this need that this monograph is written.

Where experimental data are not available to allow the accurate calculation of thermodynamic properties by the equations developed here, the engineer must have recourse to the various theoretical, semi-theoretical, and empirical correlations of thermodynamic data available. Although the existence of such correlations has been indicated from place to place, no attempt has been made to describe them in detail and no effort has been made to present a complete catalogue of them. In this regard there is no substitute for a familiarity with current literature. The general equations themselves are independent of such correlations, and remain valid as improvements are made to existing correlations.

Most of the material presented in this monograph was developed for courses of lectures to advanced students of chemical engineering. Some of it was first presented during 1958–1959 in England at King's College of the University of Durham and at the Houldsworth School of Applied Science of Leeds University. The opportunity provided by a Fulbright Grant to give attention to this subject while lecturing abroad is much appreciated. In addition, the support provided by the National Science Foundation for research in this area under my supervision has provided a stimulus for much concerted effort, and is gratefully acknowledged.

The constructive criticism of Professor J. M. Prausnitz, who reviewed the original version of this work, provided invaluable aid in the revision of the manuscript. Professor R. V. Mrazek not only made many useful suggestions but also wrote the computer programs and did many of the calculations upon which the numerical examples of this monograph are based. Finally, I would express my indebtedness to those students who by question and comment have contributed in no small measure to the final form of this monograph.

# CHAPTER 1

# FUNDAMENTAL BASIS
# OF THERMODYNAMICS

CLASSICAL thermodynamics is a network of equations, developed through the formal logic of mathematics from a very few fundamental postulates and leading to a great variety of useful deductions. In the sense that mathematics is an exact system of logic, thermodynamics is an exact science. However, as with any deductive procedure, the derived conclusions are conditioned by the limitations imposed by the fundamental postulates and depend for validity upon the truth of these postulates within the imposed limitations. One might trace the historical development of the concepts necessary to the formulation of the fundamental postulates, but this does not seem appropriate to our purposes. Rather, we take advantage of the considerable benefits of hindsight, and present these concepts in such a way that they lead most directly to the basic postulates of classical thermodynamics.

**1.1. The Nature of a Function.** A variable $F$ is said to be a *function* of $x$ and $y$, i.e., $F = f(x, y)$, if for every pair of values $(x, y)$ there exists a value for $F$. An equation connecting $F$ with $x$ and $y$ may or may not be known. The functional relationship may equally well be given graphically, for the nature of a function $F = f(x, y)$ is obviously such that a definite value of the function $F$ is associated with each point on a $y - x$ plane.† The simplest means of representation is to show lines of constant $F$ on a $y - x$ plot, as illustrated in Fig. 1-1. For a given point $(x_1, y_1)$ there is a particular value of $F$, namely $F_1$, and for another point $(x_2, y_2)$ there is also a particular value of $F$, namely $F_2$. For a change in the variables $x$ and $y$ from $(x_1, y_1)$ to $(x_2, y_2)$, no matter how accomplished, there is a particular change in $F$, given by $\Delta F = F_2 - F_1$. This constancy of $\Delta F$ for a pair of points 1 and 2, regardless of the path connecting these points on a $y - x$ plane, is a distinguishing characteristic which marks $F$ as a function of $x$ and $y$ even though an equation relating $F$ to $x$ and $y$ is not known.

† $F$ may, of course, be a function of more than two independent variables. Although this renders graphical representation more difficult, the general nature of a function is the same regardless of the number of variables it depends on.

1

A simple example is evident if we regard Fig. 1-1 as a contour map. $F$ then represents elevation, and $x$ and $y$ are the position coordinates. Clearly, if one travels from position 1 to position 2, the net change in elevation $\Delta F$ is independent of the path taken. This immediately marks the elevation $F$ as a function of the position coordinates $x$ and $y$.

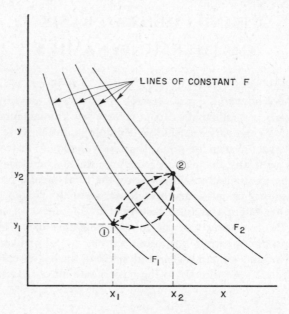

Fig. 1-1. $F$ represented as a function of $x$ and $y$.

We recognize the functional dependence of elevation on the position coordinates through experience. If we were interested in mathematics only, we could write a limitless number of equations expressing $F$ as various functions of $x$ and $y$, or alternatively we could draw an indefinite number of "contour maps" giving similar arbitrary relationships, and we might study their properties. But the problem of science and technology is to detect characteristics of our material world which are expressible as functions of measurable variables and to express these functional relationships in graphical, tabular, or equation form. The characteristic of elevation above a datum (sea level) is easily recognized, and has long been expressed as a function of position coordinates by means of contour maps.

**1.2. Properties of Simple Systems.** In the field of classical thermodynamics we are concerned with the macroscopic properties of matter and their relation to the measurable conditions of temperature, pressure, and composition. Experimentation with various materials leads us to believe that there is a large class of homogeneous fluids (both liquid and gas) whose properties depend solely on these variables. We could observe, for example, that the density of pure liquid acetone is constant for a given temperature and pressure, regardless of the past history of the experimental sample. Similarly, we would find the specific volume of an equimolal mixture of gaseous oxygen and nitrogen to be fixed for a given temperature and pressure. Were we to change the temperature or pressure, or both, of these materials, we would find a fixed change in their properties, regardless of how the change was accomplished. These observations are quite general for single-phase fluids.

However, we might well note that in setting up our experiments we may well have eliminated the effects of certain extraneous influences. In all probability we would not carry out our experiments in the presence of a strong magnetic or electrostatic field. Our samples of material would be small enough so that the effect of the earth's gravitational field would not be detected in a variation of properties from top to bottom of the sample. The sample would be stationary, not subject to shear stresses, and samples would not be subdivided into small droplets or bubbles that would make surface-tension effects important. We would undoubtedly deal, quite naturally, with what have been called *simple systems*, and our equations would then be written to apply to fluids as they exist in such simple systems. In practice, these equations are often applied in cases where extraneous influences are not entirely absent but where their effect is considered to be negligible.

This discussion has been preliminary to the statement of our first fundamental postulate, which is that *the macroscopic properties† of homogeneous fluids can be expressed as functions of temperature, pressure, and composition only*. One must keep in mind that this is a postulate which contributes to the basis upon which our network of equations is founded, and is not an absolute law of nature. Thus the ensuing equations are restricted to applications where this postulate is essentially valid, i.e., to simple systems.

**1.3. The Special Functions of Thermodynamics.** We have taken temperature, pressure, and composition as basic thermodynamic variables for homogeneous fluids. These are not regarded primarily as properties of fluids but as *conditions* imposed on them, or manifested by them by virtue of their direct measurability. What *are* the properties that we recognize

† The simple term *property* as applied to a homogeneous material (here, a fluid) should not be ambiguous. It must obviously be independent of the amount of material; otherwise it would not be a property of the *material*. Specific or molal volume is such a property. Were we to speak of properties of a system, we would find it necessary to take into account the extent of the system. The total volume of a system is a property of the system, not of the material which constitutes it. Thus the common terms, intensive and extensive property, refer respectively to a material and to a system. Properties of systems generally depend not only on temperature, pressure, and compositions of the phases, but also on the extent of the phases.

as being functions of temperature, pressure, and composition? Specific or molal volume is certainly one; we know this from experience. For any homogeneous fluid of constant composition and existing as a simple system we can write:

$$V = v(T, P).$$

We know this functional relationship to exist, but its expression for a given material by means of a table, a graph, or an equation must be based on careful experimental measurements.

What other functions of constant-composition, homogeneous fluids can be expressed in terms of temperature and pressure? We could define *arbitrarily* any number of functions of $T$ and $P$. For example, we might *define* a function $X$ as

$$X = \frac{3P^2}{VT}.$$

We could give this function a name; call it *Xtropy*. We could show lines of constant Xtropy on a $T - P$ plane for the given material. We could compute the values of $\Delta X$ for the material which would result from given changes in $T$ and $P$. The function $X$ would satisfy all the mathematical requirements of a property of the material. But from the scientific, as opposed to the purely mathematical point of view, is $X$ to be regarded as a *useful* property of the material? The scientist or engineer requires an affirmative answer to one or both of the following questions:

(a) Is $X$ directly measurable, like specific volume, and thus capable of adding to our experimental knowledge of the material?

(b) Is $X$ an *essential* function in that some generalization can be made concerning it which allows the prediction of the behavior of material systems? For example, are there common processes which occur at constant Xtropy? Since $X$ was arbitrarily defined, the answer to both questions is probably negative, and we are unlikely to consider the function $X$ a useful property of the material.

The only way to avoid completely arbitrary definitions of properties is to base their recognition on observations of the behavior of real materials. The most fundamental concept to arise from such observations is that of *energy*. The development of this concept took many centuries, and eventually led to one of the great generalizations of science: The law of conservation of energy. All this is discussed in detail in other books, and will not be further elaborated here. We merely list as postulates those principles pertinent to this work:

(a) There exists a form of energy, known as *internal energy*, $U$, which for homogeneous fluids existing as simple systems is a property of the material and is a function of temperature, pressure, and composition.

(b) The *total* energy of a system *and* its surroundings is conserved; energy may be transferred from a system to its surroundings and vice versa, it may be transformed from one form to another, but the total quantity remains constant.

The first of these postulates is requisite to the second, which through its universal acceptance has come to be known as the first law of thermodynamics. Its domain of validity has been circumscribed by the discovery of nuclear reactions in which mass is converted into energy and vice versa. Nevertheless, it remains a law valid for all other processes.

*Heat* is a word used to describe the process by which energy is transferred ("flows") under the influence of a temperature difference between a system and its surroundings. Since internal energy is the only form of energy of which temperature is a manifestation, the notion of heat is inherently tied to the concept of internal energy. However, a quantity of heat, $Q$, represents merely an amount of energy crossing the boundary of a system, and thus cannot be a property of the system.

*Work* is a word used to describe the process by which energy is transferred between a system and its surroundings as the result of the displacement of an external force. A quantity of work, $W$, again represents an amount of energy crossing the boundary of a system, and is not a property of the system.

As applied to systems of constant mass (closed systems) for which the only form of energy to experience change is its internal energy, the first law takes the familiar form:

$$\Delta U = Q - W.$$

The usual sign conventions with regard to $Q$ and $W$ have been adopted: The numerical value of $Q$ is taken as positive when heat is added to the system, while the numerical value of $W$ is taken as negative when work is done on the system.

This equation cannot be regarded as giving an explicit definition of internal energy. In fact, no such definition is known. However, the postulated existence of internal energy as a property can be tested through the use of this equation as applied to experiments with homogeneous fluids.

Consider, then, the performance of a series of experiments with a constant-composition homogeneous fluid in a piston-and-cylinder assembly. Temperature and pressure are taken as the independent variables of the system. Changes are brought about in the system by alteration of its temperature and pressure. This is accomplished by the addition or extraction of heat and by displacement of the piston within the cylinder. In all experiments the temperature and pressure are changed from $T_1$ and $P_1$ to $T_2$ and $P_2$, so that the properties of the system are altered by a constant amount. However, the *path* of the change, i.e., the relation between $T$ and $P$ during the process, is varied arbitrarily from run to run.

It is implicit in these discussions that there *be* a single value of $P$ and a single value of $T$ for the entire system at each stage of every process. The moment we write $P$ and $T$ for the system, we imply uniformity of temperature and pressure throughout the system. The only way we can ensure this uniformity during the course of our experiments is to carry them out slowly so as to avoid the generation of pressure waves in our fluids and so as to allow time for the thermal diffusivity of the system to smooth out even minute temperature variations. A system *within which* there are no non-uniformities which act as driving forces for change is said to be in a state of internal equilibrium. Processes that proceed so that displacements from internal equilibrium are always infinitesimal are said to be internally reversible. To carry out such processes in practice, we find it necessary also to keep the system very nearly in equilibrium with its surroundings. Processes that proceed so that displacements from both external and internal equilibrium are infinitesimal are called completely reversible, or more simply, reversible. The term arises from the fact that such processes can be reversed by a differential change in external conditions.

The experiments we are discussing are therefore conducted essentially reversibly. For each experiment we keep a careful account of the volume of the system, $V$, of the amount of heat, $Q_{rev}$, added or extracted, and of the work, $W_{rev}$, done on or by the system up to each intermediate set of conditions, $T$ and $P$. We emphasize the restriction to processes that are reversible by writing $Q_{rev}$ and $W_{rev}$.

We then examine the data, trying various combinations of the measured values and performing various numerical operations, to see what order, if any, can be brought out of the apparently disconnected sets of numbers.

For a given amount of material of given composition changed along various paths from a particular initial condition $(T_1, P_1)$ to a particular final condition $(T_2, P_2)$, we would first note, as would be expected, that $\Delta V = V_2 - V_1$ is constant regardless of path. This serves to confirm our earlier observation that the volume of a given amount of a homogeneous fluid (or its specific or molal volume) is a function of temperature, pressure, and composition.

Our next observation would probably be that for the same set of experiments the difference $Q_{rev} - W_{rev}$ is constant for the over-all change regardless of path. This result is expected provided our postulates regarding the existence of internal energy as a property and the conservation of energy are valid. This observation provides at least partial confirmation of these postulates, for the difference, $Q_{rev} - W_{rev}$, is seen to be the *measure* of a property change which has already been designated $\Delta U$. The restriction of reversibility here comes about from the nature of the experiments being considered, and not as a consequence of any limitation imposed by the basic postulates. The result obtained that $\Delta U = Q_{rev} - W_{rev}$ is merely a special case of the more general equation for closed systems,

$\Delta U = Q - W$, which applies for any two equilibrium states whether the process connecting them is reversible or not.

A further examination of the experimental data is then made to determine whether the existence of any additional properties is indicated. Certainly none is obvious, but if we evaluate the integral $\int_1^2 d\,W_{rev}/P$ for each run, we find it to be constant and equal to $\Delta V$. Thus

$$\Delta V = \int_1^2 \frac{d\,W_{rev}}{P}.$$

This is actually a well-known equation, far more easily arrived at through the definition of work. As a result of this definition it is immediately deduced that for a reversible expansion or compression of a fluid

$$d\,W_{rev} = P\,d\,V.$$

Hence

$$d\,V = \frac{d\,W_{rev}}{P}$$

or

$$\Delta V = \int_1^2 \frac{d\,W_{rev}}{P}.$$

The point here is that we *could* establish the existence of the property, $V$, as a result of integrations of our experimental data as indicated. Once it is shown that a single value of the integral results, regardless of the path, for given initial and final states, it becomes clear that the integral is the measure of a property change. In this case we immediately recognize the property as already known through much more direct observations.

A similar integral is $\int_1^2 d\,Q_{rev}/T$. If we evaluate this integral for each run of our set of experiments, we again find a single value for all paths. Again we have evidence of the existence of a property. However, in this instance it is not recognized as being known. Nevertheless, once the existence of a property is indicated, it is natural to give it a symbol and a name. Thus we write

$$\Delta S = \int_1^2 \frac{d\,Q_{rev}}{T},$$

where $S$ is called the *entropy*.

This result leads to an additional basic postulate: There exists a property of materials called *entropy*, $S$, which for homogeneous fluids existing as simple systems is a function of temperature, pressure, and composition. The integral given for $\Delta S$ provides a means for the calculation of changes in this property.

Just as the equation $\Delta U = Q - W$ does not explicitly define the property internal energy, so the equations $\Delta V = \int_1^2 d W_{rev}/P$ and $\Delta S = \int_1^2 d Q_{rev}/T$ cannot be considered to give explicit definitions of volume and entropy. But implicit in these three equations is the existence of three properties. This is obvious in the case of volume, for which an explicit definition in terms of directly measurable distances is known. With regard to internal energy and entropy, the situation is quite different. Classical thermodynamics furnishes no explicit definitions of these properties. Further insight can be gained only through study of statistical mechanics and molecular theory.

We have dealt so far with simple systems made up of a given amount of a homogeneous fluid. The reason for this is that the state of such systems is fixed by establishing the conditions of temperature, pressure, and composition. For *heterogeneous* simple systems made up of several phases, each in itself a simple system but existing in mutual equilibrium with the others, the state of the system depends on its temperature and pressure, on the composition of each of the phases, and on the relative amounts of the phases. It is clear that the total property of such a system is the sum of its parts. Thus one can ascribe a complete set of total properties to any equilibrium state of the system, and for a change in a closed system between two equilibrium states a unique set of property changes must result regardless of the path of the process connecting the two states. Experiments carried out on such systems yield exactly the same results as described for homogeneous fluids. It is simply more difficult to identify unique states of the system. The point of this is to generalize the equations presented for homogeneous fluids to apply to heterogeneous systems.

Thus for any closed system subject to the limitations already described, we may write the fundamental equations:

$$\Delta U = Q - W$$

and as a special case,

$$\Delta U = Q_{rev} - W_{rev}.$$

In differential form, this last equation is written:

$$d U = d Q_{rev} - d W_{rev}. \tag{1-1}$$

For reversible processes where the only force is that of fluid pressure

$$d W_{rev} = P d V. \tag{1-2}$$

For the calculation of entropy changes we have shown that

$$\Delta S = \int_1^2 \frac{d Q_{rev}}{T}.$$

It follows immediately from this that

$$dS = \frac{dQ_{rev}}{T}$$

or that

$$dQ_{rev} = T\,dS. \tag{1-3}$$

The methods of classical thermodynamics for the calculation of property values are based ultimately on Eqs. (1-1) through (1-3). This is not to suggest that direct use is commonly made of these equations for this purpose. Accurate measurements of heat and work effects in experiments such as those described are in fact very difficult. The actual methods used will be described in Chapter 3.

**1.4. The First and Second Laws of Thermodynamics.** The volume is an important thermodynamic property because it is directly measurable and can be used to provide experimental information about a system. Internal energy and entropy, on the other hand, can be determined only by indirect means. Nevertheless, these properties are essential to the science of thermodynamics, for without recognition of their existence the two great generalizations on which this science is based would be impossible.

The law of conservation of energy or the first law of thermodynamics could not be formulated without a prior postulate affirming the existence of internal energy as a property of materials. And internal energy is regarded as a property precisely for the reason that it allows this generalization to be made.

Once the existence of the entropy is postulated, it becomes necessary to determine whether any broad generalization based on this property is possible. Thus one calculates the entropy changes associated with various processes and examines the results to see whether some pattern emerges. The particular processes considered are not important, for one finds in every case that for reversible processes the *total* entropy change in system *and* surroundings resulting from the process is zero and for irreversible processes it is positive. Thus one is led to postulate that this is in general true, and we have for our final postulate a statement that has come to be known as the second law of thermodynamics: All processes proceed in such a direction that the *total* entropy change caused by the process is positive; the limiting value of zero is approached for processes which approach reversibility. Mathematically this is expressed as

$$\Delta S_{total} \geq 0.$$

It is one of the major triumphs of nineteenth-century science to have developed a principle, unsurpassed in conciseness of statement, that describes at once the directions of all processes in this vastly complex world.

The basic postulates upon which we build the science of thermodynamics are here recapitulated for convenience.

1. The macroscopic properties of homogeneous fluids existing as simple systems are functions of temperature, pressure and composition.
2. One such property is a form of energy known as internal energy.
3. Energy is conserved.
4. There exists a property called entropy. Changes in this property are calculable by the equation, $dS = dQ_{rev}/T$.
5. The total entropy change resulting from any real process is positive and approaches zero as the process approaches reversibility.

These postulates form the foundation for the development of a vast network of equations. All that is needed in addition is definition and deduction. The deductive process is purely mathematical. This deductive process and the postulates upon which it is based are ultimately subject to two tests. The network of equations which results must be internally consistent, and the consequences predicted must be in reality observed without exception. If these tests are met, then the system of logic employed and the postulates upon which it was based must be considered valid. Such tests have been applied for more than a century with complete success, so that now these postulates are regarded as laws of nature. As with all such laws, the proof of their validity lies in the absence of disproof, in the absence of contrary experience.

# CHAPTER 2

# THERMODYNAMIC PROPERTIES
# OF FLUIDS

**2.1. The Principal Thermodynamic Functions.** It was shown in the preceding chapter that for closed systems made up of phases which are themselves simple systems the following equations apply for an infinitesimal change of state of the system resulting from a reversible process in which the only force is fluid pressure.

$$\mathrm{d}U = \mathrm{d}Q_{\mathrm{rev}} - \mathrm{d}W_{\mathrm{rev}}, \tag{1-1}$$

$$\mathrm{d}W_{\mathrm{rev}} = P\,\mathrm{d}V, \tag{1-2}$$

$$\mathrm{d}Q_{\mathrm{rev}} = T\,\mathrm{d}S. \tag{1-3}$$

Hence,

$$\mathrm{d}U = T\,\mathrm{d}S - P\,\mathrm{d}V. \tag{2-1}$$

This is the basic differential equation relating the three thermodynamic properties considered so far. Since this equation relates properties only, it is not limited by the restrictions placed on the *process* considered in its derivation. However, the restrictions placed on the nature of the system still apply. Thus Eq. (2-1) is valid for *all* processes that result in a change of a *given mass of material* from one *equilibrium state* to another. Change of composition as a result of chemical reaction or mass transfer between phases is by no means excluded, provided equilibrium with respect to these processes is specified for the end states.

As a matter of convenience we now define several additional thermodynamic properties which are composites of the properties already discussed:

Enthalpy: $\qquad H = U + PV$

Helmholtz Function: $\quad A = U - TS$

Gibbs Function: $\qquad G = H - TS.$

For infinitesimal changes between equilibrium states of a given mass of material, simple differentiation gives:

$$\mathrm{d}H = \mathrm{d}U + \mathrm{d}(PV)$$

$$\mathrm{d}A = \mathrm{d}U - \mathrm{d}(TS)$$

$$\mathrm{d}G = \mathrm{d}H - \mathrm{d}(TS).$$

Combination of these equations with Eq. (2-1) yields:

$$dH = \quad T\,dS + V\,dP, \tag{2-2}$$

$$dA = -P\,dV - S\,dT, \tag{2-3}$$

$$dG = \quad V\,dP - S\,dT. \tag{2-4}$$

The same comments apply to these equations as to Eq. (2-1). Equations (2-1) through (2-4) are the basic differential equations upon which rests the entire network of equations which interrelate the thermodynamic properties of fluid systems of constant mass at equilibrium.

These equations may be written for systems of any size, and we might take the symbols, $V, U, S, H, A$, and $G$ to represent properties for the entire system regardless of size. However, for our purposes it is far more convenient to deal with symbols that represent properties on the basis of a unit amount of material, either a unit mass or a mole. Henceforth, the symbols, $V, U, S, H, A$, and $G$, will be understood to represent the properties of a system on the basis of a unit of mass, usually a mole. In the case of heterogeneous systems, the properties of a *representative* sample of unit mass, weighted in proportion to the masses of the phases, will be meant. Where it is necessary to deal with a total property of a system, we will simply multiply the unit property by the mass or total number of moles of the system. Thus $nU$ represents the total internal energy of $n$ moles of material, and $mU$ represents the internal energy of a system of mass $m$.

As a result of Eqs. (2-1) through (2-4) it is seen that the following functional relationships are always valid for closed systems in equilibrium states:

$$U = u(S, V),$$
$$H = h(S, P),$$
$$A = a(V, T),$$
$$G = g(P, T).$$

The fact that these functional relationships are valid in general does not exclude the existence of other functional relationships for particular systems. Indeed, one of our basic postulates affirms that for *homogeneous* fluids of constant composition all the thermodynamic properties are functions of temperature and pressure. But this is not true for heterogeneous or reacting systems. The general functional relationships, however, are valid for such systems. For example, a system made up of a pure liquid in equilibrium with its vapor at a given temperature exists at a particular pressure, and the internal energy of the system depends not only on these conditions but also upon the relative amounts of vapor and liquid present. Temperature and pressure in no way reflect this. However, entropy and volume do, and the relationship $U = u(S, V)$ is entirely valid. On the other hand the Gibbs function is in general a function of temperature and pressure, $G = g(T, P)$;

thus it is fixed for a given $T$ and $P$ regardless of the relative amounts of the phases.

In view of the indicated general functional relationships, we can immediately write:

$$dU = (\partial U/\partial S)_V \, dS + (\partial U/\partial V)_S \, dV, \qquad (2\text{-}5)$$

$$dH = (\partial H/\partial S)_P \, dS + (\partial H/\partial P)_S \, dP, \qquad (2\text{-}6)$$

$$dA = (\partial A/\partial V)_T \, dV + (\partial A/\partial T)_V \, dT, \qquad (2\text{-}7)$$

$$dG = (\partial G/\partial P)_T \, dP + (\partial G/\partial T)_P \, dT. \qquad (2\text{-}8)$$

Comparison of Eqs. (2-5) through (2-8) respectively with Eqs. (2-1) through (2-4) shows the following relations to be valid:

$(\partial U/\partial S)_V = T,$ $\qquad (2\text{-}9)$ $\qquad\qquad (\partial U/\partial V)_S = -P,$ $\qquad (2\text{-}10)$

$(\partial H/\partial S)_P = T,$ $\qquad (2\text{-}11)$ $\qquad\qquad (\partial H/\partial P)_S = V,$ $\qquad (2\text{-}12)$

$(\partial A/\partial V)_T = -P,$ $\qquad (2\text{-}13)$ $\qquad\qquad (\partial A/\partial T)_V = -S,$ $\qquad (2\text{-}14)$

$(\partial G/\partial P)_T = V.$ $\qquad (2\text{-}15)$ $\qquad\qquad (\partial G/\partial T)_P = -S.$ $\qquad (2\text{-}16)$

Another useful set of equations may be obtained by applying the criteria for the existence of an exact differential. If $F = f(x, y, z)$, then the exact or total differential of this function is:

$$dF = \left(\frac{\partial F}{\partial x}\right)_{y,z} dx + \left(\frac{\partial F}{\partial y}\right)_{x,z} dy + \left(\frac{\partial F}{\partial z}\right)_{x,y} dz$$

or

$$dF = L \, dx + M \, dy + N \, dz,$$

where

$$L = (\partial F/\partial x)_{y,z}, \quad M = (\partial F/\partial y)_{x,z}, \quad \text{and} \quad N = (\partial F/\partial z)_{x,y}.$$

Then

$$\left(\frac{\partial L}{\partial y}\right)_{x,z} = \frac{\partial^2 F}{\partial x \, \partial y} \quad \text{and} \quad \left(\frac{\partial M}{\partial x}\right)_{y,z} = \frac{\partial^2 F}{\partial y \, \partial x}.$$

Since the order of differentiation in mixed second derivatives is immaterial,

$$(\partial L/\partial y)_{x,z} = (\partial M/\partial x)_{y,z}.$$

Similarly,

$$(\partial L/\partial z)_{x,y} = (\partial N/\partial x)_{y,z}$$

and

$$(\partial M/\partial z)_{x,y} = (\partial N/\partial y)_{x,z}.$$

The application of these relations to Eqs. (2-1) through (2-4) yields a set of relationships known as the Maxwell equations:

$$(\partial T/\partial V)_S = -(\partial P/\partial S)_V, \qquad (2\text{-}17)$$

$$(\partial T/\partial P)_S = (\partial V/\partial S)_P, \qquad (2\text{-}18)$$

$$(\partial P/\partial T)_V = (\partial S/\partial V)_T, \qquad (2\text{-}19)$$

$$(\partial V/\partial T)_P = -(\partial S/\partial P)_T. \qquad (2\text{-}20)$$

**2.2. Some Equations for a Homogeneous Phase of Constant Composition.** We return now to a further consideration of homogeneous phases. Our basic postulate for such a phase, provided it is a simple system of constant mass, is that its properties are functions of temperature and pressure. If we consider the properties $H$ and $S$ for a unit mass of fluid, we may immediately write:

$$dH = (\partial H/\partial T)_P \, dT + (\partial H/\partial P)_T \, dP \qquad (2\text{-}21)$$

and

$$dS = (\partial S/\partial T)_P \, dT + (\partial S/\partial P)_T \, dP. \qquad (2\text{-}22)$$

Clearly, if we are to calculate changes in the properties $H$ and $S$ from these equations, we must be able to evaluate the partial derivatives $(\partial H/\partial T)_P$, $(\partial H/\partial P)_T$, etc., in terms of measurable variables.

We first define the *heat capacity at constant pressure*

$$C_P = (\partial H/\partial T)_P. \qquad (2\text{-}23)$$

This quantity has a simple physical interpretation. If a fluid of constant composition is held at constant pressure, then its temperature may be considered the only independent variable, and we can write from Eq. (2-23):

$$dH_P = C_P \, dT$$

but in general

$$dH = dU + d(PV).$$

Thus at constant pressure

$$dH_P = C_P \, dT = dU + P \, dV.$$

But

$$P \, dV = dW_{\text{rev}}.$$

Hence

$$dH_P = C_P \, dT = dU + dW_{\text{rev}}.$$

By the first law for a reversible process in a closed system

$$dU = dQ_{\text{rev}} - dW_{\text{rev}}.$$

Hence

$$dH_P = C_P \, dT = dQ_{\text{rev}}$$

or

$$C_P = (dQ_{\text{rev}}/dT)_P.$$

In words, $C_P$ is the temperature derivative of the heat added to a unit mass of fluid at constant composition and pressure in a reversible process. It is a property of the material and a function of temperature and pressure. Moreover, it can be measured directly.

Equation (2-2) is valid in general:

$$dH = T \, dS + V \, dP. \qquad (2\text{-}2)$$

If pressure is held constant and temperature is taken as the only independent variable, then any change in properties can be considered to result from a temperature change. Thus Eq. (2-2) becomes

$$(\partial H/\partial T)_P = T(\partial S/\partial T)_P.$$

Hence, in view of Eq. (2-23)

$$(\partial S/\partial T)_P = C_P/T. \tag{2-24}$$

Equation (2-2) may also be restricted to constant temperature; in which case the pressure may be regarded as the only independent variable. All property changes then come about as a result of pressure changes, and in this event Eq. (2-2) may we written

$$(\partial H/\partial P)_T = T(\partial S/\partial P)_T + V.$$

Equation (2-20) gives $(\partial S/\partial P)_T$ directly as

$$(\partial S/\partial P)_T = -(\partial V/\partial T)_P. \tag{2-25}$$

Hence

$$(\partial H/\partial P)_T = -T(\partial V/\partial T)_P + V. \tag{2-26}$$

Combination of Eqs. (2-21), (2-23), and (2-26) gives

$$dH = C_P \, dT + \left[ V - T\left(\frac{\partial V}{\partial T}\right)_P \right] dP. \tag{2-27}$$

Since $dH$ is an exact differential, we may immediately write:

$$\left(\frac{\partial C_P}{\partial P}\right)_T = \left\{ \frac{\partial [V - T(\partial V/\partial T)_P]}{\partial T} \right\}_P$$

or

$$\left(\frac{\partial C_P}{\partial P}\right)_T = -T\left(\frac{\partial^2 V}{\partial T^2}\right)_P. \tag{2-28}$$

If $H$ is constant in some process, $dH = 0$, and from Eq. (2-27)

$$\mu = \left(\frac{\partial T}{\partial P}\right)_H = \frac{T(\partial V/\partial T)_P - V}{C_P}. \tag{2-29}$$

In Eq. (2-29) $\mu$ is known as the Joule–Thomson coefficient.

Combination of Eqs. (2-22), (2-24), and (2-25) gives

$$dS = (C_P/T) \, dT - (\partial V/\partial T)_P \, dP. \tag{2-30}$$

If $S$ is constant, as in a reversible, adiabatic process, then $dS = 0$, and

$$C_P = T\left(\frac{\partial V}{\partial T}\right)_P \left(\frac{\partial P}{\partial T}\right)_S. \tag{2-31}$$

It should be noted that Eqs. (2-27) and (2-30) allow the calculation of enthalpy and entropy changes from measurements of heat capacities and $P$-$V$-$T$ data. If a datum state is selected for which $H$ and $S$ are taken as zero, these equations allow calculation of enthalpy and entropy values for constant-composition, homogeneous fluids. Once $V$, $H$, and $S$ are known, the other thermodynamic properties are readily calculated from the equations:

$$U = H - PV,$$
$$A = U - TS,$$
$$G = H - TS.$$

It is not always convenient to take temperature and pressure as the independent variables for homogeneous phases of constant composition. Since the properties of such fluids are functions of $T$ and $P$, $V = v(T, P)$. Hence the other properties can be regarded as functions of temperature and volume. Let us now consider that the properties $U$ and $S$ are functions of $T$ and $V$. If this is so, we may immediately write:

$$dU = (\partial U/\partial T)_V \, dT + (\partial U/\partial V)_T \, dV \tag{2-32}$$

and

$$dS = (\partial S/\partial T)_V \, dT + (\partial S/\partial V)_T \, dV. \tag{2-33}$$

We proceed much as before, first defining a *heat capacity at constant volume* as

$$C_V = (\partial U/\partial T)_V. \tag{2-34}$$

Again this has a simple physical interpretation. If the fluid is held at constant volume, then temperature can be regarded as the only independent variable, and we can write

$$dU_V = C_V \, dT.$$

But for a closed system at constant volume the first law reduces to

$$dU_V = dQ.$$

Thus

$$dQ = C_V \, dT$$

or

$$C_V = (dQ/dT)_V.$$

Hence $C_V$ is the temperature derivative of the heat added to a unit mass of fluid at constant composition and volume. It is a property of the material and is directly measurable.

For the case we are considering, where $T$ and $V$ are the independent variables, if $V$ is held constant then all property changes can be attributed to changes in $T$. Equation (2-1) may then be written:

$$(\partial U/\partial T)_V = T(\partial S/\partial T)_V.$$

From which we obtain

$$(\partial S/\partial T)_V = C_V/T. \tag{2-35}$$

If $T$ is held constant, $V$ becomes the only independent variable, and Eq. (2-1) becomes:

$$(\partial U/\partial V)_T = T(\partial S/\partial V)_T - P.$$

Equation (2-19) gives $(\partial S/\partial V)_T$ directly as

$$(\partial S/\partial V)_T = (\partial P/\partial T)_V. \tag{2-36}$$

Hence

$$(\partial U/\partial V)_T = T(\partial P/\partial T)_V - P. \tag{2-37}$$

Combination of Eqs. (2-32), (2-34), and (2-37) gives:

$$dU = C_V\, dT + \left[T\left(\frac{\partial P}{\partial T}\right)_V - P\right] dV. \tag{2-38}$$

Since $dU$ is an exact differential:

$$\left(\frac{\partial C_V}{\partial V}\right)_T = \left\{\frac{\partial\,[T(\partial P/\partial T)_V - P]}{\partial T}\right\}_V$$

or

$$\left(\frac{\partial C_V}{\partial V}\right)_T = T\left(\frac{\partial^2 P}{\partial T^2}\right)_V. \tag{2-39}$$

Combination of Eqs. (2-33), (2-35), and (2-36) gives:

$$dS = (C_V/T)\, dT + (\partial P/\partial T)_V\, dV. \tag{2-40}$$

If $S$ is constant, $dS = 0$, and Eq. (2-40) becomes

$$C_V = -T(\partial P/\partial T)_V\, (\partial V/\partial T)_S. \tag{2-41}$$

Equations (2-30) and (2-40) are two expressions for $dS$. For the same change in state they must be equal. Hence

$$\frac{C_P}{T}\, dT - (\partial V/\partial T)_P\, dP = \frac{C_V}{T}\, dT + (\partial P/\partial T)_V\, dV$$

or

$$dT = \left(\frac{T}{C_P - C_V}\right)\left(\frac{\partial V}{\partial T}\right)_P dP + \left(\frac{T}{C_P - C_V}\right)\left(\frac{\partial P}{\partial T}\right)_V \partial V.$$

Since $T = t(P, V)$

$$dT = (\partial T/\partial P)_V\, dP + (\partial T/\partial V)_P\, dV.$$

Thus we have two equations for $dT$ in the same independent variables. Equating coefficients of either $dP$ or $dV$ gives

$$C_P - C_V = T\left(\frac{\partial V}{\partial T}\right)_P \left(\frac{\partial P}{\partial T}\right)_V. \tag{2-42}$$

Division of Eq. (2-31) by Eq. (2-41) gives

$$\gamma = \frac{C_P}{C_V} = -\left(\frac{\partial V}{\partial T}\right)_P\left(\frac{\partial P}{\partial T}\right)_S\left(\frac{\partial T}{\partial P}\right)_V\left(\frac{\partial T}{\partial V}\right)_S = -\left(\frac{\partial V}{\partial T}\right)_P\left(\frac{\partial T}{\partial P}\right)_V\left(\frac{\partial P}{\partial V}\right)_S.$$

Since $V = v(T, P)$

$$dV = \left(\frac{\partial V}{\partial T}\right)_P dT + \left(\frac{\partial V}{\partial P}\right)_T dP.$$

If $V$ is constant, $dV = 0$, and

$$\left(\frac{\partial V}{\partial P}\right)_T = -\left(\frac{\partial V}{\partial T}\right)_P \left(\frac{\partial T}{\partial P}\right)_V.$$

The ratio of heat capacities $\gamma$ then becomes

$$\gamma = \frac{C_P}{C_V} = \left(\frac{\partial V}{\partial P}\right)_T \left(\frac{\partial P}{\partial V}\right)_S. \tag{2-43}$$

One method of evaluating the partial derivatives involving $P$, $V$, and $T$ which occur in the foregoing equations is through an *equation of state*, an equation relating $P$, $V$, and $T$. The simplest such equation is the ideal-gas law, $PV = RT$, where $R$ is the universal gas constant. A gas which obeys this relationship is said to be an ideal gas. For such a gas the foregoing equations may be greatly simplified.

If $PV = RT$, then

$$(\partial P/\partial T)_V = R/V = P/T \quad \text{and} \quad (\partial^2 P/\partial T^2)_V = 0,$$
$$(\partial V/\partial T)_P = R/P = V/T \quad \text{and} \quad (\partial^2 V/\partial T^2)_P = 0,$$
$$(\partial P/\partial V)_T = -(P/V).$$

These relations may be combined with the general equations derived in this section for homogeneous fluids to give results valid for ideal gases. Equation (2-25) becomes:

$$(\partial S/\partial P)_T = -(R/P). \tag{2-25A}$$

From Eq. (2-26) we get

$$(\partial H/\partial P)_T = 0. \tag{2-26A}$$

Hence for an ideal gas the enthalpy is independent of pressure and a function of temperature only. Equation (2-27) reduces to

$$dH = C_P\, dT \tag{2-27A}$$

an equation which is *always* valid for the calculation of enthalpy changes of an ideal gas. From Eq. (2-28)

$$(\partial C_P/\partial P)_T = 0 \tag{2-28A}$$

which shows $C_P$ for an ideal gas to be independent of pressure and a function of temperature only.

By Eq. (2-29)

$$\mu = (\partial T/\partial P)_H = 0. \tag{2-29A}$$

Thus the Joule–Thomson coefficient for an ideal gas is zero. Equation (2-30) becomes

$$dS = (C_P/T)\, dT - (R/P)\, dP. \tag{2-30A}$$

From Eq. (2-36)

$$(\partial S/\partial V)_T = R/V \tag{2-36A}$$

and from Eq. (2-37)

$$(\partial U/\partial V)_T = 0. \tag{2-37A}$$

Hence for an ideal gas $U$ is a function of temperature only. Equation (2-38) reduces to

$$dU = C_V \, dT \tag{2-38A}$$

an equation *always* valid for calculating internal energy changes of an ideal gas. Equation (2-39) gives

$$(\partial C_V/\partial V)_T = 0. \tag{2-39A}$$

Hence $C_V$ for an ideal gas is a function of temperature only. From Eq. (2-40)

$$dS = (C_V/T) \, dT + (R/V) \, dV. \tag{2-40A}$$

Equation (2-42) reduces to

$$C_P - C_V = R, \tag{2-42A}$$

which shows that for an ideal gas the difference between $C_P$ and $C_V$ is a constant. Equation (2-43) becomes

$$\gamma = -(\partial \ln P/\partial \ln V)_S. \tag{2-43A}$$

If $\gamma$ is a constant, this equation can be integrated to give

$$PV^\gamma = \text{constant}$$

for a process at constant entropy. This equation therefore holds for an ideal gas with constant heat capacities undergoing a reversible, adiabatic process. The severe limitations on this equation should be noted.

**2.3. Basic Equations for Solutions.** A homogeneous solution in an equilibrium state at a given temperature, pressure, and composition can be assigned a complete set of thermodynamic properties. Since this monograph is primarily concerned with solutions, it is convenient to represent the properties of a unit mass or a mole of solution by the symbols $V$, $U$, $S$, $C_P$, etc., unadorned by identifying subscripts or superscripts. Since solutions are a mixture of chemical species, it is often convenient to refer to the unit properties of these constituents *as they exist pure at the same temperature and pressure*. These pure-constituent properties will be denoted by a subscript, e.g., $V_i$, $U_i$, $S_i$, etc. Since a pure material is merely a solution whose mass or mole fraction in one constituent approaches unity, any equation that can be written for a solution can immediately be reduced to one applying to a pure constituent. Thus for a unit mass of a solution of given composition we can write by definition

$$H = U + PV,$$
$$A = U - TS,$$
$$G = H - TS,$$

and for a unit amount of pure constituent at the same $T$ and $P$, these equations become

$$H_i = U_i + PV_i,$$
$$A_i = U_i - TS_i,$$
$$G_i = H_i - TS_i.$$

One would hope that a simple relationship could be found to connect a property of a solution to the same properties of the pure constituents that are mixed to form it. Thus if $M$ represents any thermodynamic property of a mole of solution and if $M_i$ represents the same molal property of a constituent of the solution when pure, where both are taken at the same temperature and pressure, it would be most convenient to find that

$$M = x_1 M_1 + x_2 M_2 + x_3 M_3 + \ldots = \sum_i (x_i M_i),$$

where the $x_i$ 's represent mole fractions. Unfortunately, such a relationship proves valid only under the most unusual circumstances.

Up to this point we have limited our discussion to closed systems of fixed mass. For a consideration of the influence of composition on the thermodynamic properties of solutions, it is convenient to treat open systems in which changes of composition are accomplished through the transfer of matter to and from the system. Since the properties of a homogeneous phase are taken to be functions of temperature, pressure, and composition, a total property of a phase, say $n M$, may be expressed functionally as:

$$n M = f(T, P, n_1, n_2, n_3, \ldots),$$

where $M$ represents any molal property of the solution, $n$ is the total moles of solution, and $n_1, n_2, n_3$, etc., are the moles of the constituents which make up the solution. Clearly, $n = \sum_i n_i$.

For the moment we wish to deal exclusively with the effect on $n M$ of changes in the amounts of the constituents making up a solution. Thus throughout this section we will take $T$ and $P$ as being fixed. We can then write:

$$n M = \varphi(n_1, n_2, n_3, \ldots).$$

In addition, we know from physical evidence that if each of the $n_i$'s is doubled or tripled at constant $T$ and $P$, the total property $n M$ is doubled or tripled. Hence $n M$ is a homogeneous function[†] of first degree in the mole numbers of the constituents. Since this is the case, the total property of the

---

[†] For the function $q = q(x, y, z, \ldots)$ we have $q_1 = q(x_1, y_1, z_1, \ldots)$ and $q_2 = q(x_2, y_2, z_2, \ldots)$ for two sets of values of the independent variables. If the function is such that $q_2 = k^p q_1$ when $x_2 = k x_1$, $y_2 = k y_1$, $z_2 = k z_1$, etc., then the function is said to be homogeneous of degree $p$ in the variables $x, y, z$, etc. If $p = 1$, then we have a homogeneous function of the first degree.

solution can be functionally related to the mole numbers in a special way:

$$n M = n_1 \varphi_1 \left[ \frac{n_2}{n_1}, \frac{n_3}{n_1}, \ldots \right].$$

If we define $N_2 = n_2/n_1$, $N_3 = n_3/n_1$, etc., we can write

$$n M = n_1 \varphi_1(N_2, N_3, \ldots),$$

with respect to this relationship we obtain the following partial derivatives:

$$\frac{\partial(n M)}{\partial n_1} = \varphi_1(N_2, N_3, \ldots) + n_1 \left[ \frac{\partial \varphi_1}{\partial N_2} \frac{\partial N_2}{\partial n_1} + \frac{\partial \varphi_1}{\partial N_3} \frac{\partial N_3}{\partial n_1} + \cdots \right]$$

$$\frac{\partial(n M)}{\partial n_2} = n_1 \left[ \frac{\partial \varphi_1}{\partial N_2} \frac{\partial N_2}{\partial n_2} + \frac{\partial \varphi_1}{\partial N_3} \frac{\partial N_3}{\partial n_2} + \cdots \right]$$

$$\frac{\partial(n M)}{\partial n_3} = n_1 \left[ \frac{\partial \varphi_1}{\partial N_2} \frac{\partial N_2}{\partial n_3} + \frac{\partial \varphi_1}{\partial N_3} \frac{\partial N_3}{\partial n_3} + \cdots \right]$$

etc.

From the definitions of $N_2$, $N_3$, etc., we find:

$$\frac{\partial N_2}{\partial n_1} = -\frac{n_2}{n_1^2} \qquad \frac{\partial N_2}{\partial n_2} = \frac{1}{n_1} \qquad \frac{\partial N_2}{\partial n_3} = 0$$

$$\frac{\partial N_3}{\partial n_1} = -\frac{n_3}{n_1^2} \qquad \frac{\partial N_3}{\partial n_2} = 0 \qquad \frac{\partial N_3}{\partial n_3} = \frac{1}{n_1}.$$

Substituting these in the three above equations reduces them to:

$$\frac{\partial(n M)}{\partial n_1} = \varphi_1(N_2, N_3, \ldots) - \frac{1}{n_1} \left[ n_2 \frac{\partial \varphi_1}{\partial N_2} + n_3 \frac{\partial \varphi_1}{\partial N_3} + \cdots \right]$$

$$\frac{\partial(n M)}{\partial n_2} = \frac{\partial \varphi_1}{\partial N_2}$$

$$\frac{\partial(n M)}{\partial n_3} = \frac{\partial \varphi_1}{\partial N_3}$$

etc.

Multiplication of these partial derivatives respectively by $n_1$, $n_2$, $n_3$, etc., and summation gives:

$$n_1 \frac{\partial(n M)}{\partial n_1} + n_2 \frac{\partial(n M)}{\partial n_2} + n_3 \frac{\partial(n M)}{\partial n_3} + \ldots = n_1 \varphi_1(N_2, N_3, \ldots)$$

but

$$n_1 \varphi_1(N_2, N_3, \ldots) = n M.$$

Therefore

$$n M = n_1 \frac{\partial(n M)}{\partial n_1} + n_2 \frac{\partial(n M)}{\partial n_2} + n_3 \frac{\partial(n M)}{\partial n_3} + \cdots$$

For convenience we now define

$$\overline{M}_1 = \frac{\partial(n M)}{\partial n_1}, \quad \overline{M}_2 = \frac{\partial(n M)}{\partial n_2}, \quad \overline{M}_3 = \frac{\partial(n M)}{\partial n_3},$$

etc.

Then

$$n M = n_1 \overline{M}_1 + n_2 \overline{M}_2 + n_3 \overline{M}_3 + \cdots$$

In brief

$$n M = \sum_i (n_i \overline{M}_i), \tag{2-44}$$

where

$$\overline{M}_i = \frac{\partial(n M)}{\partial n_i}. \tag{2-45}$$

In the above equations the partial derivatives, $\partial(n M)/\partial n_i$, are taken at constant temperature, pressure, and each of the $n_i$'s except the one with respect to which differentiation is carried out. It should be remembered that our primary variables are temperature, pressure, and the mole numbers.

We have stated on the basis of physical evidence that the total property of a solution $n M$ is a homogeneous function of first degree in the mole numbers $n_i$ for a given $T$ and $P$. That is, if all the $n_i$ are doubled, $n M$ is doubled; if all the $n_i$ are tripled, $n M$ is tripled; etc. Equation (2-44) meets this requirement only if the $\overline{M}_i$'s remain unchanged upon doubling, tripling, etc., the $n_i$'s. Thus the $\overline{M}_i$'s depend not on the *absolute* amounts of the constituents present but on their *relative* amounts, that is, upon the composition of the solution. In addition, since the total property $n M$ is a function of $T$ and $P$ and since the $n_i$'s are independent of $T$ and $P$, the $\overline{M}_i$'s must also be functions of $T$ and $P$. Thus the $\overline{M}_i$'s are functions of temperature, pressure, and composition, and are intensive properties of the solution. They are, in fact, called partial molal properties, and their physical interpretation will be considered shortly.

Equation (2-44) is general, and can be written for any amount of a homogeneous phase as it exists at a particular temperature, pressure, and composition. Changes in the total property $n M$ resulting from alteration of temperature, pressure, or the numbers of moles of the constituents are obtained by direct differentiation of Eq. (2-44). This *total* differential of $n M$ is given by

$$\mathrm{d}(n M) = \sum_i (n_i \, \mathrm{d}\overline{M}_i) + \sum_i (\overline{M}_i \, \mathrm{d}n_i). \tag{2-46}$$

It should be recalled that we are considering open systems for which the effects of addition or extraction of mass must be taken into account.

For a homogeneous solution at constant $T$ and $P$ our original functional relationship was given as

$$n M = \varphi(n_1, n_2, n_3, \ldots).$$

Thus we can write

$$\mathrm{d}(n M) = \frac{\partial(n M)}{\partial n_1} \mathrm{d}n_1 + \frac{\partial(n M)}{\partial n_2} \mathrm{d}n_2 + \frac{\partial(n M)}{\partial n_3} \mathrm{d}n_3 \cdots$$

In view of the definition given by Eq. (2-45), this becomes

$$d(n\,M) = \overline{M}_1\,dn_1 + \overline{M}_2\,dn_2 + \overline{M}_3\,dn_3 + \cdots$$

or

$$d(n\,M) = \sum_i (\overline{M}_i\,dn_i). \tag{2-47}$$

If we now restrict Eq. (2-46) to constant $T$ and $P$ in accordance with the restrictions on Eq. (2-47), these two relationships can be equated. The result is

$$\sum_i (n_i\,d\overline{M}_i) = 0. \tag{2-48}$$

This is the Gibbs–Duhem equation, and is valid for all homogeneous open systems constrained to changes occurring between equilibrium states at *constant temperature and pressure*.

The proper physical interpretation of a partial molal property is clear from Eq. (2-45), which we rewrite here for constituent 1:

$$\overline{M}_1 = [\partial(n\,M)/\partial n_1]_{T,P,n_2,n_3,\ldots}$$

The partial molal property $\overline{M}_1$ is seen to be the total response of a finite system to the addition of an infinitesimal amount of constituent 1 when the process is carried out at constant $T$, $P$, $n_2$, $n_3$, etc. Since $\overline{M}_1$ is an intensive property of the solution and is thus a function of temperature, pressure, and composition, it is independent of $n$. It follows that the response of a system is independent of its size for a given $T$, $P$, and composition. For example, the total volume change of an equimolal mixture of ethanol and water is essentially the same whether a drop of ethanol is added to one liter or to ten. It is necessary, of course, that the temperature and pressure be held constant and that the amount of material added be small enough in comparison with the amount of solution so as to cause negligible composition changes in the system.

Although the physical interpretation of a partial molal property just given is precise, it is not very helpful in facilitating the use of such quantities. Far more instructive from this point of view would be an interpretation of $\overline{M}_1$ as the molal property of constituent 1 *as it exists in solution*. There is, however, serious objection to such a view on the grounds that any constituent of a solution is an intimate part of the solution and hence cannot have private properties of its own. This is undoubtedly true. Nevertheless, the equations just developed relating solution properties to partial molal properties lend themselves completely to such an interpretation. Hence we may reason logically and derive correct results on the basis that partial molal properties behave *as though* they represent the molal properties of the constituents as they exist in solution. Another way of saying essentially the same thing is to regard a partial property of a constituent as the part of the solution property attributable to its presence. Equation (2-44)

$$n\,M = \sum_i (n_i\,\overline{M}_i)$$

is then viewed merely as a statement that the total property of a solution is the sum of its parts.

If we consider the addition of a differential number of moles of constituent 1 to a solution held at constant $T$, $P$, and the mole numbers of the other constituents, Eq. (2-47) reduces to

$$d(n\,M) = \overline{M}_1\,dn_1.$$

If $\overline{M}_1$ is considered the molal property of constituent 1 in solution, then the total property change $d(n\,M)$ is merely this molal property multiplied by the number of moles added. Clearly, the size of the system, provided it is not infinitesimal, does not matter.

The Gibbs–Duhem equation

$$\sum_i \left(n_i\,d\overline{M}_i\right) = 0,$$

shows that the net result of the differential changes in constituent properties caused by addition or extraction of differential amounts of the constituents is zero. This, of course, is necessary if as shown by Eq. (2-47) the total property change of the solution is to be made up solely of the property values associated with the differential amounts of the constituents added to or taken from the system.

If we apply Eq. (2-45) to pure material $i$, then $n$ becomes $n_i$ and $M$ becomes $M_i$. Hence

$$\overline{M}_i = \frac{\partial(n_i\,M_i)}{\partial n_i} = n_i\frac{\partial M_i}{\partial n_i} + M_i.$$

But $M_i$ is a molal property of pure $i$, and is independent of the number of moles; therefore $(\partial M_i/\partial n_i) = 0$, and $\overline{M}_i = M_i$ for a pure material, as one would expect.

Equations (2-44) and (2-48) can easily be put on a mole basis by dividing through by $n$. Since $x_i = n_i/n$,

$$M = \sum_i \left(x_i\,\overline{M}_i\right), \tag{2-49}$$

$$\sum_i \left(x_i\,d\overline{M}_i\right) = 0. \tag{2-50}$$

Equation (2-50) is an alternative expression for the Gibbs–Duhem equation valid at constant temperature and pressure.

The equations of this section could equally well have been written with a unit mass rather than a mole as basis. In this event we would write $m$ in place of $n$, and the partial properties would be on a gram or pound mass basis. These are sometimes called partial specific properties.

The actual determination of numerical values for partial properties could be accomplished through direct application of the defining expression, Eq. (2-45), to experimental data. However, this is not usually done; the methods used in practice will be developed in Chapter 5.

We now wish to consider the basic thermodynamic properties which our general property $M$ can represent. They are put down systematically as follows.

(a) Volume $V$:

$$\overline{V}_i = \partial(n\,V)/\partial n_i \quad V = \sum_i (x_i\,\overline{V}_i),$$

(b) Internal energy $U$:

$$\overline{U}_i = \partial(n\,U)/\partial n_i \quad U = \sum_i (x_i\,\overline{U}_i),$$

(c) Heat capacity at constant volume $C_V$:

$$\overline{C}_{V_i} = \partial(n\,C_V)/\partial n_i \quad C_V = \sum_i (x_i\,\overline{C}_{V_i}),$$

The heat capacity at constant volume for a mole of material was defined by Eq. (2-34):

$$C_V = (\partial U/\partial T)_V.$$

For $n$ moles

$$n\,C_V = [\partial(n\,U)/\partial T]_V.$$

Differentiation with respect to $n_i$ gives

$$\frac{\partial(n\,C_V)}{\partial n_i} = \frac{\partial[\partial(n\,U)/\partial T]_V}{\partial n_i}.$$

Since the order of differentiation is immaterial, this can be written:

$$\frac{\partial(n\,C_V)}{\partial n_i} = \left\{ \frac{\partial[\partial(n\,U)/\partial n_i]}{\partial T} \right\}_V.$$

In view of the definitions of $\overline{C}_{V_i}$ and $\overline{U}_i$, this equation may be written:

$$\overline{C}_{V_i} = (\partial\overline{U}_i/\partial T)_V,$$

(d) Enthalpy $H$:

$$\overline{H}_i = \partial(n\,H)/\partial n_i \quad H = \sum_i (x_i\,\overline{H}_i).$$

Since by definition

$$n\,H = n\,U + P(n\,V)$$

$$\frac{\partial(n\,H)}{\partial n_i} = \frac{\partial(n\,U)}{\partial n_i} + P\,\frac{\partial(n\,V)}{\partial n_i}.$$

Thus

$$\overline{H}_i = \overline{U}_i + P\,\overline{V}_i,$$

(e) Heat capacity at constant pressure $C_P$:

$$\overline{C}_{P_i} = \partial(n\,C_P)/\partial n_i \quad C_P = \sum_i (x_i\,\overline{C}_{P_i}).$$

In a manner entirely analogous to the treatment of $C_V$, it can be shown that

$$\overline{C}_{P_i} = (\partial \overline{H}_i / \partial T)_P,$$

(f) Entropy $S$:

$$\overline{S}_i = \partial(n\,S)/\partial n_i \quad S = \sum_i (x_i\,\overline{S}_i),$$

(g) Helmholtz function $A$:

$$\overline{A}_i = \partial(n\,A)/\partial n_i \quad A = \sum_i (x_i\,\overline{A}_i).$$

Since by definition

$$n\,A = n\,U - T(n\,S)$$

$$\frac{\partial(n\,A)}{\partial n_i} = \frac{\partial(n\,U)}{\partial n_i} - T\frac{\partial(n\,S)}{\partial n_i}.$$

Hence

$$\overline{A}_i = \overline{U}_i - T\overline{S}_i.$$

(h) Gibbs function $G$:

$$\overline{G}_i = \partial(n\,G)/\partial n_i \quad G = \sum_i (x_i\,\overline{G}_i).$$

In the same way as for the Helmholtz function, it is easily shown that

$$\overline{G}_i = \overline{H}_i - T\,\overline{S}_i.$$

It should be clear by now that for every relationship connecting the thermodynamic properties of a pure material or a solution, there is a corresponding relation connecting the corresponding partial molal properties of a solution.

**2.4. Auxiliary Thermodynamic Functions.** A large number of thermodynamic functions could be arbitrarily defined by making combinations of the properties already discussed. In practice it is found convenient to define a limited number of such auxiliary functions. These are considered in the following paragraphs.

(a) Compressibility factor $Z$:

For a mole of solution the compressibility factor is defined by the equation

$$P\,V = Z\,R\,T \qquad (2\text{-}51)$$

and for the special case of a pure material this becomes

$$P\,V_i = Z_i\,R\,T.$$

For $n$ moles of solution

$$n\,Z = \frac{P(n\,V)}{R\,T}.$$

Partial differentiation with respect to $n_i$ yields

$$\frac{\partial(n\,Z)}{\partial n_i} = \frac{P}{R\,T}\left[\frac{\partial(n\,V)}{\partial n_i}\right].$$

In view of the definition of a partial molal property, this becomes

$$\overline{Z}_i = \frac{P\,\overline{V}_i}{R\,T}.$$

Moreover

$$Z = \sum_i (y_i\,\overline{Z}_i).$$

The compressibility factor is usually applied to gases only, and for this reason $y_i$ has been used to represent mole fraction in the above equation. For an ideal gas $P\,V = R\,T$, and $Z$, $Z_i$, and $\overline{Z}_i$ become unity. If experimental $P$-$V$-$T$ data for a pure material or for a solution are used to calculate $Z$ values, the results may be plotted on $Z$ vs. $1/V$ or on $Z$ vs. $P$ graphs as lines for constant $T$. In either case, it is found that as $P$ or $1/V$ approaches zero (when $P$ approaches zero, $V$ approaches infinity) $Z$ approaches unity. Thus the "zero-pressure" state is often spoken of as an ideal-gas state. However, this is not strictly correct, for not all attributes of an ideal gas are exhibited by a real gas at a pressure approaching zero.

(b) The residual volume $\alpha$:

For a mole of a gaseous solution the residual volume is defined by the equation

$$\alpha = \frac{R\,T}{P} - V \tag{2-52}$$

and for the special case of a pure material this becomes

$$\alpha_i = \frac{R\,T}{P} - V_i.$$

For $n$ moles of a solution we may write

$$n\alpha = \frac{n\,R\,T}{P} - n\,V.$$

Thus

$$\frac{\partial(n\alpha)}{\partial n_i} = \frac{R\,T}{P}\left(\frac{\partial n}{\partial n_i}\right) - \frac{\partial(n\,V)}{\partial n_i}.$$

But $\partial n/\partial n_i = 1$, because all the $n_i$'s are independent. Therefore

$$\overline{\alpha}_i = \frac{R\,T}{P} - \overline{V}_i \qquad \alpha = \sum_i (y_i\,\overline{\alpha}_i).$$

The relationship between the residual volume and the compressibility factor is shown as follows:

3*

Since
$$V = ZRT/P$$

$$\alpha = \frac{RT}{P} - \frac{ZRT}{P} = \frac{RT}{P}(1 - Z).$$  (2-53)

In the limit as $P$ approaches zero, $Z$ approaches unity, and we have

$$\lim_{P \to 0} \alpha = RT \lim_{P \to 0}\left(\frac{1 - Z}{P}\right) = -RT(\partial Z/\partial P)_T^*,$$

where we have applied l'Hôpital's rule to evaluate the indeterminate quantity. The asterisk indicates the limiting value as $P$ approaches zero.

Thus
$$\alpha^* = -RT(\partial Z/\partial P)_T^*.$$

We see that the limiting value of $\alpha$ as $P$ approaches zero is finite, and is in fact directly related to the slope of the $Z$ vs. $P$ isotherm at zero pressure.

(c) Fugacity $f$:

For a pure material $i$ we define the fugacity so that for variations of pressure at constant temperature the following equation is always true for either gases or liquids:

$$dG_i = RT \, d\ln f_i \text{ (const } T\text{)}.$$  (2-54)

To complete the definition, we specify that

$$\lim_{P \to 0} \frac{f_i}{P} = \frac{f_i^*}{P^*} = 1.$$  (2-55)

That is, we include in our definition of fugacity the specification that the fugacity becomes equal to the pressure as $P$ approaches zero. This state is of course always gaseous.

For a pure material, Eq. (2-15) can be written

$$dG_i = V_i \, dP \text{ (const } T\text{)}.$$

Combining this with Eq. (2-54), we have

$$RT \, d\ln f_i = V_i \, dP$$

or for a gas

$$RT \, d\ln f_i = Z_i \, RT \, d\ln P.$$

Integration from $P^*$ to $P$ at constant temperature gives

$$\ln\frac{f_i}{f_i^*} = \int_{P^*}^{P} Z_i \, d\ln P.$$

If we apply this equation to an ideal gas, $Z_i$ is unity and

$$\ln\frac{f_i}{f^*} = \ln\frac{P}{P^*}.$$

But $f_i^* = P^*$, where the asterisk denotes values at a pressure approaching zero. Hence for an ideal gas $f_i = P$.

For a solution we proceed in the same fashion and write by way of definition:

$$dG = RT\,d\ln f \quad (\text{const } T) \tag{2-56}$$

and

$$\lim_{P \to 0} \frac{f}{P} = \frac{f^*}{P^*} = 1. \tag{2-57}$$

Again it is easily shown that for an ideal gas $f = P$.

For a constituent of a solution we proceed in an analogous manner, and write by definition:

$$d\bar{G}_i = RT\,d\ln \hat{f}_i \quad (\text{const } T), \tag{2-58}$$

where $\hat{f}_i$ is called the fugacity of component $i$ in solution. However, as will be shown presently, $\hat{f}_i$ is not a partial molal property. For this reason we have placed the sign ($\,\hat{}\,$) rather than a bar over the symbol. Equation (2-54) for a pure material is merely a special case of Eq. (2-58).

The definition of $\hat{f}_i$ is completed by arbitrarily specifying that

$$\lim_{P \to 0} \frac{\hat{f}_i}{x_i P} = \frac{\hat{f}_i^*}{x_i P^*} = 1. \tag{2-59}$$

Equation (2-59) is supposedly analogous to Eq. (2-55) for a pure material. However, there is virtually no direct experimental justification for this analogy. Yet much depends on it, as the discerning reader will see in subsequent chapters. The one obvious requirement that Eq. (2-59) must meet is that it reduce to Eq. (2-55) as $x_i$ approaches unity. This it clearly does. But so would other expressions, such as $\hat{f}_i/x_i^2 P$, $\hat{f}_i/x_i^3 P$, etc. The justification for Eq. (2-59) appears to be indirect in that its use leads to a set of self-consistent equations, none of which is at odds with experimental observation. It is not difficult to show that one consequence of these equations is that for an ideal gas $\hat{f}_i = y_i P$, which quantity is called partial pressure.

At constant temperature the fugacity of a constituent in solution depends on both pressure and composition. Equation (2-58) is therefore written to allow integration over changes in both pressure and composition. General integration at constant $T$ yields simply

$$\bar{G}_{i_2} - \bar{G}_{i_1} = RT\ln(\hat{f}_{i_2}/\hat{f}_{i_1}).$$

In other words, Eq. (2–58) may be integrated between any two states of constituent $i$ at the same temperature. For example, if $P$ is held constant along with $T$, and the composition changes from pure $i$ to $x_i$, then Eq. (2-58) integrates to:

$$\bar{G}_i - G_i = RT\ln\frac{\hat{f}_i}{f_i}.$$

As a special case of this, if integration is for a constant pressure equal to $P^*$, where $P^*$ is a pressure approaching zero, the above equation becomes

$$\overline{G}_i^* - G_i^* = R T \ln \frac{\hat{f}_i^*}{f_i^*} = R T \ln \frac{x_i \, P^*}{P^*}$$

or

$$\overline{G}_i^* - G_i^* = R T \ln x_i. \tag{2-60}$$

Although $\hat{f}_i$ is a property of constituent $i$ as it exists in solution, it is *not* a partial molal property, because $\partial(nf)/\partial n_i \neq \hat{f}_i$. However, $f$ and $\hat{f}_i$ are related. This is shown as follows: By Eq. (2-56) for a solution,

$$\mathrm{d}G = R T \mathrm{d} \ln f.$$

Integration at constant temperature and composition from the zero-pressure state to a state at finite pressure $P$ gives:

$$G - G^* = R T \ln f - R T \ln P^*.$$

For $n$ moles of solution this may be written:

$$n G - n G^* = n R T \ln f - n R T \ln P^*.$$

Differentiation of this general equation at constant $T$ and $P$ gives

$$\frac{\partial(n \, G)}{\partial n_i} - \frac{\partial(n \, G^*)}{\partial n_i} = R T \frac{\partial(n \ln f)}{\partial n_i} - R T \ln P^*$$

or

$$\overline{G}_i - \overline{G}_i^* = R T \frac{\partial(n \ln f)}{\partial n_i} - R T \ln P^*. \tag{A}$$

Now by Eq. (2-58) for constituent $i$ in solution

$$\mathrm{d}\overline{G}_i = RT \mathrm{d} \ln \hat{f}_i.$$

Integration between $P^*$ and $P$ at constant temperature and composition gives

$$\overline{G}_i - \overline{G}_i^* = R T \ln \frac{\hat{f}_i}{x_i \, P^*}$$

or

$$\overline{G}_i - \overline{G}_i^* = R T \ln \frac{\hat{f}_i}{x_i} - R T \ln P^*. \tag{B}$$

Comparison of Eqs. (A) and (B) shows that

$$\ln \frac{\hat{f}_i}{x_i} = \frac{\partial(n \ln f)}{\partial n_i}. \tag{2-61}$$

Hence $\ln(\hat{f}_i/x_i)$ is related to $\ln f$ as a partial molal quantity. Thus in view of Eq. (2-49) we can write

$$\ln f = \sum_i \left( x_i \ln \frac{\hat{f}_i}{x_i} \right), \tag{2-62}$$

(d) Fugacity coefficient $\varphi$:

By definition, the fugacity coefficient of a constituent in solution is

$$\hat{\varphi}_i = \frac{\hat{f}_i}{x_i P}. \tag{2-63}$$

For a pure material this becomes

$$\varphi_i = \frac{f_i}{P}. \tag{2-64}$$

For a solution the fugacity coefficient is defined analogously:

$$\varphi = f/P. \tag{2-65}$$

In view of Eq. (2-62) and the above definitions we can write

$$\ln(P\,\varphi) = \sum_i (x_i \ln P \,\hat{\varphi}_i)$$

or

$$\ln\varphi + \ln P = \sum_i (x_i \ln \hat{\varphi}_i) + \sum_i (x_i \ln P).$$

But

$$\sum_i (x_i \ln P) = (\ln P) \sum_i x_i = \ln P.$$

Therefore

$$\ln\varphi = \sum_i (x_i \ln \hat{\varphi}_i). \tag{2-66}$$

Clearly $\ln\hat{\varphi}_i$ is related to $\ln\varphi$ as a partial molal property.

(e) Activity coefficient $\gamma_i$:

By definition, the activity coefficient of a constituent in solution is

$$\gamma_i = \frac{\hat{f}_i}{x_i f_i^0}, \tag{2-67}\dagger$$

where $f_i^0$ is the fugacity of constituent $i$ in some convenient *standard state*. Within certain limitations the standard state for a constituent may be arbitrarily selected. The primary limitation is that the temperature of the standard state must *always* be that of the solution. Thus the temperature of the standard state varies with the solution temperature. The standard state of constituent $i$ in any particular application must be taken at a fixed, though arbitrary, composition of the solution. This composition may be, but need not be, the same for all constituents. One common standard state composition is that of the constituent at a mole fraction of unity, that is, the pure constituent. The pressure of the standard state may be

---

† An even more general definition of the activity coefficient would allow choice of the composition variable. Thus composition could be given by molality, weight fraction, etc., rather than by mole fraction. However, mole fraction is the variable almost universally used with solutions of non-electrolytes.

arbitrarily selected at a constant value, for example, at atmospheric pressure; or it may be specified to vary in some arbitrarily chosen way with the pressure, composition, or temperature of the solution. Frequently, the standard-state pressure is taken as the solution pressure, and hence varies with the solution pressure. At other times it is taken as a vapor pressure, and thus varies with the solution temperature. It should also be noted that hypothetical or fictitious states are sometimes employed as standard states. Skill in the selection of convenient standard states and an understanding of their correct uses comes only with practice.

An activity coefficient is meaningless unless it is accompanied by a detailed description of the standard state to which it refers. Since the term applies to a constituent in solution, consistency would require that we place the sign ($\hat{}$) over the symbol $\gamma$. However, there is no need for this device here. For a pure constituent, the right-hand side of Eq. (2-67) reduces to $f_i/f_i^0$, and this quantity is called an *activity*, not an activity coefficient. Hence the activity for a pure material is given by

$$a_i = \frac{f_i}{f_i^0}.$$

For a constituent in solution we write

$$\hat{a}_i = \frac{\hat{f}_i}{f_i^0}.$$

Clearly

$$\gamma_i = \frac{\hat{a}_i}{x_i}.$$

A very common standard state is that of the pure constituent at the temperature and pressure of the solution and in the same physical state. We will consider this case in some detail. For this standard state, Eq. (2-67) becomes

$$\gamma_i = \frac{\hat{f}_i}{x_i f_i}, \tag{2-68}$$

where $f_i$ is the fugacity of pure $i$ at the temperature and pressure of the solution. For a pure material this equation reduces to unity.

If Eq. (2-58) is integrated at constant temperature and composition for a pressure change from $P^*$ to $P$, the result is

$$\bar{G}_i - \bar{G}_i^* = R T \ln \frac{\hat{f}_i}{x_i P^*}.$$

For pure $i$ at the same temperature and for the same pressure change the above equation becomes

$$G_i - G_i^* = R T \ln \frac{f_i}{P^*}.$$

Subtracting the latter from the former gives

$$\bar{G}_i - G_i - (\bar{G}_i^* - G_i^*) = R T \ln \frac{\hat{f}_i}{x_i f_i}.$$

In view of Eqs. (2-60) and (2-68), this becomes

$$\bar{G}_i - G_i - R T \ln x_i = R T \ln \gamma_i. \tag{2-69}$$

The activity coefficient based on a standard state of the pure constituent at the solution temperature and pressure and in the same physical state is related to the fugacity coefficient as follows:

$$\gamma_i = \frac{\hat{f}_i}{x_i f_i} = \frac{\hat{f}_i / x_i P}{f_i / P} = \frac{\hat{\varphi}_i}{\varphi_i}$$

or

$$\ln \gamma_i = \ln \hat{\varphi}_i - \ln \varphi_i. \tag{2-70}$$

Throughout this monograph, when the symbol $\gamma_i$ is used without comment as to the standard state, it will be this quantity that is intended.

Table 2-1 summarizes the various thermodynamic properties which our general symbol $M$ can represent.

TABLE 2-1. THERMODYNAMIC PROPERTIES

| Name | Solution property (unit basis) $M$ | Pure component property $M_i$ | Partial property $\bar{M}_i$ |
|---|---|---|---|
| Volume | $V$ | $V_i$ | $\bar{V}_i$ |
| Residual volume | $\alpha$ | $\alpha_i$ | $\bar{\alpha}_i$ |
| Compressibility factor | $Z$ | $Z_i$ | $\bar{Z}_i$ |
| Internal energy | $U$ | $U_i$ | $\bar{U}_i$ |
| Heat capacity at const $V$ | $C_V$ | $C_{V_i}$ | $\bar{C}_{V_i}$ |
| Enthalpy | $H$ | $H_i$ | $\bar{H}_i$ |
| Heat capacity at const $P$ | $C_P$ | $C_{P_i}$ | $\bar{C}_{P_i}$ |
| Entropy | $S$ | $S_i$ | $\bar{S}_i$ |
| Helmholtz function | $A$ | $A_i$ | $\bar{A}_i$ |
| Gibbs function | $G$ | $G_i$ | $\bar{G}_i$ |
| Fugacity | $\ln f$ | $\ln f_i$ | $\ln(\hat{f}_i / x_i)$ |
| Fugacity coefficient | $\ln \varphi$ | $\ln \varphi_i$ | $\ln \hat{\varphi}_i$ |

**2.5. Special Equations for the Gibbs Function and Related Properties.** We noted in Section 2.1 that the Gibbs function for a closed system in equilibrium states is always a function of $T$ and $P$. It is this functional relationship which makes $G$ a particularly useful thermodynamic property, for temperature and pressure are very convenient primary variables.

For an open system the Gibbs function depends not only on $T$ and $P$ but also on the mole numbers of the constituents making up the solution. Thus in general

$$n\,G = g(P, T, n_1, n_2, n_3, \ldots).$$

It follows that

$$\mathrm{d}(n\,G) = \frac{\partial(n\,G)}{\partial P}\,\mathrm{d}P + \frac{\partial(n\,G)}{\partial T}\,\mathrm{d}T + \frac{\partial(n\,G)}{\partial n_1}\,\mathrm{d}n_1 + \frac{\partial(n\,G)}{\partial n_2}\,\mathrm{d}n_2 + \cdots$$

But by Eq. (2-15)†, $\partial(n\,G)/\partial P = n\,V$, and by Eq. (2-16)†, $\partial(n\,G)/\partial T = -n\,S$, and by Eq. (2-45), $\partial(n\,G)/\partial n_i = \overline{G}_i$. Therefore

$$\mathrm{d}(n\,G) = n\,V\,\mathrm{d}P - n\,S\,\mathrm{d}T + \sum_i (\overline{G}_i\,\mathrm{d}n_i). \tag{2-71}$$

It is universal practice to abbreviate $\overline{G}_i$ by $\mu_i$, and to call $\mu_i$ the chemical potential. Thus for the Gibbs function Eq. (2-44) is written

$$n\,G = \sum_i (n_i\,\mu_i)$$

and Eq. (2-45) becomes

$$\mu_i = \partial(n\,G)/\partial n_i.$$

Hence Eq. (2-71) may be written

$$\mathrm{d}(n\,G) = n\,V\,\mathrm{d}P - n\,S\,\mathrm{d}T + \sum_i (\mu_i\,\mathrm{d}n_i). \tag{2-72}$$

By direct differentiation we find

$$\mathrm{d}(\mu_i\,n_i) = \mu_i\,\mathrm{d}n_i + n_i\,\mathrm{d}\mu_i.$$

If we sum over all components

$$\sum_i \mathrm{d}(\mu_i\,n_i) = \sum_i (\mu_i\,\mathrm{d}n_i) + \sum_i (n_i\,\mathrm{d}\mu_i)$$

or

$$\sum_i (\mu_i\,\mathrm{d}n_i) = \mathrm{d}\sum_i (\mu_i\,n_i) - \sum_i (n_i\,\mathrm{d}\mu_i)$$

or

$$\sum_i (\mu_i\,\mathrm{d}n_i) = \mathrm{d}(n\,G) - \sum_i (n_i\,\mathrm{d}\mu_i).$$

If the last equation is substituted into Eq. (2-72) we get

$$n\,V\,\mathrm{d}P - n\,S\,\mathrm{d}T = \sum_i (n_i\,\mathrm{d}\mu_i).$$

Division by $n$ puts this equation on a mole basis:

$$V\,\mathrm{d}P - S\,\mathrm{d}T = \sum_i (x_i\,\mathrm{d}\mu_i). \tag{2-73}$$

---

† Equations (2-15) and (2-16) were derived for closed systems. Though not specifically stated, it is clear that the partial derivatives of these equations are taken with all mole numbers constant. Hence they meet exactly the requirements of the partial derivatives indicated here. Multiplication by $n$, which is held constant, clearly does not alter their validity.

Equation (2-73) is the unrestricted form of the Gibbs–Duhem equation as it applies to the Gibbs function. Starting with this equation, we now develop additional generalized forms of the Gibbs–Duhem equation which are particularly useful.

Equation (2-58) can be written

$$d\mu_i = RT\, d\ln\hat{f_i} \quad (\text{const } T).$$

This equation takes into account variations in $\mu_i$ as a result of pressure and composition changes *at constant temperature*, and therefore cannot be substituted into Eq. (2-73) for the general case where $d\mu_i$ is the total differential of $\mu_i$ as a result of changes in temperature as well as in pressure and composition.

If we imagine that constituent $i$ is changed from its actual state in solution to a pure ideal gas at the same temperature and pressure, the above equation integrates for this change to give

$$G_i^{id} - \mu_i = RT\ln f_i^{id} - RT\ln\hat{f_i}.$$

It should be noted that for a pure material $\mu_i$ becomes $G_i$, and in this case, $G_i^{id}$. We have already shown that for an ideal gas the fugacity equals the pressure. Thus $f_i^{id} = P$, and

$$\mu_i - G_i^{id} = RT\ln\hat{f_i} - RT\ln P. \tag{2-74}$$

General differentiation of Eq. (2-74) gives

$$d\mu_i = dG_i^{id} + RT\, d\ln\hat{f_i} + R\ln\hat{f_i}\, dT - RT\, d\ln P - R\ln P\, dT.$$

In this equation $d\mu_i$ is the required total differential. Simplification can be effected by the following substitutions. By Eq. (2-4) we have

$$dG_i^{id} = V_i^{id}\, dP - S_i^{id}\, dT$$

or

$$dG_i^{id} = \frac{RT}{P}\, dP - S_i^{id}\, dT = RT\, d\ln P - S_i^{id}\, dT$$

and by Eq. (2-74)

$$R\ln\hat{f_i}\, dT - R\ln P\, dT = \frac{\mu_i - G_i^{id}}{T}\, dT.$$

Therefore

$$d\mu_i = -S_i^{id}\, dT + RT\, d\ln\hat{f_i} + \frac{\mu_i - G_i^{id}}{T}\, dT$$

or since $S_i^{id} + G_i^{id}/T = H_i^{id}/T$ by the defining equation for the Gibbs function,

$$d\mu_i = -(H_i^{id}/T)\, dT + (\mu_i/T)\, dT + RT\, d\ln\hat{f_i}.$$

If this equation is now multiplied through by $x_i$ and summed over all constituents, we have

$$\sum_i (x_i \, \mathrm{d}\mu_i) = \frac{-\sum_i (x_i \, H_i^{\mathrm{id}})}{T} \, \mathrm{d}T + \frac{\sum_i (x_i \, \mu_i)}{T} \, \mathrm{d}T + RT \sum_i (x_i \, \mathrm{d} \ln \hat{f}_i).$$

In this equation $\sum_i (x_i \, \mu_i)$ can be replaced by $G$, the molal Gibbs function for the solution, and as will be shown in Chapter 4 $\sum_i (x_i \, H_i^{\mathrm{id}})$ can be replaced by $H^{\mathrm{id}}$, the molal enthalpy of an ideal-gas solution of the given composition at the given temperature and pressure. Thus

$$\sum_i (x_i \, \mathrm{d}\mu_i) = -(H^{\mathrm{id}}/T) \, \mathrm{d}T + (G/T) \, \mathrm{d}T + RT \sum_i (x_i \, \mathrm{d} \ln \hat{f}_i).$$

Combination of this equation with Eq. (2-73) gives

$$V \, \mathrm{d}P - S \, \mathrm{d}T = -(H^{\mathrm{id}}/T) \, \mathrm{d}T + (G/T) \, \mathrm{d}T + RT \sum_i (x_i \, \mathrm{d} \ln \hat{f}_i).$$

Since $S + G/T = H/T$ by the definition of $G$, this equation can be rearranged to give

$$\frac{V}{RT} \, \mathrm{d}P + \frac{(H^{\mathrm{id}} - H)}{RT^2} \, \mathrm{d}T = \sum_i (x_i \, \mathrm{d} \ln \hat{f}_i).$$

In this equation $H^{\mathrm{id}} - H$ is the difference between the enthalpy of an ideal-gas solution and the enthalpy of the actual solution, both for the same composition and at the same temperature and pressure. This difference is called the enthalpy deviation and is abbreviated $\Delta H'$. Thus the above equation is written

$$\frac{V}{RT} \, \mathrm{d}P + \frac{\Delta H'}{RT^2} \, \mathrm{d}T = \sum_i (x_i \, \mathrm{d} \ln \hat{f}_i). \tag{2-75}$$

Equation (2-75) is the exact form of the Gibbs–Duhem equation relating pressure, temperature, and the fugacities for *any* liquid or gaseous phase.

It can be written in another form by a simple substitution.

$$\mathrm{d}\left(x_i \ln \frac{\hat{f}_i}{x_i}\right) = x_i \, \mathrm{d} \ln \hat{f}_i - x_i \, \mathrm{d} \ln x_i + \ln \frac{\hat{f}_i}{x_i} \, \mathrm{d}x_i.$$

Summation over all constituents gives

$$\mathrm{d} \sum_i \left(x_i \ln \frac{\hat{f}_i}{x_i}\right) = \sum_i (x_i \, \mathrm{d} \ln \hat{f}_i) - \sum_i (x_i \, \mathrm{d} \ln x_i) + \sum_i \left(\ln \frac{\hat{f}_i}{x_i} \, \mathrm{d}x_i\right).$$

But

$$\sum_i (x_i \, \mathrm{d} \ln x_i) = \sum_i \mathrm{d}x_i = 0,$$

because $\sum_i x_i = 1$, and by Eq. (2-62),

$$\sum_i \left(x_i \ln \frac{\hat{f}_i}{x_i}\right) = \ln f.$$

Therefore

$$\sum_i \left( x_i \, d\ln \hat{f}_i \right) = d\ln f - \sum_i \left( \ln \frac{\hat{f}_i}{x_i} \, dx_i \right).$$

Substitution in Eq. (2-75) yields

$$d\ln f = \frac{V}{RT} \, dP + \frac{\Delta H'}{RT^2} \, dT + \sum_i \left( \ln \frac{\hat{f}_i}{x_i} \, dx_i \right). \qquad (2\text{-}76)\dagger$$

Equations (2-75) and (2-76) can of course be written for the special case of a fluid at constant composition, in which case they both reduce to the same expression:

$$d\ln f = \frac{V}{RT} \, dP + \frac{\Delta H'}{RT^2} \, dT. \qquad (2\text{-}77)$$

Another analogous set of equations is readily obtained by substituting for the fugacities in terms of fugacity coefficients. By definition $\hat{\varphi}_i = \hat{f}_i / x_i P$. Therefore

$$\ln \hat{\varphi}_i = \ln \hat{f}_i - \ln x_i - \ln P$$

and

$$d\ln \hat{\varphi}_i = d\ln \hat{f}_i - d\ln x_i - d\ln P.$$

Multiplying through by $x_i$ and summing over all constituents gives

$$\sum_i (x_i \, d\ln \hat{f}_i) = \sum_i (x_i \, d\ln \hat{\varphi}_i) + \sum_i (x_i \, d\ln x_i) + \sum_i (x_i \, d\ln P).$$

But

$$\sum_i (x_i \, d\ln x_i) = 0$$

and

$$\sum_i (x_i \, d\ln P) = (d\ln P)(\sum_i x_i) = d\ln P.$$

Thus

$$\sum_i \left( x_i \, d\ln \hat{f}_i \right) = \sum_i (x_i \, d\ln \hat{\varphi}_i) + \frac{dP}{P}.$$

Substitution in Eq. (2-75) gives

$$\left( \frac{V}{RT} - \frac{1}{P} \right) dP + \frac{\Delta H'}{RT^2} \, dT = \sum_i (x_i \, d\ln \hat{\varphi}_i).$$

But

$$\frac{V}{RT} - \frac{1}{P} = \frac{1}{RT} \left( V - \frac{RT}{P} \right) = \frac{-\alpha}{RT},$$

where $\alpha$ is the residual volume as defined by Eq. (2-52). Therefore

$$\frac{-\alpha}{RT} \, dP + \frac{\Delta H'}{RT^2} \, dT = \sum_i (x_i \, d\ln \hat{\varphi}_i). \qquad (2\text{-}78)$$

---

† One of the $dx_i$'s can be eliminated from this equation through the relation $\sum_i dx_i = 0$. All the remaining variables are then independent. This procedure is illustrated on p. 80 for another equation of similar form. In Eq. (2-76) as it stands the variables are not all independent; hence certain mathematical operations on it are excluded.

Similarly, transformation of Eq. (2-76) yields

$$d \ln \varphi = \frac{-\alpha}{RT} dP + \frac{\Delta H'}{RT^2} dT + \sum_i (\ln \hat{\varphi}_i \, dx_i). \qquad (2\text{-}79)\dagger$$

For a fluid at constant composition Eqs. (2-78) and (2-79) both reduce to

$$d \ln \varphi = \frac{-\alpha}{RT} dP + \frac{\Delta H'}{RT^2} dT. \qquad (2\text{-}80)$$

The purpose of this section has been the development of Eqs. (2-75) through (2-80) in the most direct fashion possible. They are general equations, and form the basis for much of what follows in this monograph. The reason for this is that singly and in combination they represent a most concise means of storing much information about the thermodynamic behavior of fluids. It should be noted that while Eqs. (2-75), (2-76), and (2-77) are commonly applied to either liquids or gases, Eqs. (2-78), (2-79), and (2-80) are usually applied only to gases or vapors.

**2.6. Another Expression for the Chemical Potential.** It has already been pointed out that it is not always convenient to use temperature and pressure as primary variables. However, these are special variables with respect to the Gibbs function, as shown by the general functional equation

$$n G = g(P, T, n_1, n_2, n_3, \ldots).$$

Our particular attention to this function has led to the emphasis of $P$ and $T$ as primary variables. But temperature and volume (or density) are for practical reasons often more suitable variables than temperature and pressure.

Temperature and volume are the special variables of the Helmholtz function. Thus we have the general functional relationship

$$n A = a(T, n V, n_1, n_2, n_3, \ldots).$$

It follows that

$$d(n A) = \frac{\partial(n A)}{\partial T} dT + \frac{\partial(n A)}{\partial(n V)} d(n V) + \frac{\partial(n A)}{\partial n_1} dn_1 + \frac{\partial(n A)}{\partial n_2} dn_2 + \cdots$$

As a result of Eqs. (2-13) and (2-14) we may write

$$d(n A) = -n S \, dT - P \, d(n V) + \sum_i \left[ \frac{\partial(n A)}{\partial n_i} \right]_{T,\,(n V),\, n_{k \neq i}} dn_i. \qquad (2\text{-}81)$$

From the basic definitions of $G$ and $A$, we get

$$G = A + P V$$

and

$$n G = n A + P(n V).$$

<hr />

† The footnote on page 37 applies to this equation as well as to Eq. (2-76).

Therefore

$$d(n\,G) = d(n\,A) + P\,d(n\,V) + n\,V\,dP.$$

Combining this equation with Eq. (2-72), we have

$$d(n\,A) = -n\,S\,dT - P\,d(n\,V) + \sum_i (\mu_i\,dn_i). \qquad (2\text{-}82)$$

Equations (2-82) and (2-81) may be compared term by term, for both give $d(n\,A)$ as a function of the same independent variables. As a result, we have

$$\mu_i = \left[\frac{\partial (n\,G)}{\partial n_i}\right]_{T,\,P,\,n_{k\neq i}} = \left[\frac{\partial (n\,A)}{\partial n_i}\right]_{T,\,(n\,V),\,n_{k\neq i}}. \qquad (2\text{-}83)$$

The choice of which expression to use for determining values for $\mu_i$ depends on which set of primary variables is more convenient.

CHAPTER 3

# BEHAVIOR
# OF CONSTANT-COMPOSITION FLUIDS

**3.1. Thermodynamic Properties from $P$-$V$-$T$ Data.** For the calculation of the thermodynamic properties of constant-composition fluids, both liquid and gaseous, the most common experimental measurements are of $P$-$V$-$T$ data for the single phases and of vapor pressures to relate the properties of vapor and liquid phases in equilibrium. The designation constant-composition includes pure materials.

The properties of homogeneous fluids may be considered functions of temperature and pressure. However, $P$-$V$-$T$ data are used to determine the influence of pressure only. So for the moment we will consider the property changes with pressure of a pure material or constant-composition solution along an isotherm. For gases at constant temperature, Eq. (2-80) becomes:

$$d \ln\varphi = \frac{-\alpha}{RT} dP. \tag{3-1}$$

Integrating at constant $T$ from the zero-pressure state to a state at finite pressure $P$, we have

$$\ln\varphi - \ln\varphi^* = -\frac{1}{RT}\int_0^P \alpha \, dP.$$

But $\varphi^* = \dfrac{f^*}{P^*} = 1$; therefore

$$\ln\varphi = -\frac{1}{RT}\int_0^P \alpha \, dP. \tag{3-2}$$

Since $\alpha = (RT/P) - V$, values of $\alpha$ as a function of $P$ at a given temperature $T$ can be calculated from $P$-$V$-$T$ data. Moreover, the value of $\alpha$ as pressure approaches zero is finite, so no difficulty arises in evaluation of the integral. Values of $\ln\varphi$ can therefore be calculated as a function of pressure for various constant temperatures, and a plot of $\ln\varphi$ vs. $P$ with $T$ as a parameter can be constructed. Cross plots can then be made of $\ln\varphi$ vs. $T$ with $P$ as parameter.

At constant pressure, Eq. (2-80) may be written

$$\left(\frac{\partial \ln \varphi}{\partial T}\right)_P = \frac{\Delta H'}{RT^2}$$

or

$$\Delta H' = RT^2 \left(\frac{\partial \ln \varphi}{\partial T}\right)_P. \tag{3-3}$$

Thus values of $\Delta H'$ can be determined at a series of constant temperatures by taking slopes to the curves of $\ln \varphi$ vs. $T$. We now have values of $\ln \varphi$ and $\Delta H'$ as functions of pressure at various constant temperatures.

Since by definition $G = H - TS$, then also $G^{id} = H^{id} - TS^{id}$. By difference we get for a given temperature and pressure

$$G^{id} - G = H^{id} - H - T(S^{id} - S)$$

or

$$G^{id} - G = \Delta H' - T\Delta S', \tag{3-4}$$

where $\Delta S'$ is the entropy deviation, defined in a fashion analogous to the enthalpy deviation. By Eq. (2-56), $dG = RT\, d \ln f$ at constant temperature. Integration of this equation from the real-gas state to the ideal-gas state gives

$$G^{id} - G = RT \ln \frac{P}{f} = -RT \ln \varphi.$$

Therefore Eq. (3-4) becomes

$$-RT \ln \varphi = \Delta H' - T\Delta S'$$

or

$$\Delta S' = \frac{\Delta H'}{T} + R \ln \varphi. \tag{3-5}$$

By Eq. (3-5) we can now calculate values of the entropy deviation as a function of pressure for various temperatures from the previously determined values of $\ln \varphi$ and $\Delta H'$.

All that remains is to show how the ideal-gas values $H^{id}$ and $S^{id}$ are determined as functions of temperature and pressure, for

$$H = H^{id} - \Delta H' \tag{3-6}$$

and

$$S = S^{id} - \Delta S'. \tag{3-7}$$

Since $V$ is known from the primary $P$-$V$-$T$ data, all other properties can then be calculated from their defining equations.

For an ideal gas by Eq. (2-27A)

$$d H^{id} = C_P^{id}\, dT,$$

where $H^{id}$ and $C_P^{id}$ are shown to be functions of temperature only in Chapter 2. Thus

$$H^{id} - H_0^{id} = \int_{T_0}^{T} C_P^{id}\, dT, \tag{3-8}$$

where $H_0^{id}$ is an arbitrarily selected value of the ideal-gas-state enthalpy at an arbitrarily selected temperature $T_0$. Once a value of $H_0^{id}$ is selected all values of $H^{id}$ are calculable by Eq. (3-8) provided $C_P^{id}$ is known as a function of temperature. Such a relationship is often provided by statistical calculations based on spectroscopic measurements or alternatively by direct heat capacity measurements on gases at very low pressures, where the heat capacity approaches the ideal-gas value. We will assume here that such data are available and that $C_P^{id}$ is known to us as a function of temperature.

For an ideal gas, by Eq. (2-30A)

$$d\,S^{id} = \frac{C_P^{id}}{T}\,dT - \frac{R}{P}\,dP.$$

In integral form this becomes

$$S^{id} - S_0^{id} = \int_{T_0}^{T} \frac{C_P^{id}}{T}\,dT - R\int_{P_0}^{P} \frac{dP}{P}, \tag{3-9}$$

where $S_0^{id}$ is an arbitrarily selected value of the ideal-gas state entropy at the arbitrarily selected conditions $T_0$ and $P_0$.

Combining Eq. (3-8) with (3-6) and Eq. (3-9) with (3-7) we get

$$H - H_0^{id} = \int_{T_0}^{T} C_P^{id}\,dT - \Delta H' \tag{3-10}$$

and

$$S - S_0^{id} = \int_{T_0}^{T} \frac{C_P^{id}}{T}\,dT - R\ln\frac{P}{P_0} - \Delta S'. \tag{3-11}$$

Once the temperature and pressure, $T_0$ and $P_0$, of the ideal-gas state that is to serve as the *reference* state for the material are selected, the right-hand sides of Eqs. (3-10) and (3-11) can be evaluated from ideal-gas heat capacities and $P$-$V$-$T$ data. Values of $(H - H_0^{id})$ and $(S - S_0^{id})$ can then be tabulated or plotted as functions of $T$ and $P$. The selection of a numerical value for $H_0^{id}$ and for $S_0^{id}$ is arbitrary. Frequently, $H_0^{id}$ and $S_0^{id}$ are chosen so as to make $H$ and $S$ zero in some predetermined real state of the material. Once selected, these values are constant, and do not affect property *changes* of the material.

The methods described are used for gases from the zero-pressure state up to the pressure at which condensation begins, i.e., the dew point, or if the temperature is above the critical temperature, they are used to the ultimate pressure for which $P$-$V$-$T$ data are available. For convenience, calculations are invariably made along isotherms.

For a pure vapor the dew point occurs at the vapor pressure. When this pressure is reached along an isotherm, the property being represented generally changes abruptly from that observed for the vapor phase to that observed for the liquid phase after condensation at constant temperature and pressure. For example, the specific volume of saturated liquid $V_i^L$ is very different from that for saturated vapor $V_i^V$; there is a discrete enthalpy change from $H_i^L$ to $H_i^V$, and a discrete entropy change from $S_i^L$ to $S_i^V$. The exception is the Gibbs function. We noted in Section 2.1 that as a result of Eq. (2-4) the Gibbs function for systems at equilibrium is always given by $G = g(T, P)$. This is true even for heterogeneous systems. We know from experience that when a pure material evaporates or condenses at constant temperature, the pressure also remains constant. Thus for such a process $dG_i = 0$, and this can only mean that $G_i^L = G_i^V$. Also, from Eq. (2–54) we have

$$dG_i = RT\,d\ln f_i = 0.$$

Hence $f_i^L = f_i^V$ for liquid and vapor states of pure $i$ in equilibrium.

Equation (2-77) may be written both for a liquid phase and for a vapor phase of pure $i$:

$$d\ln f_i^V = \frac{V_i^V}{RT}dP + \frac{H_i^{\text{id}} - H_i^V}{RT^2}dT,$$

$$d\ln f_i^L = \frac{V_i^L}{RT}dP + \frac{H_i^{\text{id}} - H_i^L}{RT^2}dT.$$

For phases in equilibrium, the pressure and temperature are the same and $f_i^V = f_i^L$. Subtraction therefore gives

$$0 = \frac{V_i^V - V_i^L}{RT}dP - \frac{H_i^V - H_i^L}{RT^2}dT$$

or

$$\frac{dP}{dT} = \frac{\Delta H_i^{\text{Vap}}}{T\Delta V_i^{\text{Vap}}}, \tag{3-12}$$

where $dP/dT$ is the slope of the vapor pressure curve at the particular temperature being considered,

$$\Delta H_i^{\text{Vap}} = H_i^V - H_i^L,$$

the latent heat of vaporization, and

$$\Delta V_i^{\text{Vap}} = V_i^V - V_i^L,$$

the volume change of vaporization. This is the famous Clapeyron equation, which allows calculation of $H_i^V - H_i^L$ from $P$-$V$-$T$ measurements and knowledge of the vapor-pressure curve:

$$H_i^V - H_i^L = \Delta H^{\text{Vap}} = T(V_i^V - V_i^L)(dP/dT). \tag{3-13}$$

Since $P$ and $T$ are constant during the vaporization process, Eq. (2-2) becomes $\Delta H^{\text{Vap}} = T\Delta S^{\text{Vap}}$. Hence the entropy of vaporization is given by

$$S_i^V - S_i^L = \Delta S^{\text{Vap}} = \Delta H^{\text{Vap}}/T. \tag{3-14}$$

4*

Thus once the vapor-pressure curve is established and saturated liquid and vapor volumes are measured for a pure material, the enthalpy and entropy values of liquid and vapor are connected by Eqs. (3-13) and (3-14).

For the liquid phase Eqs. (3-2), (3-3), and (3-5) are still valid and could be applied to the calculation of liquid properties, but are not commonly used. This procedure would make the Clapeyron equation for pure materials unnecessary. Since the properties of liquids change only slowly with pressure, it is generally more convenient to apply Eqs. (2-25) and (2-26) along an isotherm from the saturated liquid state to "sub-cooled" liquid states. Integration of these equations for constant-composition liquids gives:

$$S - S^L = - \int_{P_s}^{P} \left( \frac{\partial V}{\partial T} \right)_P \mathrm{d}P \qquad \text{(const } T) \qquad (3\text{-}15)$$

and

$$H - H^L = \int_{P_s}^{P} \left[ V - T \left( \frac{\partial V}{\partial T} \right)_P \right] \mathrm{d}P \qquad \text{(const } T), \qquad (3\text{-}16)$$

where the superscript $L$ designates the saturated liquid state and $P_s$ is the liquid saturation pressure (vapor pressure) for the isotherm in question. These equations allow the extension of isotherms into the liquid region provided $P$-$V$-$T$ data for the liquid are known.

Thus we have developed the general equations which allow calculation of the thermodynamic properties of constant-composition fluids in the gaseous and liquid regions from $P$-$V$-$T$ data, vapor pressure data, and ideal-gas heat capacities. Other methods of calculation from the same data are certainly possible, but none is more direct. From such calculations tables of thermodynamic data are readily tabulated and thermodynamic diagrams may be prepared.

The experimental determination of $P$-$V$-$T$ data may be accomplished by various means, the most common of which are reviewed by Rowlinson.[†] The alternatives to $P$-$V$-$T$ measurements for gases are very limited, because the types of experimental measurement which provide entry into the network of equations relating the thermodynamic properties are few in number. The direct measurement of heat capacities and other thermal quantities is a possibility, as is the measurement of Joule–Thomson coefficients. However, practical difficulties have worked against the use of such methods, and they are seldom used. It seems safe to say that calculations of the thermodynamic properties of pure gases are usually based on experimental $P$-$V$-$T$ data, although other measurements are sometimes used to test the accuracy of results.

[†] S. Flügge (ed.), *Encyclopedia of Physics*, Vol. XII, pp. 1–72, Springer-Verlag, Berlin, 1958.

**3.2. Equations of State.** Equations (3-2) and (3-3) for the calculation of the effect of pressure on thermodynamic properties are based on the assumption that $T$ and $P$ are the most convenient primary variables. For direct graphical or numerical computation procedures this is probably true. It is also true if one makes use of an *equation of state* explicit in volume to represent the $P$-$V$-$T$ data. Such expressions are usually empirical. The earliest and simplest resulted from the combination of Boyle's and Charles' laws, and is known as the ideal-gas law, $PV = RT$. Many attempts to find a more realistic relation of fluid volume to the conditions of temperature and pressure have been made since the pioneering work of van der Waals prior to 1873. The object of all such efforts has been to find an equation suitable in form for all materials, but which allows for differences between materials in the assignment of values to the constants appearing in the equation. Hundreds of such equations have been proposed, but none has proved entirely satisfactory.

The only equation of state which has been shown to have exact physical significance on a molecular scale is the virial expansion for gases, which in its proper form gives the compressibility factor $Z$ as a power series in density or $1/V$:

$$Z = 1 + \frac{B}{V} + \frac{C}{V^2} + \frac{D}{V^3} + \cdots \tag{3-17}$$

The coefficients $B, C, D$, etc., are known as virial coefficients, with $B$ designated as the second virial coefficient, $C$, the third, etc. For a given material they are functions of temperature only.

Since $Z = PV/RT$, the virial equation is seen to be explicit in $P$ rather than $V$, and does not therefore lend itself conveniently to the use of $P$ and $T$ as primary variables. This no doubt accounts for the long and unfortunate neglect of this equation by engineers. With the present availability of computing machines computational inconvenience is of little importance and is far outweighed by the great utility of this equation. Hence we will consider its use in detail.

The virial equation can be developed by the methods of statistical mechanics, from which the virial coefficients take on physical significance as reflecting the molecular interactions of particular numbers of molecules. Thus it has been shown that the second virial coefficient accounts for interactions between pairs of molecules. If $B$ represents the second virial coefficient for a gaseous solution of $n$ constituents, it is given exactly by

$$B = \sum_i^n \sum_j^n y_i \, y_j \, B_{ij}. \tag{3-18}$$

For a binary solution consisting of constituents 1 and 2, this equation becomes:

$$B = y_1^2 \, B_{11} + 2y_1 \, y_2 \, B_{12} + y_2^2 \, B_{22}, \tag{3-19}$$

where $y$ is used to represent mole fraction in gaseous systems. The coefficients $B_{11}$ and $B_{22}$ are the second virial coefficients for the pure gases 1 and 2 at the temperature of the solution, and $B_{12}$ is known as the interaction or cross coefficient. All are functions of temperature only. Experimental values of $B_{12}$ are calculated from Eq. (3-19). It is convenient to define an additional factor $\delta_{12}$ by the equation

$$\delta_{12} = 2B_{12} - B_{11} - B_{22}. \tag{3-20}$$

Combination of Eqs. (3-19) and (3-20) gives

$$B = y_1 B_{11} + y_2 B_{22} + y_1 y_2 \delta_{12}. \tag{3-21}$$

The third virial coefficient accounts for interactions among triples of molecules. If $C$ represents the third virial coefficient for a gaseous solution of $n$ constituents, it is given by

$$C = \sum_i^n \sum_j^n \sum_k^n y_i y_j y_k C_{ijk}. \tag{3-22}$$

For a binary solution of constituents 1 and 2, this reduces to:

$$C = y_1^3 C_{111} + 3y_1^2 y_2 C_{112} + 3y_1 y_2^2 C_{122} + y_2^3 C_{222}. \tag{3-23}$$

The coefficients $C_{111}$ and $C_{222}$ are the third virial coefficients of the pure gases 1 and 2, and $C_{112}$ and $C_{122}$ are the cross coefficients. Again they are functions of temperature only.

As before, additional factors may be defined:

$$\left. \begin{aligned} \delta_{112} &= 3C_{112} - 2C_{111} - C_{222}, \\ \delta_{122} &= 3C_{122} - C_{111} - 2C_{222}. \end{aligned} \right\} \tag{3-24}$$

Equations (3-23) and (3-24) combine to give

$$C = y_1 C_{111} + y_2 C_{222} + y_1 y_2 (y_1 \delta_{112} + y_2 \delta_{122}). \tag{3-25}$$

One could continue in a like fashion with the higher virial coefficients. However, virtually nothing is known about the virial coefficients beyond the third. Fortunately, the virial equation truncated to the second term is a highly reliable equation of state at low pressures. The second term of the virial equation represents no more than a first-order correction to the ideal-gas law, and as such provides an entirely suitable extension to the simplest of $P$-$V$-$T$ expressions for low pressures.

Truncated to three terms, the virial equation, as we shall see, represents data accurately to moderate pressures, and is therefore entirely adequate for the vast majority of engineering applications.

Since the basis of the virial equation is rooted in statistical mechanics, it is in principle possible to calculate the virial coefficients from considerations of the intermolecular potential functions. The possibility of a theoretical approach to the calculation of the virial coefficients gives the virial equation a tremendous advantage over all empirical or semi-empirical equations of state. Much progress has already been made along these lines, and engineers must become aware of such developments. Classical thermodynamics is limited in the information it can provide, and progress beyond its limitations must come from the considerations of statistical mechanics and molecular theory. However, these subjects are not within the scope of this monograph. A detailed treatment is given by Hirschfelder, Curtiss, and Bird.†

The second and third virial coefficients can of course be determined from experimental $P$-$V$-$T$ data. However, this must be done with caution. If one has volumetric data for a gas along an isotherm and over a considerable pressure range, a simple fitting of an equation of the form

$$Z = 1 + \frac{B}{V} + \frac{C}{V^2} + \frac{D}{V^3} + \cdots$$

to the data may yield coefficients $B$, $C$, $D$, etc., which are quite unrelated to the virial coefficients of theoretical significance that we have been considering. A far more satisfactory procedure is first to truncate the virial equation to three terms and to rearrange it as follows:

$$(Z - 1)(V) = B + \frac{C}{V}. \tag{3-26}$$

This equation shows that if the truncated virial equation is to represent the data, then a plot of $(Z - 1)(V)$ vs. $1/V$ for an isotherm must be a straight line. If a straight line is obtained, its intercept at $1/V = 0$ is $B$ and its slope is $C$.††

Experience with reliable data shows that Eq. (3-26) is in fact valid up to moderate pressures. Thus the function $(Z - 1)(V)$, which can be shown to be equal to $-Z\alpha$, is a particularly valuable one for smoothing $P$-$V$-$T$ data and for extrapolation of data to zero pressure, i.e., to $1/V = 0$. It seems safe to say that data which do not approach linearity on a $(Z - 1)(V)$ vs. $1/V$ plot as $1/V$ becomes small are incorrect. The quantity $(Z - 1)(V)$ becomes very sensitive to small experimental errors as $1/V$ or $P$ approaches zero. Hence data for very low pressures can be expected to scatter, and this throws greater weight on the data at higher pressures. Nevertheless, the direct smoothing of $Z$ values or of $\alpha$ values is not nearly so reliable as the method recommended here, for the reason that Eq. (3-26) is known from both theory and experience to be a reliable guide.

Figure 3-1 will serve as an example. Data for nitrogen at 340°F from two different compilations are shown. The circles are calculated from smoothed values of $Z$ as reported by Sage and Lacey.§ The solid line is

† J. O. Hirschfelder, C. F. Curtiss, and R. B. Bird, *Molecular Theory of Gases and Liquids*, John Wiley, New York, 1954.

†† Strictly, $C$ is the limiting value of the slope on this plot as $1/V$ approaches zero.

§ B. H. Sage and W. N. Lacey, Monograph, API Research Project 37, "Thermodynamic Properties of the Lighter Hydrocarbons and Nitrogen", American Petroleum Institute, New York, 1950.

based on data tabulated in Circular 564 of the U.S. Bureau of Standards†
at pressures from 0.01 to 100 atm. The Bureau of Standards compilation
shows that the virial equation truncated after three terms is valid for nitrogen
at 340°F (444.25°K) up to 100 atm. Although the values of Sage and Lacey
at pressures above 140 atm. appear to be essentially consistent with the
NBS values (as indicated by the dashed curve), their values at lower pressures

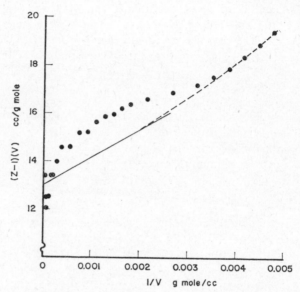

Fig. 3-1. Smoothing plot for *P-V-T* data. Nitrogen isotherm at 340°F. Circles
from Sage and Lacey. Solid line from NBS compilation.

were obviously not obtained by smoothing in accordance with the virial
equation. The NBS data are obviously to be preferred within the pressure
range where they are given.

Figure 3-2 shows experimental data for the nitrogen–n-butane system
at 370°F as given by Evans and Watson.†† The points represent experimental
values. Data are available for five compositions. Lines representing values
for the pure constituents are also shown. The one for nitrogen is based
on the NBS compilation,§ and the one for n-butane, on data of Sage and
Lacey.§§ For pure butane the truncated virial equation holds only in the
region where the solid line is shown. The second and third virial coefficients
for the mixtures and pure constituents as determined from these graphs
are shown as points on Fig. 3-3, which gives the composition dependence

† Hilsenrath *et al.*, *Tables of Thermal Properties of Gases*, National Bureau of Stan-
dards Circular 564, Washington, 1955. Pergamon Press, 1960.
†† R. B. Evans III and G. M. Watson, *Chem. and Eng. Data Series*, **1**, 67 (1956).
§ Op. cit.
§§ Op. cit.

of the virial coefficients. The curves on this graph are calculated from Eqs. (3-21) and (3-25) by use of the constants given with Fig. 3-3. The required cross virial coefficients were determined so as to give the most reasonable fit of the curves to the points. The suitability of the forms of

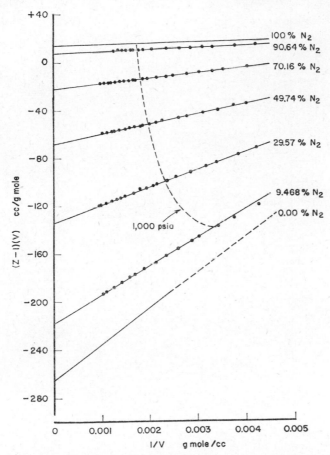

FIG. 3-2. Smoothing plots for nitrogen–n-butane data at 370°F, used for determination of second and third virial coefficients.

the equations giving the composition dependence of mixture virial coefficients is apparent from Fig. 3-3.

Another example is shown in Fig. 3-4 where the data reported by McKetta and coworkers† for $SO_2$ are plotted for three temperatures. The isotherm at 157.5°C is the critical isotherm; that at 50°C is well below the critical, and terminates at the two-phase boundary at 8.484 atm.; the one at 250°C

† T. L. Kang, L. J. Hirth, K. A. Kobe, and J. J. McKetta, *J. Chem. and Eng. Data*, **6**, 220 (1961).

is well above the critical. The virial coefficients determined by means of this graph were used with the virial equation to calculate compressibility factors for the purpose of comparison with experimental values. This comparison is shown in Fig. 3-5. For the 50°C isotherm no deviations between

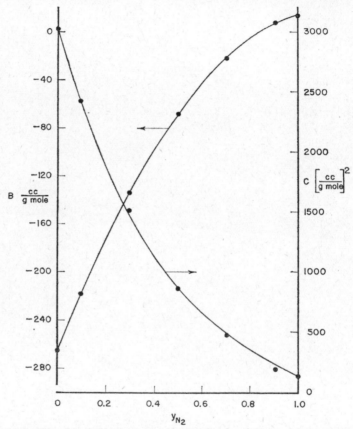

FIG. 3-3. Second and third virial coefficients for the nitrogen–n-butane system at 370°F. Nitrogen is constituent 1; n-butane is constituent 2. Circles represent values from experimental $P$-$V$-$T$ data. The curves are calculated through the use of the following constants:

$$
\begin{aligned}
B_{11} &= \phantom{-}14 & C_{222} &= \phantom{-}30{,}250 \\
B_{22} &= -\phantom{0}265 & \delta_{112} &= -18{,}000 \\
\delta_{12} &= \phantom{-}232 & \delta_{122} &= -40{,}000 \\
C_{111} &= \phantom{-}1300 &
\end{aligned}
$$

experimental and calculated values of $Z$ are detectable on the graph. For the critical isotherm and the isotherm at the higher temperature, agreement is seen to be excellent up to densities of about two-thirds the critical density. The pressure range depends on the isotherm considered.

The shape of the critical isotherm on this type of plot is in marked contrast to that observed when $Z$ is plotted against $P$ rather than $1/V$. The single direction of curvature of the isotherms on a $Z$ vs. $1/V$ plot is what allows a quadratic equation in $1/V$ to fit the data over a considerable range. A similar expansion of $Z$ as a power series in $P$ has nevertheless found considerable use:

$$Z = 1 + B'P + C'P^2 + D'P^3 + \cdots \tag{3-27}$$

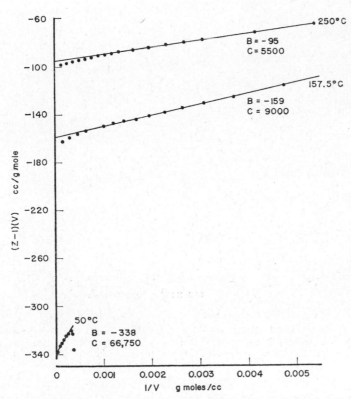

FIG. 3-4. Smoothing plots for $SO_2$ data for determination of second and third virial coefficients. Units of $B$ are cc/g mole. Units of $C$ are $(\text{cc/g mole})^2$.

However, this expansion when truncated to the same number of terms as the virial expansion does not usually represent data over so wide a range of pressures as the virial. Its sole advantage, and it is no longer an important one, is that it is explicit in volume. This makes easier the calculation of volume and other thermodynamic properties at given values of $T$ and $P$.

The expansions in $P$ and in $1/V$ can be related. However, a term by term comparison of truncated series is not possible.† In the limit as $P$ and $1/V$

† For a detailed treatment of the relationship between these two expansions see: Leo Epstein, *J. Chem. Phys.* **20**, 1981 (1952); Putnam and Kilpatrick, *ibid.* **21**, 951 (1953).

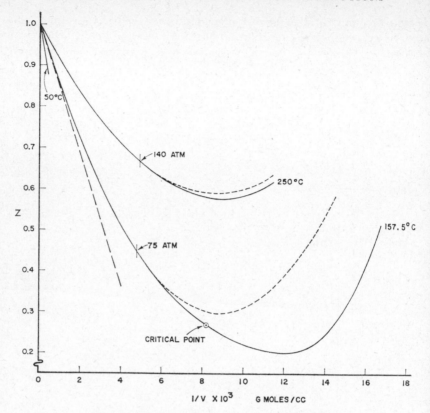

FIG. 3-5. Compressibility factor vs. Density for $SO_2$.
——— Experimental data; ------ Calculated from the virial expansion,
Eq. (3-17), truncated to three terms; ----- Calculated for the critical
isotherm from the virial expansion truncated to two terms.

approach zero, the two expansions must become identical. This is the basis for
the determination of the relations between $B$ and $B'$, between $C$ and $C'$, etc.
    Since
$$V = ZRT/P,$$
Eq. (3-17) can be written
$$\frac{(Z-1)}{P} = \frac{B}{ZRT} + \frac{CP}{(ZRT)^2} + \frac{DP^2}{(ZRT)^3} + \cdots$$

Differentiation with respect to pressure at constant temperature gives:

$$\frac{\partial\left(\dfrac{Z-1}{P}\right)}{\partial P} = \frac{-B}{Z^2RT}\left(\frac{\partial Z}{\partial P}\right) + \frac{C}{(ZRT)^2}\left[1 - \frac{2P}{Z}\left(\frac{\partial Z}{\partial P}\right)\right]$$
$$+ \frac{DP}{(ZRT)^3}\left[2 - \frac{3P}{Z}\left(\frac{\partial Z}{\partial P}\right)\right].$$

Taking the limit of the first of these equations as pressure approaches zero, we get:

$$\lim_{P \to 0} \left( \frac{Z - 1}{P} \right) = \frac{B}{RT}.$$

If the expansion for $Z$ is written directly in $P$, that is, Eq. (3-27), the limit of $(Z - 1)/P$ as $P$ approaches zero is obviously

$$\lim_{P \to 0} \left( \frac{Z - 1}{P} \right) = B'.$$

Application of l'Hôpital's rule shows this limit also to be $(\partial Z / \partial P)_T$. Thus we have

$$B' = \frac{B}{RT} = \lim_{P \to 0} \left( \frac{\partial Z}{\partial P} \right)_T. \qquad (3\text{-}28)\dagger$$

Making use of this equation, we take the limit of the second equation derived above:

$$\lim_{P \to 0} \frac{\partial \left( \dfrac{Z - 1}{P} \right)}{\partial P} = \frac{-B^2}{(RT)^2} + \frac{C}{(RT)^2} = \frac{C - B^2}{(RT)^2}.$$

But from Eq. (3-27)

$$\frac{\partial \left( \dfrac{Z - 1}{P} \right)}{\partial P} = C' + 2D' P + \cdots$$

and

$$\lim_{P \to 0} \frac{\partial \left( \dfrac{Z - 1}{P} \right)}{\partial P} = C'.$$

Thus

$$C' = \frac{C - B^2}{(RT)^2}. \qquad (3\text{-}29)$$

We can now write Eq. (3-27) as

$$Z = 1 + \frac{BP}{RT} + \frac{(C - B^2)}{(RT)^2} P^2 + \cdots \qquad (3\text{-}30)$$

This gives $Z$ as a power series in $P$ with the constants written in terms of the true virial coefficients. This equation has the advantages of being explicit in $V$ and at the same time of having coefficients with theoretical significance. However, it is no better than the original expansion in $P$ on which it is based.

† Comparison of this equation with the one for $\alpha^*$ on page 28 shows that

$$B = B' RT = RT \left( \frac{\partial Z}{\partial P} \right)_T^* = -\alpha^*.$$

The virial expansion and Eq. (3-30) can be used in conjunction with Eqs. (3-2), (3-3), and (3-5) for the calculation of the pressure dependency of the thermodynamic properties of gases. Substituting in Eq. (3-2) for $\alpha$ as given by Eq. (2-53) we have

$$\ln \varphi = \int_0^P (Z - 1) \frac{dP}{P} \quad \text{(const } T\text{)}. \tag{3-31}$$

The most convenient substitution for $(Z - 1)$ that we can make here is by Eq. (3-30) truncated to three terms:

$$\ln \varphi = \int_0^P \left[ \frac{B}{RT} + \frac{(C - B^2)}{(RT)^2} P \right] dP.$$

Integration gives:

$$\ln \varphi = \frac{BP}{RT} + \left( \frac{C - B^2}{2} \right) \left( \frac{P}{RT} \right)^2. \tag{3-32}$$

Although this equation is easily derived, its range of validity is limited to that of Eq. (3-27). A better expression results from use of the true virial expansion. What is needed for this is a convenient rearrangement of the quantity $(Z - 1) \frac{dP}{P}$ in Eq. (3-31).

Since $PV = ZRT$, then at constant $T$

$$PdV + VdP = RTdZ.$$

Rearrangement gives

$$\frac{dP}{P} = \frac{dZ}{Z} - \frac{dV}{V}.$$

Therefore

$$(Z - 1) \frac{dP}{P} = (Z - 1) \frac{dZ}{Z} - (Z - 1) \frac{dV}{V}$$

or

$$(Z - 1) \frac{dP}{P} = dZ - d \ln Z + (Z - 1)(V) \, d \left( \frac{1}{V} \right).$$

But by Eq. (3-26)

$$(Z - 1)(V) = B + C/V.$$

Hence

$$\ln \varphi = \int_0^P (Z - 1) \frac{dP}{P} = \int_1^Z dZ - \int_0^{\ln Z} d \ln Z + \int_0^{1/V} \left[ B + C \left( \frac{1}{V} \right) \right] d \left( \frac{1}{V} \right).$$

Integration gives

$$\ln \varphi = Z - 1 - \ln Z + \frac{B}{V} + \frac{C}{2V^2}. \tag{3-33}$$

Substitution for $Z - 1$ by the virial equation gives an equivalent form of this expression:

$$\ln\varphi = -\ln Z + \frac{2B}{V} + \frac{3C}{2V^2}. \tag{3-34}$$

An approximate form of this equation may be obtained by expanding $\ln Z$.

$$\ln Z = \ln\left[1 + \frac{B}{V} + \frac{C}{V^2}\right].$$

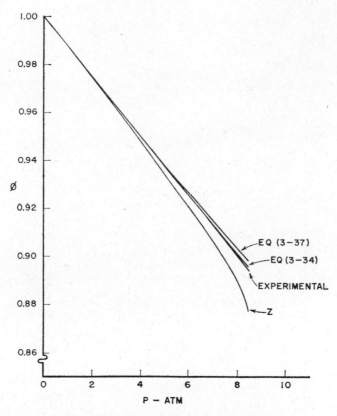

FIG. 3-6. Fugacity coefficients for $SO_2$ at 50°C.

Since $\ln(1 + x) = x - x^2/2$ for small values of $x$

$$\ln Z = \frac{B}{V} + \frac{C}{V^2} - \frac{B^2}{2V^2}, \tag{3-35}$$

where terms containing powers on $V$ higher than the second have been dropped. Substitution in Eq. (3-34) gives

$$\ln\varphi = \frac{B}{V} + \frac{B^2 + C}{2V^2}. \tag{3-36}$$

Further approximations are possible for low pressures where the virial equation truncated to just two terms is essentially valid. Similar truncation of Eq. (3-32) gives

$$\ln\varphi = \frac{B\,P}{R\,T} \qquad (3\text{-}37)$$

an equation very commonly used for low pressures. In addition, comparison

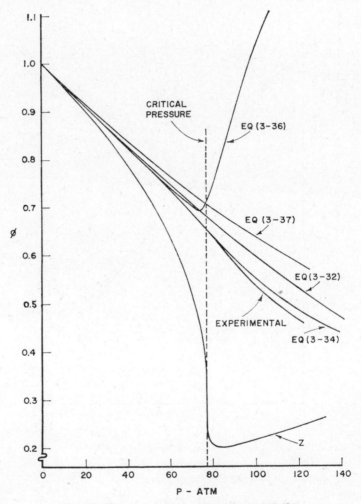

FIG. 3-7. Fugacity coefficients for $SO_2$ at 157.5°C.

of Eqs. (3-35) and (3-36) shows that $\varphi$ should become equal to $Z$ at low pressures where the second-order terms become negligible.

Results calculated from these various expressions are compared in Figs. 3-6, 3-7, and 3-8 for the $SO_2$ data previously illustrated in Figs. 3-4 and 3-5. The virial coefficients used were determined from Fig. 3-4 and are given there. Also shown are results calculated by graphical integration of the experimental data by Eq. (3-31). These are labeled experimental values.

Figure 3-6 giving results for $SO_2$ at 50°C extends to a pressure of only 8.5 atm. At these low pressures Eqs. (3-32), (3-34), and (3-36) all give essen-

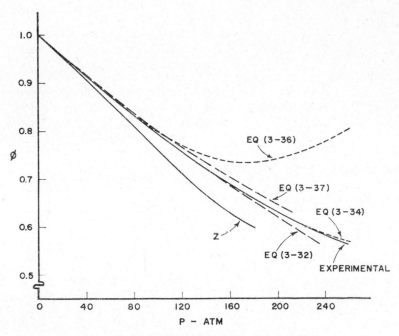

FIG. 3-8. Fugacity coefficients for $SO_2$ at 250°C.

tially the same results; so only Eq. (3-34) is shown in the figure. It deviates only slightly from the experimental curve as the saturation pressure is approached. Equation (3-37) is also seen to be a good approximation at these pressures. At pressures up to 2 atm., $\varphi$ is seen to be essentially the same as $Z$.

Figure 3-7 shows results for the critical isotherm. Equation (3-34) is seen to be essentially valid up to the critical pressure. Equation (3-36) gives excellent results up to 50 atm., but fails completely near the critical pressure. The other equations are seen to be valid up to pressures which depend on the degree of approximation represented.

For $SO_2$ at 250°C, Eq. (3-34) gives excellent agreement with experimental values at least to 200 atm. Equation (3-36) again behaves badly at higher pressures. The superiority of Eq. (3-34) at higher pressures is clearly evident from both Figs. 3-7 and 3-8. There is no really good reason to use approximate equations if accurate values of $B$ and $C$ are available. Where only the second virial coefficient is known, Eq. (3-37) is both simple and accurate at low pressures. As a good approximation it may be used to moderate pressures.

We turn now to the calculation of other properties through use of the virial equation. We would like to make use of Eq. (3-34) for $\ln\varphi$, because it has been demonstrated to be the best of the equations based on the virial expansion. However, it cannot be easily used with Eq. (3-3) for the development of an expression for $\Delta H'$. We return instead to Eq. (2-77):

$$d\ln f = \frac{V}{RT}dP + \frac{\Delta H'}{RT^2}dT.$$

If temperature and volume are taken as independent variables, then changes at constant volume must come about solely as a result of temperature changes. Under these conditions the above equation can be written:

$$\left(\frac{\partial \ln f}{\partial T}\right)_V = \frac{V}{RT}\left(\frac{\partial P}{\partial T}\right)_V + \frac{\Delta H'}{RT^2}.$$

Since $PV = ZRT$

$$V\left(\frac{\partial P}{\partial T}\right)_V = RT\left(\frac{\partial Z}{\partial T}\right)_V + RZ$$

or

$$\frac{V}{RT}\left(\frac{\partial P}{\partial T}\right)_V = \left(\frac{\partial Z}{\partial T}\right)_V + \frac{Z}{T}.$$

Our first equation now becomes

$$\frac{\Delta H'}{RT^2} = \left(\frac{\partial \ln f}{\partial T}\right)_V - \left(\frac{\partial Z}{\partial T}\right)_V - \frac{Z}{T}. \qquad (3\text{-}38)$$

From Eq. (3-34) we get

$$\ln f = \ln\frac{P}{Z} + \frac{2B}{V} + \frac{3C}{2V^2}.$$

But

$$P/Z = RT/V.$$

Therefore

$$\ln f = \ln\frac{RT}{V} + \frac{2B}{V} + \frac{3C}{2V^2}$$

and

$$\left(\frac{\partial \ln f}{\partial T}\right)_V = \frac{1}{T} + \frac{2}{V}\frac{dB}{dT} + \frac{3}{2V^2}\frac{dC}{dT}. \qquad (3\text{-}39)$$

Direct differentiation of the virial equation gives

$$\left(\frac{\partial Z}{\partial T}\right)_V = \frac{1}{V}\frac{dB}{dT} + \frac{1}{V^2}\frac{dC}{dT}.$$

Combining this equation and Eq. (3-39) with Eq. (3-38) gives

$$\frac{\Delta H'}{RT} = -(Z-1) + \frac{T}{V}\frac{dB}{dT} + \frac{T}{2V^2}\frac{dC}{dT}.$$

Substitution for $Z - 1$ by the virial equation gives finally

$$\frac{\Delta H'}{RT} = \frac{T}{V}\left[\frac{dB}{dT} - \frac{B}{T}\right] + \frac{T}{V^2}\left[\frac{1}{2}\frac{dC}{dT} - \frac{C}{T}\right]. \qquad (3\text{-}40)$$

From Eq. (3-5) we have

$$\frac{\Delta S'}{R} = \frac{\Delta H'}{RT} + \ln\varphi.$$

Substitution for $\Delta H'/RT$ and for $\ln\varphi$ by Eqs. (3-40) and (3-34) gives

$$\frac{\Delta S'}{R} = -\ln Z + \frac{T}{V}\left[\frac{dB}{dT} + \frac{B}{T}\right] + \frac{1}{2}\frac{T}{V^2}\left[\frac{dC}{dT} + \frac{C}{T}\right]. \qquad (3\text{-}41)$$

For low pressures simplified forms of these equations are adequate. We may make the following approximations.

(a) Neglect the third-virial coefficient terms,
(b) Substitute $P/R$ for $T/V$,
(c) Substitute $B/V$ for $\ln Z$ in accordance with Eq. (3-35) at small values of $1/V$.

These reduce Eqs. (3-40) and (3-41) to

$$\frac{\Delta H'}{RT} = \frac{P}{R}\left[\frac{dB}{dT} - \frac{B}{T}\right] \qquad (3\text{-}42)$$

and

$$\frac{\Delta S'}{R} = \frac{P}{R}\left(\frac{dB}{dT}\right). \qquad (3\text{-}43)$$

Thus we see that for low pressures the enthalpy and entropy deviations for gases are readily calculated to a good approximation from a knowledge of just the second virial coefficient as a function of temperature.

At high pressures the truncated virial equation is inadequate, and equations of greater complexity must be used. Among the many equations that have been proposed for this purpose, the two following indicate the wide range in complexity of modern equations of state. Like the virial equation, both are explicit in $P$.

The Benedict–Webb–Rubin equation† contains eight constants, and represents a high degree of complexity. On the other hand it is capable of representing the $P$-$V$-$T$ behavior of many gases to high accuracy over a reasonable range of conditions:

$$P = \frac{RT}{V} + \frac{B_0 RT - A_0 - C_0/T^2}{V^2} + \frac{bRT - a}{V^3} + \frac{a\alpha}{V^6}$$

$$+ \frac{c}{V^3 T^2}\left(1 + \frac{\gamma}{V^2}\right)e^{-\gamma/V^2}, \qquad (3\text{-}44)$$

† M. Benedict, G. B. Webb, and L. C. Rubin, *J. Chem. Phys.* **8**, 334 (1940).

where $A_0$, $B_0$, $C_0$, $a$, $b$, $c$, $\alpha$, and $\gamma$ are constants. The determination of these constants for a particular gas requires a considerable amount of data, and the procedure is involved. A large number of significant figures must be carried in numerical computations because the successive terms in Eq. (3-44) do not necessarily diminish in importance. Thus the net result of combination of the terms is often a relatively small number resulting from the difference of two larger ones. These problems can certainly be overcome with the use of modern computers, but even so, complexity is a distinct disadvantage.

The Redlich and Kwong equation† contains two constants and is an example of a modern equation of state of minimum complexity. It is relatively easy to use, applies over a very wide range of conditions, but does not give results of high accuracy:

$$P = \frac{RT}{V - b} - \frac{a}{T^{0.5} V(V + b)}. \tag{3-45}$$

One advantage of a two-constant equation of state is that approximate values of the constants can be determined from the critical constants. These relationships are found by imposing the conditions for the existence of the critical point on the equation of state. These are

$$(\partial P / \partial V)_{Tc} = 0 \quad \text{and} \quad (\partial^2 P / \partial V^2)_{Tc} = 0.$$

Applied to the Redlich and Kwong equation, these conditions lead to the following equations:

$$a = 0.4278 R^2 T_c^{2.5} / P_c$$
$$b = 0.0867 R T_c / P_c.$$

Expressions for $\ln \varphi$, $\Delta H'$, and $\Delta S'$ can be determined through the use of any equation of state in a manner analogous to that demonstrated with the virial equation. For a complex equation of state such as the Benedict–Webb–Rubin equation the results can be very accurate, but the computations are involved. For a simpler equation like that of Redlich and Kwong the calculations can be more readily carried out, but the results are not likely to be accurate.

When one is using $P$-$V$-$T$ data at high pressure for the purpose of calculating thermodynamic properties, a useful procedure is to calculate the major part of the desired quantity by a simple equation of state and to determine the remainder by graphical methods. This in effect allows one to work with residuals from an equation of state rather than with deviations from the ideal-gas law. For this purpose we define:

$$\delta Z = Z - Z_{eq}$$

or

$$Z = Z_{eq} + \delta Z, \tag{3-46}$$

† Otto Redlich and J. N. S. Kwong, *Chem. Rev.* **44**, 233 (1949).

where $Z$ represents an experimental value of the compressibility factor and $Z_{eq}$ is a value calculated by means of an equation of state at the same temperature and pressure.

By way of illustration, we will consider the calculation of $\ln\varphi$ values from experimental data through the use of the residuals $\delta Z$. Combination of Eqs. (3-1) and (2-53) gives

$$d\ln\varphi = (Z - 1)\frac{dP}{P}.$$

Substitution for $Z$ by Eq. (3-46) gives:

$$d\ln\varphi = (Z_{eq} - 1)\frac{dP}{P} + \frac{\delta Z}{P}dP.$$

Integration from $P'$ to $P$ gives

$$\ln\varphi = \ln\varphi' + \int_{P'}^{P}(Z_{eq} - 1)\frac{dP}{P} + \int_{P'}^{P}\frac{\delta Z}{P}dP. \tag{3-47}$$

The first integral on the right is evaluated through use of an equation of state and the second integral by graphical methods. With a properly chosen equation of state the residual term can be made small so that graphical integration is facilitated.

The lower pressure limit in Eq. (3-47) $P'$ can, of course, be taken as zero, in which case $\ln\varphi'$ is also zero. However, the low-pressure region is difficult to treat in this way, because empirical equations often do not provide a reliable guide for extrapolation to zero pressure, and at the same time $\delta Z/P$ becomes indeterminate. The recommended procedure is to use the virial equation from zero pressure to the highest pressure for which it represents the data. That is, use Eq. (3-34) for the direct calculation of $\ln\varphi$ values up to $P'$. Above this pressure Eq. (3-47) may be employed together with any convenient empirical equation of state.

Once $\ln\varphi$ values are determined, Eqs. (3-3) and (3-5) are available for the calculation of $\Delta H'$ and $\Delta S'$ values. One does not appreciate what is involved in the construction of accurate thermodynamic tables until he attempts the calculations. Even with the simplest procedures that have been devised, the calculational task is formidable. It should be clear also that before calculations can begin extensive data of high accuracy must be available. Furthermore, once one understands the nature of these calculations, he will have a much clearer notion of the uncertainties which must inevitably appear in the results.

**3.3. Qualitative Representation of Behavior.** It is useful to know in a qualitative way how the thermodynamic properties of pure materials vary with temperature and pressure. With respect to temperature, no difficulty arises. By Eqs. (2-23) and (2-24)

$$(\partial H/\partial T)_P = C_P \quad \text{and} \quad (\partial S/\partial T)_P = C_P/T.$$

Since $C_P$ must be positive for any stable phase, both the enthalpy and entropy always increase with temperature at constant pressure for all homogeneous fluids in equilibrium states.

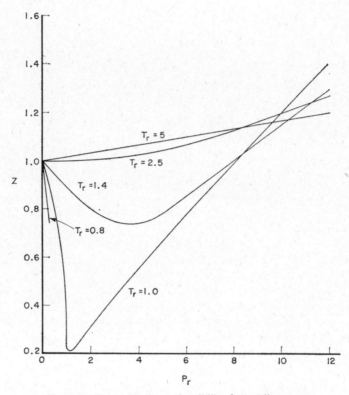

FIG. 3-9. Generalized compressibility factor diagram.

The effect of pressure at constant temperature is not so easy to generalize. By Eq. (2-20)

$$(\partial S/\partial P)_T = -(\partial V/\partial T)_P.$$

Since $(\partial V/\partial T)_P$ is almost always positive, entropy almost always decreases with increasing pressure at constant temperature. Only in rare instances, as in the case of water between 0 and 4°C, is the opposite true. For gases $(\partial V/\partial T)_P$ is found to be positive, and entropy decreases as $P$ increases. Since $PV = ZRT$,

$$\left(\frac{\partial V}{\partial T}\right)_P = \frac{R}{P}\left[T\left(\frac{\partial Z}{\partial T}\right)_P + Z\right]. \tag{3-48}$$

As $P$ approaches zero, $Z \to 1$ and $(\partial Z/\partial T)_P \to 0$. Thus

$$\left(\frac{\partial V}{\partial T}\right)_{P*} = \frac{R}{P*} \to \infty.$$

Thus as $P \to 0$, $(\partial S/\partial P)_T \to -\infty$, and the entropy of gases approaches $+\infty$ as $P \to 0$, provided the entropy at finite pressure is taken to be finite.

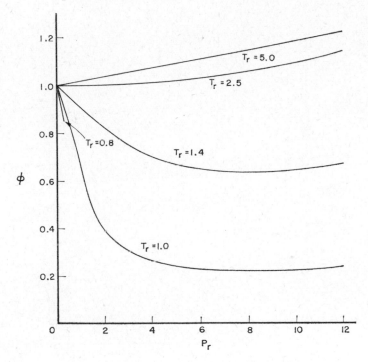

FIG. 3-10. Generalized fugacity coefficient diagram.

By Eq. (2-26)

$$\left(\frac{\partial H}{\partial P}\right)_T = -T\left(\frac{\partial V}{\partial T}\right)_P + V.$$

If $(\partial V/\partial T)_P$ and $V$ are both positive, the sign of $(\partial H/\partial P)_T$ is not evident from this equation. Qualitative delineation of the region for which this quantity is positive from the region for which it is negative is best accomplished by invoking the principle of corresponding states.

One of the consequences of this principle is that to a fair approximation the compressibilities of all gases are the same at the same reduced temperature and pressure. That is, $Z$ is the same function of $T_r$ and $P_r$ for all gases:

$$Z = z(T_r, P_r),$$

where

$$T_r = T/T_c,$$
$$P_r = P/P_c,$$
$$T_c = \text{critical temperature,}$$
$$P_c = \text{critical pressure.}$$

Thus

$$P = P_c P_r, \quad \text{and} \quad dP = P_c \, dP_r.$$

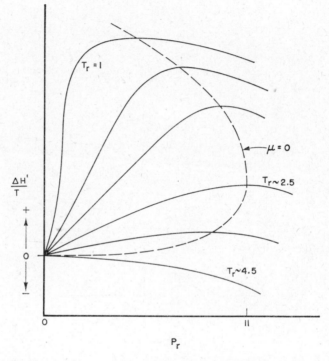

FIG. 3-11. Sketch of generalized enthalpy deviation diagram. Dashed line is the inversion curve.

Substitution for $P$ and $dP$ in Eq. (3-31) gives

$$\ln \varphi = \int_0^{P_r} (Z - 1) \frac{dP_r}{P_r} \quad \text{(const } T_r\text{).} \tag{3-49}$$

Because of the principle of corresponding states, a generalized plot of $Z$ vs. $P_r$ with $T_r$ as parameter can be drawn to represent approximately the $P$-$V$-$T$ behavior of all gases, as shown in Fig. 3-9. Data from this plot allow integration of Eq. (3-49) and the preparation of a generalized plot of $\varphi$ vs. $P_r$ with $T_r$ as parameter, as illustrated in Fig. 3-10.

By Eq. (3-3)

$$\frac{\Delta H'}{T} = R T \left(\frac{\partial \ln \varphi}{\partial T}\right)_P.$$

Since $T = T_c T_r$,

$$(\partial T/\partial T_r)_P (1/T_c) = 1.$$

Therefore

$$\frac{\Delta H'}{T} = R T_c T_r \left(\frac{d \ln \varphi}{\partial T}\right)_P \left(\frac{\partial T}{\partial T_r}\right)_P \left(\frac{1}{T_c}\right)$$

or

$$\frac{\Delta H'}{T} = R T_r \left(\frac{\partial \ln \varphi}{\partial T_r}\right)_{P_r}. \tag{3-50}$$

Equation (3-50) allows the development of a generalized diagram giving $\Delta H'/T$ as a function of $P_r$ with $T_r$ as parameter, as indicated in Fig. 3-11.

Equation (2-29) may be combined with Eq. (2-26) to give

$$\mu = \left(\frac{\partial T}{\partial P}\right)_H = \frac{-(\partial H/\partial P)_T}{C_P},$$

where $\mu$ is the Joule–Thomson coefficient. Also, combination of the equation $V = Z R T/P$ and Eq. (3-48) with Eq. (2-26) leads to

$$\left(\frac{\partial H}{\partial P}\right)_T = \frac{-R T^2}{P} \left(\frac{\partial Z}{\partial T}\right)_P. \tag{3-51}$$

Therefore

$$\mu = \left(\frac{\partial T}{\partial P}\right)_H = \frac{-(\partial H/\partial P)_T}{C_P} = \frac{R T^2}{C_P P} \left(\frac{\partial Z}{\partial T}\right)_P. \tag{3-52}$$

It is seen from Eq. (3-52) that when $(\partial Z/\partial T)_P$ is zero, then $(\partial H/\partial P)_T$ and $\mu$ are also zero. When $(\partial Z/\partial T)_P$ is positive, $\mu$ is also positive while $(\partial H/\partial P)_T$ is negative. When $(\partial Z/\partial T)_P$ is negative, $\mu$ is negative and $(\partial H/\partial P)_T$ is positive. Since the value of zero for these quantities separates the regions of positive values from those of negative values, it is clear that the states for which zero values are obtained are of some significance. They are in fact known as Joule–Thomson inversion points, and the locus of inversion points divides the appropriate diagrams into regions of positive and negative values of $(\partial Z/\partial T)_P$, $(\partial H/\partial P)_T$, and $\mu$.

Figure 3-12 is a cross-plot of the familiar generalized compressibility-factor diagram showing lines of constant $P_r$. The loci of minima and maxima join at a point of inflection, and together form the inversion curve. Below this curve $(\partial Z/\partial T_r)_{P_r}$ and hence $(\partial Z/\partial T)_P$ and $\mu$ are always positive; above it they are negative. A plot of the values of $T_r$ vs. $P_r$ which exist along this curve results in the tongue of Fig. 3-13. Inside this curve $\mu$ is positive and $(\partial H/\partial P)_T$ is negative. Outside of it the reverse is true. Hence the region inside this generalized inversion curve represents approximately the values of $T_r$ and $P_r$ for which $(\partial H/\partial P)_T$ is negative for all gases, and the region outside indicates the conditions for which $(\partial H/\partial P)_T$

is positive. For most gases at common conditions of $T$ and $P$, $T_r$ and $P_r$ are such that their states lie within the inversion curve. Hence $(\partial H/\partial P)_T$ is normally negative, and enthalpy increases with decreasing pressure at constant $T$. Exceptions are hydrogen, helium, and neon, which at common temperatures exist at $T_r$ values well above 5. For these gases enthalpy usually decreases with decreasing pressure.

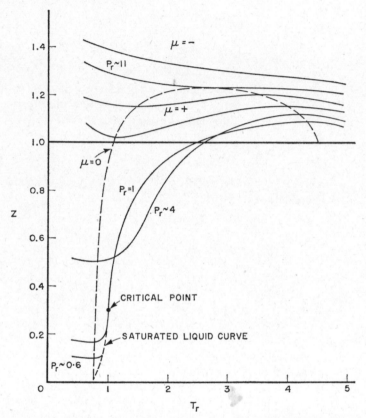

FIG. 3-12. Sketch of cross-plot of generalized compressibility factor diagram. Dashed line is the inversion curve.

Since $\mu = (\partial T/\partial P)_H$, lines of constant enthalpy must have a positive slope inside the inversion curve of Fig. 3-13; they must be zero as they cross the inversion curve; and they must be negative outside the inversion curve. This is indicated by the isenthalps shown. Since a throttling or Joule–Thomson expansion occurs at constant enthalpy, these isenthalps represent the paths of such an expansion. If one's object is to reduce the temperature of a gas by throttling from a high pressure to a low one, it is clearly a disadvantage to compress the gas to a pressure above that given by the inversion curve at a given temperature.

The dashed curve shown in Fig. 3-11 is the locus of maxima of the constant-temperature curves. It is also the inversion curve. This is shown from Eq. (3-51):

$$\left(\frac{\partial H}{\partial P}\right)_T = \frac{-RT^2}{P}\left(\frac{\partial Z}{\partial T}\right)_P.$$

For an ideal gas $(\partial H^{\text{id}}/\partial P)_T = 0$. Therefore

$$\left(\frac{\partial H^{\text{id}}}{\partial P}\right)_T - \left(\frac{\partial H}{\partial P}\right)_T = \left(\frac{\partial \Delta H'}{\partial P}\right)_T = \frac{RT^2}{P}\left(\frac{\partial Z}{\partial T}\right)_P,$$

or

$$\left[\frac{\partial(\Delta H'/T)}{\partial P}\right]_T = \frac{RT}{P}\left(\frac{\partial Z}{\partial T}\right)_P.$$

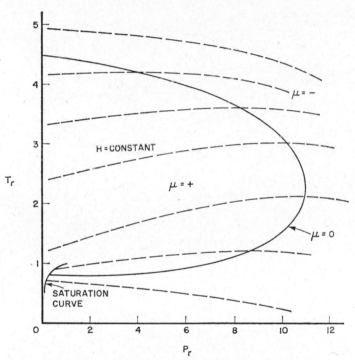

FIG. 3-13. Inversion curve on generalized coordinates.

When $(\partial Z/\partial T)_P$ is zero, as it is along the inversion curve, $\left[\dfrac{\partial(\Delta H'/T)}{\partial P}\right]_{T'}$ is also zero, and this condition corresponds to the maxima of Fig. 3-11.

Another useful correlation arises as a result of the principle of corresponding states. As seen from Eq. (3-28) the second virial coefficient of a pure gas is given by

$$B = RT\left(\frac{\partial Z}{\partial P}\right)_T^*.$$

Thus

$$\left(\frac{\partial Z}{\partial P_r}\right)_{T_r}^* = P_c \left(\frac{\partial Z}{\partial P}\right)_T^* = \frac{P_c B}{RT} = \frac{P_c B}{RT_c T_r}.$$

But it is clear from Fig. 3-9 that the limiting slope as $P \to 0$ for an isotherm is a function solely of the reduced temperature.

Thus

$$\left(\frac{\partial Z}{\partial P_r}\right)_{T_r}^* = t(T_r).$$

As a result, we have

$$\frac{P_c B}{RT_c T_r} = t(T_r)$$

or

$$\frac{B}{RT_c/P_c} = \tau(T_r). \tag{3-53}$$

We also note that

$$RT_c/P_c = V_c/Z_c,$$

where $Z_c$ is the critical compressibility factor. Hence Eq. (3-53) can be written

$$B/V_c = Z_c\, \tau(T_r).$$

If $Z_c$ is considered a constant, this becomes

$$B/V_c = \psi(T_r). \tag{3-54}$$

Equations (3-53) and (3-54) indicate two possible generalized correlations of second virial coefficients of pure gases. Both are found in the literature.

The various generalized correlations just discussed are valid only to a first approximation. Much effort has been put into attempts to improve these generalizations by including a third parameter in addition to $P_r$ and $T_r$. Considerable success has been achieved by Pitzer† and his coworkers and by Hougen†† and his colleagues.

---

† For a rather complete account of Pitzer's correlations, see G. N. Lewis, and M. Randall, *Thermodynamics*, 2nd ed., as revised by K. S. Pitzer and L. Brewer, Appendix 1, McGraw-Hill, New York, 1961.

†† The correlations developed by Hougen *et al.* are given in O. A. Hougen, K. M. Watson, and R. A. Ragatz, *Chemical Process Principles*, 2nd ed., Part II, "Thermodynamics", Chapter 14, John Wiley, New York 1959.

# CHAPTER 4

# PROPERTY CHANGES OF MIXING

**4.1. General Equations.** Throughout this chapter we will be concerned with the mixing of pure materials to form a solution under conditions of constant temperature and pressure. Although a solution property is *not* in general given by the equation

$$M = \sum_i (x_i M_i),$$

where the $M_i$'s are the properties of the pure constituents at the solution temperature and pressure, an equation of this form can be made valid by the inclusion of a correction term:

$$M = \sum_i (x_i M_i) + \varDelta M. \tag{4-1}$$

This equation actually defines $\varDelta M$, the property change which results when pure materials are mixed at constant $T$ and $P$ to form one mole of solution. Ordinarily the pure materials and the solution which they form are considered to exist as the same kind of phase (liquid or gas), even though this may require the assumption of a hypothetical state for one or more of the pure materials.

By Eq. (2-49)

$$M = \sum_i (x_i \overline{M}_i), \tag{2-49}$$

and this is also a general equation for the molal property of a solution. It may therefore be combined with Eq. (4-1) to give

$$\varDelta M = \sum_i [x_i(\overline{M}_i - M_i)]$$

or

$$\varDelta M = \sum_i (x_i \overline{\varDelta M}_i). \tag{4-2}$$

Here we have defined $\overline{\varDelta M}_i = \overline{M}_i - M_i$. This quantity represents the property change of a mole of constituent $i$ as a result of mixing at constant $T$ and $P$. It can also be regarded as the partial molal property change resulting from mixing, i.e., the part of the total property change attributable to the presence of component $i$. The proof that $\overline{\varDelta M}_i$ is in fact a partial quantity with respect to $\varDelta M$ is as follows. By Eq. (4-1)

$$\varDelta M = M - \sum_i (x_i M_i).$$

69

Then

$$n \, \Delta \, M = n \, M - \sum_{i} (n_i \, M_i).$$

If $j$ represents a particular constituent included in the set $i$, then

$$\frac{\partial (n \, \Delta \, M)}{\partial n_j} = \frac{\partial (n \, M)}{\partial n_j} - \sum_{i} \left( M_i \frac{\partial n_i}{\partial n_j} \right).$$

But all the $n_i$'s are independent; therefore $(\partial \, n_i / \partial \, n_j)$ is zero for each term except the one for which $i = j$, in which case it is unity. Thus

$$\frac{\partial (n \, \Delta \, M)}{\partial n_j} = \frac{\partial (n \, M)}{\partial n_j} - M_j$$

or by the basic definition of a partial quantity, Eq. (2-45),

$$\overline{\Delta \, M_j} = \overline{M}_j - M_j.$$

Since $j$ could be any of the constituents $i$, we can write

$$\overline{\Delta \, M_i} = \overline{M}_i - M_i. \tag{4-3}$$

Equation. (4-2) is therefore entirely analogous to Eq. (2-49). The Gibbs–Duhem equation also applies to these quantities. It is entirely analogous to and follows directly from Eq. (2-50). Thus at constant $T$ and $P$:

$$\sum_{i} \left( x_i \, \mathrm{d} \, \overline{\Delta M_i} \right) = 0. \tag{4-4}$$

**4.2. Ideal Solutions.** An ideal solution is defined as a solution for which $\hat{f}_i = x_i f_i$ or for which $\gamma_i = 1$ for all constituents at all temperatures, pressures, and compositions.† Thus for an ideal solution Eq. (2-69) reduces to:

$$\overline{G}_i^{\mathrm{id}} - G_i = R \, T \ln x_i. \tag{4-5}$$

This may also be written

$$\overline{\Delta \, G_i^{\mathrm{id}}} = R \, T \ln x_i.$$

By Eq. (4-2) we may also write

$$\Delta \, G^{\mathrm{id}} = R \, T \sum_{i} (x_i \ln x_i). \tag{4-6}$$

---

† The expression $\hat{f}_i = x_i f_i$ is known as the Lewis and Randall rule. In this equation $f$ is the fugacity of pure $i$ at the temperature and pressure of the solution and in the same physical state as the solution. This leads to no difficulty as long as pure $i$ is stable under these conditions. However, situations frequently arise, particularly when phase equilibrium is involved, where pure $i$ is stable in a different physical state than that of the solution. This leads to the concept of hypothetical states, for which $f_i$ is taken as the value it would assume if pure $i$ did exist at the prescribed conditions. Although this concept is widely accepted, it is not altogether satisfactory, because it is seldom clear how the value of $f_i$ should be calculated for a state that does not exist.

Differentiation of Eq. (4-5) with respect to $P$ at constant $T$ and composition gives:

$$\frac{\partial \bar{G}_i^{id}}{\partial P} - \frac{\partial G_i}{\partial P} = 0.$$

But by Eq. (2-15), $(\partial G_i/\partial P) = V_i$, and analogously for a component in solution $(\partial \bar{G}_i/\partial P) = \bar{V}_i$. Thus

$$\bar{V}_i^{id} - V_i = 0$$

or

$$\overline{\Delta V_i^{id}} = 0$$

and

$$\bar{V}_i^{id} = V_i.$$

As a result of Eq. (4-2), it is also evident that $\Delta V^{id} = 0$. If follows immediately that

$$\bar{\alpha}_i^{id} - \alpha_i = \overline{\Delta \alpha_i^{id}} = 0 \quad \text{and} \quad \Delta \alpha^{id} = 0$$

and that

$$\bar{Z}_i^{id} - Z_i = \overline{\Delta Z_i^{id}} = 0 \quad \text{and} \quad \Delta Z^{id} = 0.$$

Differentiation of Eq. (4-5) with respect to temperature at constant $P$ and composition gives:

$$\frac{\partial \bar{G}_i^{id}}{\partial T} - \frac{\partial G_i}{\partial T} = R \ln x_i.$$

By Eq. (2-16), $(\partial G_i/\partial T) = - S_i$, and analogously for a constituent in solution $(\partial \bar{G}_i/\partial T) = - \bar{S}_i$. Thus

$$\bar{S}_i^{id} - S_i = - R \ln x_i$$

and

$$\overline{\Delta S_i^{id}} = - R \ln x_i.$$

By Eq. (4-2)

$$\Delta S^{id} = - R \sum_i (x_i \ln x_i).$$

Since

$$G_i = H_i - T S_i \quad \text{and} \quad \bar{G}_i^{id} = \bar{H}_i^{id} - T \bar{S}_i^{id},$$

we get by difference

$$\bar{G}_i^{id} - G_i = \bar{H}_i^{id} - H_i - T(\bar{S}_i^{id} - S_i)$$

or

$$\overline{\Delta G_i^{id}} = \overline{\Delta H_i^{id}} - T \overline{\Delta S_i^{id}}.$$

But by Eq. (4-5), $\overline{\Delta G_i^{id}} = RT \ln x_i$, and we have just shown that $\overline{\Delta S_i^{id}} = - R \ln x_i$. Thus it follows for an ideal solution that

$$\overline{\Delta H_i^{id}} = \bar{H}_i^{id} - H_i = 0$$

and by Eq. (4-2) that $\Delta H^{id} = 0$.

As a consequence of this it follows immediately that

$$\frac{\partial \bar{H}_i^{id}}{\partial T} - \frac{\partial H_i}{\partial T} = \bar{C}_{P_i}^{id} - C_{P_i} = \overline{\varDelta C}_{P_i}^{id} = 0$$

and that $\varDelta C_P^{id} = 0$.

Since

$$U_i = H_i - P V_i \quad \text{and} \quad \bar{U}_i^{id} = \bar{H}_i^{id} - P \bar{V}_i^{id},$$

$$\bar{U}_i^{id} - U_i = \bar{H}_i^{id} - H_i - P(\bar{V}_i^{id} - V_i)$$

or

$$\overline{\varDelta U}_i^{id} = \overline{\varDelta H}_i^{id} - P(\overline{\varDelta V}_i^{id}).$$

Since $\overline{\varDelta H}_i^{id}$ and $\overline{\varDelta V}_i^{id}$ are zero, $\overline{\varDelta U}_i^{id} = 0$ also. Furthermore $\varDelta U^{id} = 0$. Again it follows that $\bar{C}_{V_i}^{id} - C_{V_i} = \overline{\varDelta C}_{V_i}^{id} = 0$ and $\varDelta C_V^{id} = 0$.

In summary, for an ideal solution

| | | |
|---|---|---|
| $\bar{V}_i^{id} = V_i$ | $\overline{\varDelta V}_i^{id} = 0$ | $\varDelta V^{id} = 0$ |
| $\bar{\alpha}_i^{id} = \alpha_i$ | $\overline{\varDelta \alpha}_i^{id} = 0$ | $\varDelta \alpha^{id} = 0$ |
| $\bar{Z}_i^{id} = Z_i$ | $\overline{\varDelta Z}_i^{id} = 0$ | $\varDelta Z^{id} = 0$ |
| $\bar{U}_i^{id} = U_i$ | $\overline{\varDelta U}_i^{id} = 0$ | $\varDelta U^{id} = 0$ |
| $\bar{C}_{V_i}^{id} = C_{V_i}$ | $\overline{\varDelta C}_{V_i}^{id} = 0$ | $\varDelta C_V^{id} = 0$ |
| $\bar{H}_i^{id} = H_i$ | $\overline{\varDelta H}_i^{id} = 0$ | $\varDelta H^{id} = 0$ |
| $\bar{C}_{P_i}^{id} = C_{P_i}$ | $\overline{\varDelta C}_{P_i}^{id} = 0$ | $\varDelta C_P^{id} = 0$ |
| $\bar{S}_i^{id} = S_i - R \ln x_i$ | $\overline{\varDelta S}_i^{id} = - R \ln x_i$ | $\varDelta S^{id} = - R \sum_i (x_i \ln x_i)$ |
| $\bar{G}_i^{id} = G_i + R T \ln x_i$ | $\overline{\varDelta G}_i^{id} = R T \ln x_i$ | $\varDelta G^{id} = R T \sum_i (x_i \ln x_i)$ |

With respect to property changes of mixing, an ideal gas is merely a special case of the ideal solution, because

$$\gamma_i = \frac{\hat{f}_i}{y_i f_i} = \frac{y_i P}{y_i P} = 1$$

for an ideal gas at all temperatures, pressures, and compositions. Thus all of the above equations are valid for a solution which is an ideal gas. For a gas $y_i$ is usually used to represent mole fraction.

The behavior of real gases at a pressure approaching zero is a special case of interest. It is frequently stated that gases approach ideality as the pressure approaches zero. In many respects this is true, and with the exception of $\varDelta V$ (and therefore $\varDelta \alpha$) the property changes of mixing in the zero-pressure state are the ideal-gas or ideal-solution values. However, experimental data generally show $\varDelta V$ to be finite and not zero at zero pressure.

The reason is that volume becomes infinite at zero pressure; hence $\Delta V^*$ is the difference between infinite quantities, and experimental data show it to be finite and usually non-zero.

By Eq. (2-60) for the zero-pressure state

$$\bar{G}_i^* - G_i^* = \overline{\Delta G_i^*} = R T \ln y_i \qquad (2\text{-}60)$$

and by Eq. (4-2)

$$\Delta G^* = R T \sum_i (y_i \ln y_i).$$

Differentiation of Eq. (2-60) with respect to $T$ at the constant pressure, $P^* \rightarrow 0$, gives

$$\frac{\partial \bar{G}_i^*}{\partial T} - \frac{\partial G_i^*}{\partial T} = R \ln y_i.$$

In view of Eq. (2-16) this becomes

$$-\bar{S}_i^* + S_i^* = R \ln y_i.$$

Thus

$$\overline{\Delta S_i^*} = - R \ln y_i$$

and

$$\Delta S^* = - R \sum_i (y_i \ln y_i)$$

which is the ideal-gas value.

Since

$$\Delta G^* = \Delta H^* - T \Delta S^*$$

$$R T \sum_i (y_i \ln y_i) = \Delta H^* + R T \sum_i (y_i \ln y_i)$$

or

$$\Delta H^* = 0 \quad \text{as for an ideal gas.}$$

Also

$$\Delta U^* = \Delta H^* - P^* \Delta V^*.$$

Since $\Delta H^* \rightarrow 0$ when $P^* \rightarrow 0$, $\Delta U^* \rightarrow 0$ as for an ideal gas, even though $\Delta V^*$ is finite.

**4.3. Excess Properties of Solutions.** An *excess* property is defined as the difference between the actual property and the property which one would obtain for an ideal solution.† There are four possible excess properties, designated as follows by the superscript $E$:

$$\bar{M}_i^E = \bar{M}_i - \bar{M}_i^{\text{id}}$$

$$M^E = M - M^{\text{id}}$$

$$\overline{\Delta M_i^E} = \overline{\Delta M_i} - \overline{\Delta M_i^{\text{id}}}$$

$$\Delta M^E = \Delta M - \Delta M^{\text{id}}.$$

---

† Most authors limit the consideration of excess properties to saturated phases. This is not the intent here, for they have a much wider applicability.

Actually $\overline{M}_i^E \equiv \overline{\Delta\,M}_i^E$ and $M^E \equiv \Delta\,M^E$ as can be shown as follows: By definition

$$\overline{M}_i^E \equiv \overline{M}_i - \overline{M}_i^{\mathrm{id}}.$$

Hence

$$\overline{M}_i^E \equiv (\overline{M}_i - M_i) - (\overline{M}_i^{\mathrm{id}} - M_i)$$

and

$$\overline{M}_i^E \equiv \overline{\Delta\,M}_i - \overline{\Delta\,M}_i^{\mathrm{id}}$$

or finally

$$\overline{M}_i^E \equiv \overline{\Delta\,M}_i^E \quad \text{Q.E.D.}$$

Also by definition

$$M^E \equiv M - M^{\mathrm{id}}.$$

Hence

$$M^E \equiv \Big[ M - \sum_i (x_i\,M_i) \Big] - \Big[ M^{\mathrm{id}} - \sum_i (x_i\,M_i) \Big]$$

and

$$M^E \equiv \Delta\,M - \Delta\,M^{\mathrm{id}}$$

or finally

$$M^E \equiv \Delta\,M^E \quad \text{Q.E.D.}$$

Thus $\overline{\Delta\,M}_i^E$ and $\Delta\,M^E$ are the only excess properties we will use. However, their identity with $\overline{M}_i^E$ and $M^E$ respectively should be kept in mind.

The $\overline{\Delta\,M}_i^E$ values are related to corresponding values of $\Delta\,M^E$ as partial molal properties. This is shown as follows:

$$\frac{\partial\,(n\Delta\,M^E)}{\partial n_i} = \frac{\partial\,(n\,M^E)}{\partial n_i} = \frac{\partial\,(n\,M)}{\partial n_i} - \frac{\partial\,(n\,M^{\mathrm{id}})}{\partial n_i} = \overline{M}_i - \overline{M}_i^{\mathrm{id}} = \overline{M}_i^E.$$

Since

$$\overline{M}_i^E \equiv \overline{\Delta\,M}_i^E,$$

$$\frac{\partial\,(n\Delta\,M^E)}{\partial n_i} = \overline{\Delta\,M}_i^E,$$

which is the required relationship for the existence of a partial molal property. Hence

$$\Delta\,M^E = \sum_i \big( x_i\,\overline{\Delta\,M}_i^E \big). \tag{4-7}$$

When $M$ represents the properties $V, \alpha, Z, U, C_V, H$, and $C_P, \overline{\Delta\,M}_i^{\mathrm{id}} = 0$ and $\Delta\,M^{\mathrm{id}} = 0$. Hence for these functions

$$\overline{\Delta\,M}_i^E = \overline{\Delta\,M}_i \quad \text{and} \quad \Delta\,M^E = \Delta\,M$$

and the excess properties do not represent new properties for these variables. For example, $\overline{\Delta\,V}_i^E = \overline{\Delta\,V}_i,\ \Delta\,V^E = \Delta\,V,\ \overline{\Delta\,H}_i^E = \overline{\Delta\,H}_i$, and $\Delta\,H^E = \Delta\,H$. However, for the functions which involve entropy, the excess properties represent distinctly different functions. Hence

$$\overline{\Delta\,S}_i^E = \overline{\Delta\,S}_i - \overline{\Delta\,S}_i^{\mathrm{id}} = \overline{\Delta\,S}_i + R\ln x_i \tag{4-8}$$

and

$$\Delta\,S^E = \Delta\,S - \Delta\,S^{\mathrm{id}} = \Delta\,S + R\sum_i (x_i \ln x_i). \tag{4-9}$$

In addition

$$\overline{\Delta G_i^E} = \overline{\Delta G_i} - \overline{\Delta G_i^{id}} = \overline{\Delta G_i} - R T \ln x_i \qquad (4\text{-}10)$$

and

$$\Delta G^E = \Delta G - \Delta G^{id} = \Delta G - R T \sum_i (x_i \ln x_i). \qquad (4\text{-}11)$$

By Eq. (2-69)

$$\overline{G}_i - G_i - R T \ln x_i = R T \ln \gamma_i$$

or

$$\overline{\Delta G_i} - R T \ln x_i = R T \ln \gamma_i$$

or finally

$$\overline{\Delta G_i^E} = R T \ln \gamma_i. \qquad (4\text{-}12)$$

This may also be written

$$\ln \gamma_i = \frac{\overline{\Delta G_i^E}}{R T}. \qquad (4\text{-}13)$$

Combined with Eq. (4-12), Eq. (4-7) becomes

$$\Delta G^E = R T \sum_i (x_i \ln \gamma_i)$$

or

$$\frac{\Delta G^E}{R T} = \sum_i (x_i \ln \gamma_i). \qquad (4\text{-}14)$$

In view of Eqs. (4-13) and (4-14) it is clear that $\ln \gamma_i$ is related to $\Delta G^E / R T$ as a partial molal property.

In addition, we have from Eq. (2-70)

$$\ln \gamma_i = \ln \hat{\varphi}_i - \ln \varphi_i. \qquad (2\text{-}70)$$

This corresponds to the general equation,

$$\overline{\Delta M_i} = \overline{M}_i - M_i.$$

As a result of Eq. (2-70) we may write

$$\sum_i (x_i \ln \gamma_i) = \sum_i (x_i \ln \hat{\varphi}_i) - \sum_i (x_i \ln \varphi_i).$$

But by Eq. (2-66)

$$\ln \varphi = \sum_i (x_i \ln \hat{\varphi}_i). \qquad (2\text{-}66)$$

Therefore

$$\sum_i (x_i \ln \gamma_i) = \ln \varphi - \sum_i (x_i \ln \varphi_i) = \Delta \ln \varphi. \qquad (4\text{-}15)$$

Here the last equality corresponds to the general relation, Eq. (4-1),

$$M - \sum_i (x_i M_i) = \Delta M.$$

Combination of Eqs. (4-14) and (4-15) gives:

$$\frac{\Delta G^E}{R T} \equiv \Delta \ln \varphi \equiv \sum_i \left( x_i \frac{\overline{\Delta G_i^E}}{R T} \right) \equiv \sum_i (x_i \ln \gamma_i). \qquad (4\text{-}16)$$

Thus $\ln \gamma_i$ is also related to $\Delta \ln \varphi$ as a partial molal property.

6*

Table 4-1 summarizes the various functions used for solutions, and shows their interrelationships.

It should be noted that the Gibbs–Duhem equation at constant $T$ and $P$ applies to the partial molal excess properties of mixing. This follows directly from Eq. (4-4),

$$\sum_i (x_i \, d\overline{\Delta M_i}) = 0.$$

For if this is true then

$$\sum_i (x_i \, d\overline{\Delta M_i^{id}}) = 0$$

is a special case. Combination gives

$$\sum_i [x_i \, d(\overline{\Delta M_i} - \overline{\Delta M_i^{id}})] = 0$$

or

$$\sum_i (x_i \, d\overline{\Delta M_i^E}) = 0. \tag{4-17}$$

As a special case of Eq. (4-17) we have at constant $T$ and $P$:

$$\sum_i (x_i \, d\ln\gamma_i) = 0. \tag{4-18}$$

We have proceeded from a consideration of a mixture property $M$ to a treatment of $\Delta M$ and finally of $\Delta M^E$. Clearly, we have a choice of dealing with $M$, $\Delta M$, or $\Delta M^E$ values. It is often advantageous to treat mixture data in terms of $\Delta M^E$ (which is actually the same as $\Delta M$ except for the entropy and related functions), because this is the smallest and most sensitive measure of mixture properties in relation to the pure-constituent properties. Experimental data are always easily converted to excess properties, and mixture data are always easily calculated from excess values, provided pure-constituent data are available at the same temperature and pressure.

**4.4. Special Equations for the Gibbs Function and Related Properties.** As was noted in Section 2.5, the Gibbs function is particularly useful because of its primary dependence on the variables $T$ and $P$. We are now in a position to extend the equations developed in Section 2.5 to property changes of mixing. We start with Eq. (2-75):

$$\frac{V}{RT} \, dP + \frac{(H^{id} - H)}{RT^2} \, dT = \sum_i (x_i \, d\ln\hat{f}_i). \tag{2-75}†$$

In addition, for a constant-composition solution Eq. (2-77) gives

$$d\ln f = \frac{V}{RT} \, dP + \frac{H^{id} - H}{RT^2} \, dT. \tag{2-77}$$

† The superscript ($^{id}$) here refers to ideal gases.

For constant composition we may also write

$$d \ln f = \left(\frac{\partial \ln f}{\partial P}\right)_T dP + \left(\frac{\partial \ln f}{\partial T}\right)_P dT.$$

Comparison of these two equations shows

$$\left(\frac{\partial \ln f}{\partial P}\right)_T = \frac{V}{RT}$$

and

$$\left(\frac{\partial \ln f}{\partial T}\right)_P = \frac{H^{id} - H}{RT^2}.$$

For $n$ moles we have

$$\left[\frac{\partial(n \ln f)}{\partial P}\right]_T = \frac{(nV)}{RT}$$

and

$$\left[\frac{\partial(n \ln f)}{\partial T}\right]_P = \frac{nH^{id} - nH}{RT^2}.$$

Differentiation of the first of these expressions with respect to $n_i$ gives

$$\frac{\partial[\partial(n \ln f)/\partial P]_T}{\partial n_i} = \left\{\frac{\partial[\partial(n \ln f)/\partial n_i]}{\partial P}\right\}_T = \frac{\partial(nV)/\partial n_i}{RT}.$$

Equation (2-61) shows that

$$\partial(n \ln f)/\partial n_i = \ln(\hat{f}_i/x_i).$$

Also, $\partial(nV)/\partial n_i = \bar{V}_i$. The last equality of the preceding expression may therefore be written

$$\left[\frac{\partial \ln(\hat{f}_i/x_i)}{\partial P}\right]_T = \frac{\bar{V}_i}{RT}.$$

Since we are discussing constant-composition solutions, this becomes:

$$\left(\frac{\partial \ln \hat{f}_i}{\partial P}\right)_T = \frac{\bar{V}_i}{RT}.$$

Similarly

$$\frac{\partial[\partial(n \ln f)/\partial T]_P}{\partial n_i} = \left\{\frac{\partial[\partial(n \ln f)/\partial n_i]}{\partial T}\right\}_P = \frac{\partial(nH^{id})/\partial n_i - \partial(nH)/\partial n_i}{RT^2}.$$

This reduces to

$$\left[\frac{\partial \ln(\hat{f}_i/x_i)}{\partial T}\right]_P = \left(\frac{\partial \ln \hat{f}_i}{\partial T}\right)_P = \frac{H_i^{id} - \bar{H}_i}{RT^2}.$$

Now, $\ln \hat{f}_i$ for a constituent in a constant-composition solution is clearly a function of temperature and pressure. Hence at constant composition:

$$d \ln \hat{f}_i = \left(\frac{\partial \ln \hat{f}_i}{\partial P}\right)_T dP + \left(\frac{\partial \ln \hat{f}_i}{\partial T}\right)_P dT.$$

Substitution in this equation for the partial derivatives gives for constant composition:

$$d \ln \hat{f}_i = \frac{\bar{V}_i}{RT} dP + \frac{H_i^{id} - \bar{H}_i}{RT^2} dT.$$

The equation for pure $i$ is a special case of this and may be written down immediately:

$$d \ln f_i = \frac{V_i}{RT} dP + \frac{H_i^{id} - H_i}{RT^2} dT.$$

Standard states were discussed briefly in Section 2.4. It was pointed out there, that the standard state of constituent $i$ in any particular application is always taken as the state of $i$ as it exists in a solution of fixed, but arbitrary, composition. The temperature of the standard state is always that of the system, and hence may vary. The pressure of the standard state may be fixed or it may vary in some arbitrarily specified way. Thus we see that the equations we have just developed for fixed composition may be applied in general to the fugacity of a constituent in its standard state. Thus for the standard state, taken either as a constituent in solution or as a pure material, we may write:

$$d \ln f_i^0 = \frac{V_i^0}{RT} dP_i^0 + \frac{H_i^{id} - H_i^0}{RT^2} dT, \tag{4-19}$$

where the sign ($^0$) indicates a property for the standard state. This sign does not appear on $T$, because this is always the solution temperature. However, the standard state pressure need not be the solution pressure and may be different for different constituents. Thus we have used $P_i^0$.

Multiplication of Eq. (4-19) by $x_i$ and summation over all constituents gives

$$\frac{\sum_i (x_i V_i^0 dP_i^0)}{RT} + \frac{\sum_i (x_i H_i^{id}) - \sum_i (x_i H_i^0)}{RT^2} dT = \sum_i (x_i d \ln f_i^0).$$

Subtraction of this equation from Eq. (2-75) gives

$$\frac{V dP - \sum_i (x_i V_i^0 dP_i^0)}{RT} + \frac{\sum_i (x_i H_i^0) - H}{RT^2} dT = \sum_i \left( x_i d \ln \frac{\hat{f}_i}{f_i^0} \right).$$

Because of the fact that $\sum_i \left( x_i d \ln \frac{1}{x_i} \right) = 0$, then

$$\sum_i [x_i d \ln (\hat{f}_i / f_i^0)] = \sum_i (x_i d \ln \gamma_i)$$

and

$$\frac{V dP - \sum_i (x_i V_i^0 dP_i^0)}{RT} + \frac{\sum_i (x_i H_i^0) - H}{RT^2} dT = \sum_i (x_i d \ln \gamma_i), \tag{4-20}$$

where $\gamma_i$ is the activity coefficient as defined by $\hat{f}_i / x_i f_i^0$.

Equation (4-20) allows for the widest possible choice of standard states, which may be real or hypothetical. Although an infinite variety of standard states may be chosen, convenience dictates that only a limited number be used in practice. Such variety as is found in practice is prompted largely by the application of activity coefficients to problems in phase equilibrium. We will therefore postpone any detailed discussion of standard states until we are ready to consider these applications.

For solutions not at saturation conditions and for vapor–liquid equilibrium at low pressures, the usual standard state is that of the pure component at the solution temperature and pressure. In this case $P_i^0 = P$, $V_i^0 = V_i$, $H_i^0 = H_i$, $f_i^0 = f_i$, and Eq. (4-20) becomes

$$\frac{\Delta V}{RT} dP - \frac{\Delta H}{RT^2} dT = \sum_i (x_i \, d\ln\gamma_i), \qquad (4\text{-}21)$$

where $\gamma_i = \hat{f}_i / x_i f_i$ and $\Delta V$ and $\Delta H$ have their usual meanings. Equation (4-21) applies to any homogeneous solution in an equilibrium state (but not necessarily in equilibrium with another phase), provided that $\Delta V$, $\Delta H$, and the $\ln\gamma_i$'s are all taken with respect to the pure constituents at the same temperature and pressure. Usually they are considered to be in the same physical state as the solution, but they may also be taken as existing in their real states at this $T$ and $P$ when this is a different phase from that of the solution.

Equation (4-21) may be transformed by noting that

$$d(x_i \ln\gamma_i) = x_i \, d\ln\gamma_i + \ln\gamma_i \, dx_i.$$

Thus

$$\sum_i (x_i \, d\ln\gamma_i) = d \sum_i (x_i \ln\gamma_i) - \sum_i (\ln\gamma_i \, dx_i).$$

Since

$$\sum_i (x_i \ln\gamma_i) = \Delta G^E / RT,$$

$$\sum_i (x_i \, d\ln\gamma_i) = d(\Delta G^E / RT) - \sum_i (\ln\gamma_i \, dx_i).$$

Substitution into Eq. (4-21) gives

$$d\left(\frac{\Delta G^E}{RT}\right) = \frac{\Delta V}{RT} dP - \frac{\Delta H}{RT^2} dT + \sum_i (\ln\gamma_i \, dx_i). \qquad (4\text{-}22)$$

Another form of this equation is obtained by expanding the differential on the left-hand side:

$$d\left(\frac{\Delta G^E}{RT}\right) = \frac{-\Delta G^E}{RT^2} dT + \frac{1}{RT} d(\Delta G^E).$$

Therefore

$$d(\Delta G^E) = \Delta V \, dP + \left(\frac{\Delta G^E - \Delta H}{T}\right) dT + RT \sum_i (\ln\gamma_i \, dx_i)$$

or

$$d(\Delta G^E) = \Delta V \, dP - \Delta S^E \, dT + RT \sum_i (\ln\gamma_i \, dx_i). \qquad (4\text{-}23)$$

The summation terms of Eqs. (4-22) and (4-23) include all the $x_i$'s even though they are not all independent. If one of the $x_i$'s is eliminated, then the equation is written in terms of independent variables and is more useful.

If we take $j$ as a particular constituent and let $k$ represent the general constituent other than $j$, we can write

$$x_j + \sum_k x_k = \sum_i x_i = 1.$$

Hence

$$dx_j = -\sum_k (dx_k).$$

The term $\sum_i (\ln\gamma_i \, dx_i)$ then becomes

$$\begin{aligned}
\sum_i (\ln\gamma_i \, dx_i) &= \sum_k (\ln\gamma_k \, dx_k) + \ln\gamma_j \, dx_j \\
&= \sum_k (\ln\gamma_k \, dx_k) - \ln\gamma_j \sum_k (dx_k) \\
&= \sum_k (\ln\gamma_k \, dx_k) - \sum_k (\ln\gamma_j \, dx_k) \\
&= \sum_k [(\ln\gamma_k - \ln\gamma_j) \, dx_k] \\
&= \sum_k \left( \ln \frac{\gamma_k}{\gamma_j} \, dx_k \right).
\end{aligned}$$

Substitution into Eqs. (4-22) and (4-23) gives

$$d(\Delta G^E / RT) = \frac{\Delta V}{RT} dP - \frac{\Delta H}{RT^2} dT + \sum_{k \neq j} \left( \ln \frac{\gamma_k}{\gamma_j} \, dx_k \right) \qquad (4\text{-}24)$$

and

$$d(\Delta G^E) = \Delta V \, dP - \Delta S^E \, dT + RT \sum_{k \neq j} \left( \ln \frac{\gamma_k}{\gamma_j} \, dx_k \right). \qquad (4\text{-}25)$$

Equations (4-24) and (4-25) find application in the thermodynamics of vapor–liquid equilibrium. This topic is considered in Chapter 6. In addition, they summarize a considerable amount of information about the interrelations among the thermodynamic properties of solutions.

**4.5. Experimental Measurements and the Calculation of Property Changes of Mixing.** At constant temperature and composition both Eqs. (4-24) and (4-25) show that

$$d(\Delta G^E) = \Delta V \, dP.$$

Integration from the zero-pressure state to that at a finite pressure gives:

$$\Delta G^E = \int_0^P \Delta V \, dP \qquad (\text{const } T \text{ and composition}), \qquad (4\text{-}26)$$

since $\Delta G^E$ is zero in the zero-pressure state.

Once values of $\Delta G^E$ are calculated at various pressures by Eq. (4-26) for fixed temperatures and compositions, $\Delta S^E$ values may be determined by the equation resulting from restriction of Eq. (4-25) to constant pressure and composition:

$$\Delta S^E = -\left(\frac{\partial \Delta G^E}{\partial T}\right). \qquad (4\text{-}27)$$

We also know that

$$\Delta H = \Delta G^E + T \Delta S^E. \qquad (4\text{-}28)$$

Thus if values of $\Delta V$ are measured directly as a function of temperature and pressure for a constant-composition solution, the other property changes of mixing for the solution can be calculated by Eqs. (4-26), (4-27), and (4-28).

These equations are valid in general, and apply even though the integration of Eq. (4-26) traverses the two-phase region from the gaseous to the liquid state. In this event $\Delta V$ must always represent $V - \sum_i (x_i V_i)$, where $V$ is the molal volume of the system and the $V_i$'s are the pure-constituent molal volumes in their *real* states at the system temperature and pressure.

As a matter of fact, Eqs. (4-26) and (4-27) are most commonly applied to the gas phase. In this case the primary variable usually employed is $\Delta Z$ rather than $\Delta V$. We see from Table 4-1 that

$$\Delta V = R T (\Delta Z / P).$$

Thus Eq. (4-26) becomes

$$\frac{\Delta G^E}{R T} = \int_0^P \frac{\Delta Z}{P} \, dP. \qquad (4\text{-}29)$$

By Eq. (4-16):

$$\Delta \ln \varphi = \Delta G^E / R T. \qquad (4\text{-}30)$$

Therefore

$$\Delta \ln \varphi = \int_0^P \frac{\Delta Z}{P} \, dP. \qquad (4\text{-}31)$$

This gives a direct method for the calculation of $\Delta \ln \varphi$ values from experimental data, and is an alternative to the use of the defining equation for $\Delta \ln \varphi$:

$$\Delta \ln \varphi = \ln \varphi - \sum_i (y_i \ln \varphi_i). \qquad (4\text{-}32)$$

Use of this equation to give $\Delta \ln \varphi$ values requires prior calculation of the $\ln \varphi$ values for the mixtures themselves and for the pure constituents by methods discussed in Chapter 3. If $\Delta \ln \varphi$ values are calculated directly by Eq. (4-31), then Eq. (4-32) can be used to give $\ln \varphi$ values. Values of $\ln \varphi_i$ must of course be determined by the methods of Chapter 3.

For an example of the use of Eq. (4-31) let us return to the nitrogen–n-butane system. We have first calculated values of $Z$ at even values of pressure by the virial equation for the nitrogen–butane mixture containing 49.74% nitrogen and for pure nitrogen and pure butane at 370°F for pressures up to 600 psia. The virial equation with the constants given in Fig. 3-3 has been shown to hold at these conditions. Values of $\Delta Z/P$ for the 49.74% nitrogen mixture were then computed and are plotted vs. pressure in Fig. 4-1.

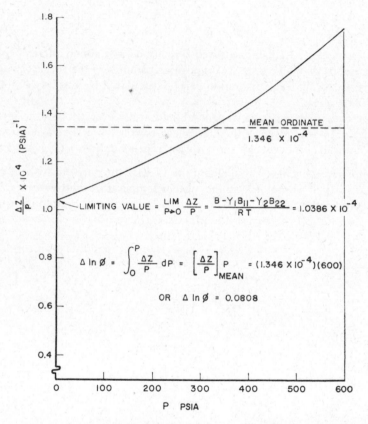

FIG. 4-1. Graphical integration for $\Delta \ln \varphi$. Nitrogen–n-butane system at 370°F, 49.74% $N_2$.

The mean ordinate of this curve between zero pressure and 600 psia as determined by the graphical equivalent of Simpson's rule is $1.346 \times 10^{-4}$ (psia)$^{-1}$. This gives a value of the integral and hence of $\Delta \ln \varphi$ equal to 0.0808 at 370°F and 600 psia.

Another relationship comes from Eq. (4-24) when it is restricted to constant pressure and composition:

$$\frac{\Delta H}{R T^2} = \frac{-\partial(\Delta G^E / R T)}{\partial T}.$$

In view of Eq. (4-30), this can be written

$$\frac{\Delta H}{R T^2} = \frac{- \partial (\Delta \ln \varphi)}{\partial T}. \tag{4-33}$$

In addition Eqs. (4-28) and (4-30) combine to give

$$\Delta S^E = \frac{\Delta H}{T} - R(\Delta \ln \varphi). \tag{4-34}$$

Equations (4-31), (4-33), and (4-34) are alternatives to Eqs. (4-26), (4-27), and (4-28) for the calculation of property changes of mixing, and are primarily applicable to gaseous systems. It might be noted that the compressibility factor and the fugacity coefficient are not commonly used for liquids.

At low pressures volumetric data for gases may be represented by the simplest form of the virial equation, i.e., Eq. (3-30) truncated to contain only the first two terms of the expansion:

$$Z = 1 + B P / R T.$$

This may also be written

$$V = R T / P + B.$$

For a pure material it becomes

$$V_i = R T / P + B_{ii}.$$

For a binary

$$\Delta V = V - y_1 V_1 - y_2 V_2.$$

Therefore

$$\Delta V = \frac{RT}{P} + B - y_1 \left( \frac{RT}{P} + B_{11} \right) - y_2 \left( \frac{RT}{P} + B_{22} \right).$$

This reduces immediately to

$$\Delta V = B - y_1 B_{11} - y_2 B_{22}.$$

But by Eq. (3-21)

$$B - y_1 B_{11} - y_2 B_{22} = y_1 y_2 \delta_{12}.$$

Thus

$$\Delta V = y_1 y_2 \delta_{12} \tag{4-35}$$

and is independent of pressure.†

Substitution for $\Delta V$ in Eq. (4-26) gives

$$\Delta G^E = \int_0^P y_1 y_2 \delta_{12} \, dP = y_1 y_2 \delta_{12} P. \tag{4-36}$$

Equations (4-27) and (4-28) then reduce to:

$$\Delta S^E = - y_1 y_2 P (d \delta_{12} / d T) \tag{4-37}$$

and

$$\Delta H = y_1 y_2 P \left( \delta_{12} - T \frac{d \delta_{12}}{d T} \right) = y_1 y_2 P \frac{d (\delta_{12}/T)}{d(1/T)}. \tag{4-38}$$

---

† For an ideal solution $\Delta V$ and hence $\delta_{12}$ are zero. From Eq. (3-20) we see that this can be true only if $B_{12} = (\frac{1}{2})(B_{11} + B_{22})$.

It is seen that although $\Delta V$ is independent of $P$ where the simplest form of the virial expression is valid, $\Delta G^E$, $\Delta S^E$, and $\Delta H$ are all directly proportional to $P$ at constant temperature and composition.

The importance of property changes of mixing as thermodynamic properties results partly from the fact that $\Delta V$ and $\Delta H$ are directly measurable and hence represent experimental observations that provide additional entries into the network of equations relating thermodynamic properties. For pure materials one measures volumes as a function of temperature and pressure, or perhaps certain thermal quantities such as heat capacities and latent heats, or possibly Joule–Thomson coefficients. One can make the same measurements for constant-composition solutions. However, for solutions the alternative of measuring property changes of mixing presents itself. And because such measurements are usually simpler and subject to less error than total property measurements, they are to be preferred.

For gaseous solutions the most obvious property change to observe is $\Delta V$. Thus one takes $P$-$\Delta V$-$T$ data for solutions of various compositions, and Eqs. (4-26), (4-27), and (4-28) or their equivalents are used to calculate other property changes of mixing. Since the integration of Eq. (4-26) must always be carried from $P = 0$ to the pressures for which values are required, data must be taken over the entire pressure range and down to pressures as low as possible. It should be noted that in general $\Delta V$ is finite at zero pressure rather than zero. Measurements of $\Delta V$ at low pressures allow the direct calculation of $\delta_{12}$ by Eq. (4-35). If values for $B_{11}$ and $B_{22}$ are known, the interaction second virial coefficient $B_{12}$ is readily calculated.

Once property changes of mixing are known they may be converted to the properties of the solution by application of the fundamental relationship, Eq. (4-1):

$$M = \sum (x_i M_i) + \Delta M.$$

The properties of the pure constituents at the same $T$ and $P$ must of course be available.

The enthalpy change of mixing $\Delta H$ can also be determined for gases directly by experiment. This is probably most conveniently accomplished by carrying out a flow process in such a way that $\Delta H$ is equal to the quantity of heat required to maintain isothermal conditions during constant-pressure mixing. The name *heat of mixing* usually given to $\Delta H$ arises from this circumstance. Measurements of this kind are rare, but some attention has recently been given to them. Making use of the properties of an exact differential, we find from Eq. (4-24): $\partial \Delta H / \partial P = \Delta V - T(\partial \Delta V / \partial T)$. This may be transformed for a given solution as follows:

$$\left[ \frac{\partial (\Delta V/T)}{\partial T} \right]_P = \frac{-1}{T^2} \left( \frac{\partial \Delta H}{\partial P} \right)_T. \tag{4-39}$$

Integration at constant pressure (and composition) gives

$$\frac{\Delta V}{T} - \frac{\Delta V_0}{T_0} = -\int_{T_0}^{T} \frac{1}{T^2} \left(\frac{\partial \Delta H}{\partial P}\right)_T dT,$$

where $T_0$ is some arbitrarily selected base temperature and $\Delta V_0$ is the volume change of mixing at that temperature and at the pressure and composition of integration. If sufficient $\Delta H$ data are available, the integral on the right-hand side of this equation can be evaluated. However, it is clear that values of $\Delta V$ are calculable only if $\Delta V_0$ is known from some other measurements. Thus if volume changes of mixing are known as a function of pressure and composition at a single temperature $T_0$, room temperature, for example, then these results can be extended by heat-of-mixing measurements. Once the $P$-$\Delta V$-$T$ data are generated, the other property changes of mixing are of course calculable.

For liquids, volume measurements are relatively simple as long as conditions of temperature and pressure are not extreme, and either direct volume measurements on solutions or observations of volume changes of mixing can be made. However, such measurements are not readily carried down to a pressure approaching zero as is the case with gases, for this would require taking data through the two-phase and vapor regions. Thus volume measurements on liquids alone are not sufficient for the calculation of their thermodynamic properties, and the experimental treatment of liquid solutions is quite different from that for gases. For liquids not close to the critical point the thermodynamic properties are only weakly dependent on pressure, and this is true also of the property changes of mixing. Thus for most practical purposes one is content to take data at normal pressures and to determine merely the influence of temperature and composition on the thermodynamic properties. Where the influence of pressure cannot be ignored, approximate methods may be used, as indicated below, for making corrections to the results available at normal pressures, except in the neighborhood of the critical point.

In addition to volumes, the heat of mixing $\Delta H$ is directly measurable for liquid solutions. The effect of pressure is given by Eq. (4-39), and it is usually applied in some approximate form such as:

$$\Delta H_2 - \Delta H_1 = -T^2 \left[\frac{d(\Delta V/T)}{dT}\right](P_2 - P_1) \qquad (\text{const } T),$$

where the effect of pressure on the derivative is ignored as a second-order effect.

Even with data for $\Delta V$ and $\Delta H$ as functions of temperature and composition for the liquid phase alone, one still cannot calculate $\Delta S$ or $\Delta G$. For these, additional data are required, and they usually take the form of phase-equilibrium data. This topic is the subject of Chapter 6.

The measurements just described are rarely made for systems more complex than binary solutions. Even for ternary solutions the data required for a complete description of the thermodynamic property changes of mixing are many times those required for a binary solution, and it becomes impractical to try to accumulate such data. Thus it is virtually mandatory that data for ternary and higher solutions be *calculated* from data for the constituent binaries and pure constituents. However, this is not a problem in thermodynamics but in statistical mechanics, for its solution depends on a consideration of molecular interactions. Suffice it to say here that the development of methods for the prediction of property changes of mixing for higher-order solutions from binary and pure-constituent data looks promising. However, a minimal amount of data on higher-order systems may well be required for the calculation of accurate values for their properties. This is one of the major unsolved problems which should receive attention in the laboratories around the world which devote at least part of their energies to the determination of the thermodynamic properties of solutions.

# CHAPTER 5

# PARTIAL MOLAL PROPERTIES

**5.1. Calculation from Experimental Data.** Although Eq. (2-45) gives a mathematical definition of a partial molal quantity, it is not a particularly useful relationship in practice for the purpose of calculation of partial molal properties from experimental data. Much more convenient would be an equation relating the partial quantities to molal properties of solutions and to mole fractions, for with these variables results from different experimental measurements are always on the same basis. The derivation of such an equation depends on the fact that for a given temperature and pressure the molal property of a solution is a function of composition, i.e., a function of the mole fractions of the constituents present. Thus for constant $T$ and $P$

$$M = m(x_1, x_2, \ldots, x_n).\tag{5-1}$$

Since $\sum_i x_i = 1$ for any solution, all the $x_i$'s of Eq. (5-1) are not independent.

Thus $M$ may be considered a function (but a different one) of $n-1$ mole fractions, since one mole fraction may always be considered a dependent variable.

If we let $x_j$ be the dependent mole fraction, then

$$M = M(x_1, x_2, \ldots, x_{j-1}, x_{j+1}, \ldots, x_n).\tag{5-2}$$

Component $j$ is then the constituent whose mole fraction is considered a dependent variable, and we choose to make it the particular constituent on which we wish to focus attention. It can of course be any constituent. We let the subscript $k$ designate the general constituent other than $j$. Then

$$n = \sum_k (n_k) + n_j.\tag{5-3}$$

Since $n_j$ and the $n_k$'s are all independent

$$\partial n / \partial n_j = 1.\tag{5-4}$$

As applied to component $j$, Eq. (2-45) becomes

$$\overline{M}_j = \partial(n\,M)/\partial n_j.$$

But in view of Eq. (5-4) this can be expanded to give

$$\overline{M}_j = M + n\left(\frac{\partial M}{\partial n_j}\right).\tag{5-5}$$

The functional relationship of Eq. (5-2) allows us to write:

$$\frac{\partial M}{\partial n_j} = \sum_k \left[ \left( \frac{\partial M}{\partial x_k} \right) \left( \frac{\partial x_k}{\partial n_j} \right) \right].$$    (5-6)

Since

$$x_k = n_k/n$$

$$\frac{\partial x_k}{\partial n_j} = -\frac{n_k}{n^2} \left( \frac{\partial n}{\partial n_j} \right) + \frac{1}{n} \left( \frac{\partial n_k}{\partial n_j} \right).$$

But $(\partial n_k/\partial n_j) = 0$, and by Eq. (5-4), $(\partial n/\partial n_j) = 1$. Therefore

$$\frac{\partial x_k}{\partial n_j} = -\frac{n_k}{n^2} = -\frac{x_k}{n}.$$    (5-7)

Combination of Eqs. (5-6) and (5-7) gives

$$\frac{\partial M}{\partial n_j} = -\sum_k \left[ \frac{x_k}{n} \left( \frac{\partial M}{\partial x_k} \right) \right].$$

Since $n$ is the same in all terms of the summation, we may write

$$n \left( \frac{\partial M}{\partial n_j} \right) = -\sum_k \left[ x_k \left( \frac{\partial M}{\partial x_k} \right) \right].$$    (5-8)

Combination of this equation with Eq. (5-5) gives

$$\overline{M}_j = M - \sum_k \left[ x_k \left( \frac{\partial M}{\partial x_k} \right) \right].$$

With regard to this equation, the original functional relationship, Eq. (5-2), upon which it is based must be kept in mind. Thus while $j$ may represent any particular constituent, $x_j$ has been eliminated as a variable. Thus the summation over all other constituents $k$ does not include $j$. Moreover the partial derivatives $(\partial M/\partial x_k)$, are taken with all mole fractions held constant save $x_j$ and the particular $x_k$ with respect to which one takes the derivative. In addition we have specified constant temperature and pressure. All this may be indicated by writing the equation with somewhat more cumbersome notation:

$$\overline{M}_j = M - \sum_{k \neq j} \left[ x_k \left( \frac{\partial M}{\partial x_k} \right)_{T,P,x_r \neq k,j} \right].$$    (5-9)

The use of this equation requires prior knowledge of the molal property $M$ at various compositions for a given system. Property values for a constant-composition material are determined by the methods described in Chapter 3.

In the same way as $\overline{M}_j$ is related to $M$, $\overline{\Delta M}_j$ is related to $\Delta M$. Thus the relation analogous to Eq. (5–9) is:

$$\overline{\Delta M}_j = \Delta M - \sum_{k \neq j} \left[ x_k \left( \frac{\partial \Delta M}{\partial x_k} \right)_{T,P,x_r \neq k,j} \right].$$    (5-10)

In addition, $\overline{\varDelta M_j^E}$ is related to $\varDelta M^E$ as a partial molal property. Thus we have still another equation of the same form:

$$\overline{\varDelta M_j^E} = \varDelta M^E - \sum_{k \neq j} \left[ x_k \left( \frac{\partial \varDelta M^E}{\partial x_k} \right)_{T, P, x_{r \neq k, j}} \right]. \tag{5-11}$$

Equations (5-9), (5-10), and (5-11) are the ones used for calculation of partial molal property values from experimental data. Their application to binary systems will be considered in detail later.

The equations just developed have the disadvantage that they are un-symmetric on account of the elimination of the mole fraction $x_j$ as a variable. Actually, it is not necessary to do this, and an alternative set of equations can be derived by retaining all compositions as variables, even though they are not all independent. Thus the following functional relationship is certainly valid at constant $T$ and $P$:

$$M = m(x_1, x_2, \ldots, x_j, \ldots, x_n). \tag{5-12}$$

Here constituent $j$ is still a particular constituent and we will let $k$ designate the general constituent other than $j$. Thus $n = \sum_k (n_k) + n_j$. However, $x_j$ is now taken as a variable along with all the $x_k$'s. We proceed much as before. In fact, Eqs. (5-4) and (5-5) are still valid.

The functional relationship of Eq. (5-12) allows us to write:

$$\frac{\partial M}{\partial n_j} = \left( \frac{\partial M}{\partial x_j} \right) \left( \frac{\partial x_j}{\partial n_j} \right) + \sum_k \left[ \left( \frac{\partial M}{\partial x_k} \right) \left( \frac{\partial x_k}{\partial n_j} \right) \right]. \tag{5-13}$$

Since $x_j = n_j/n$ and $x_k = n_k/n$

$$\frac{\partial x_j}{\partial n_j} = \frac{1}{n} - \frac{n_j}{n^2} = \frac{1}{n} \left( 1 - \frac{n_j}{n} \right) = \frac{1 - x_j}{n} \tag{5-14}$$

and

$$\frac{\partial x_k}{\partial n_j} = - \frac{n_k}{n^2} = - \frac{x_k}{n} \tag{5-15}$$

Substitution of Eqs. (5-14) and (5-15) into Eq. (5-13) gives:

$$\frac{\partial M}{\partial n_j} = \left( \frac{1 - x_j}{n} \right) \left( \frac{\partial M}{\partial x_j} \right) - \sum_k \left[ \left( \frac{x_k}{n} \right) \left( \frac{\partial M}{\partial x_k} \right) \right]$$

or since $n$ is the same in all terms,

$$n \left( \frac{\partial M}{\partial n_j} \right) = \frac{\partial M}{\partial x_j} - x_j \left( \frac{\partial M}{\partial x_j} \right) - \sum_k \left[ x_k \left( \frac{\partial M}{\partial x_k} \right) \right]$$

If now we take $i$ to represent all constituents including $j$ as well as the $k$'s, the last two terms of this equation can be included in a single summation as follows:

$$n \left( \frac{\partial M}{\partial n_j} \right) = \frac{\partial M}{\partial x_j} - \sum_i \left[ x_i \left( \frac{\partial M}{\partial x_i} \right) \right]. \tag{5-16}$$

Combination of Eqs. (5-16) and (5-5) gives:

$$\overline{M}_j = M + \frac{\partial M}{\partial x_j} - \sum_i \left[ x_i \left( \frac{\partial M}{\partial x_i} \right) \right]. \tag{5-17}$$

The summation in Eq. (5-17) is over all constituents including $j$, and the partial derivatives are taken with all mole fractions held constant except the particular $x_i$ with respect to which differentiation is carried out. Physically, of course, it is impossible to vary just one mole fraction, for the equation $\sum_i (x_i) = 1$ must always be satisfied. Equation (5-17) can therefore not be applied to the calculation of partial molal properties directly from experimental observations. However, this equation and its partial derivatives do have mathematical significance, and because of its symmetry this form of equation is convenient for mathematical derivations and for analytical treatment of data. Thus if data are first fitted by an analytical expression, Eq. (5-17) can be used to operate on it.

It may be of interest to compare Eqs. (5-9) and (5-17). Equation (5-17) may be rearranged as follows:

$$\overline{M}_j = M + \frac{\partial M}{\partial x_j} - x_j \left( \frac{\partial M}{\partial x_j} \right) - \sum_{k \neq j} \left[ x_k \left( \frac{\partial M}{\partial x_k} \right) \right]$$

$$\overline{M}_j = M + (1 - x_j) \left( \frac{\partial M}{\partial x_j} \right) - \sum_{k \neq j} \left[ x_k \left( \frac{\partial M}{\partial x_k} \right) \right]$$

$$\overline{M}_j = M + \left( \sum_{k \neq j} x_k \right) \left( \frac{\partial M}{\partial x_j} \right) - \sum_{k \neq j} \left[ x_k \left( \frac{\partial M}{\partial x_k} \right) \right]$$

$$\overline{M}_j = M + \sum_{k \neq j} \left[ x_k \left( \frac{\partial M}{\partial x_j} \right) \right] - \sum_{k \neq j} \left[ x_k \left( \frac{\partial M}{\partial x_k} \right) \right]$$

or finally

$$\overline{M}_j = M - \sum_{k \neq j} \left[ x_k \left( \frac{\partial M}{\partial x_k} - \frac{\partial M}{\partial x_j} \right) \right].$$

Comparison with Eq. (5-9) shows, since all the $x_k$'s $(k \neq j)$ are independent, that

$$\left( \frac{\partial M}{\partial x_k} \right)_{x_r \neq k, j} = \frac{\partial M}{\partial x_k} - \frac{\partial M}{\partial x_j}.$$

**5.2. Use of an Equation of State.** An equation of state normally expresses the $P$-$V$-$T$ relationship for a pure material or for a constant-composition solution. However, if the constants in such an equation can be related to composition, then the equation of state represents the $P$-$V$-$T$-$x$ behavior of a solution. The only equation of state for which the composition dependence of the constants has a sound basis in theory is the virial equation for gases, Eq. (3-17), for which $B$ and $C$ are given as functions of composition by Eqs. (3-18) and (3-22). This equation has been shown to be valid for gases up to moderate pressures. For binary gaseous solutions, Eqs. (3-21) and (3-25) give convenient expressions for $B$ and $C$.

By way of example we will now apply Eq. (5-17) to the calculation of $\ln\hat{\varphi}_1$ and $\ln\hat{\varphi}_2$ for the case of a binary gaseous solution at low pressure where $\ln\varphi$ is given by Eq. (3-37):

$$\ln\varphi = \frac{BP}{RT}. \tag{3-37}$$

Similarly for pure $i$:

$$\ln\varphi_i = \frac{B_{ii}P}{RT}. \tag{5-18}$$

According to Eq. (3-21) for a binary system $B$ is given by

$$B = y_1 B_{11} + y_2 B_{22} + y_1 y_2 \delta_{12}. \tag{3-21}$$

Equation (5-17) written for the fugacity coefficient in terms of gaseous mole fractions $y_i$ becomes:

$$\ln\hat{\varphi}_j = \ln\varphi + \frac{\partial\ln\varphi}{\partial y_j} - \sum_i \left(y_i \frac{\partial\ln\varphi}{\partial y_i}\right). \tag{5-19}$$

For a binary system made up of constituents 1 and 2,

$$\ln\hat{\varphi}_1 = \ln\varphi + \frac{\partial\ln\varphi}{\partial y_1} - y_1 \frac{\partial\ln\varphi}{\partial y_1} - y_2 \frac{\partial\ln\varphi}{\partial y_2}$$

or

$$\ln\hat{\varphi}_1 = \ln\varphi + (1 - y_1)\frac{\partial\ln\varphi}{\partial y_1} - y_2 \frac{\partial\ln\varphi}{\partial y_2}$$

or finally

$$\ln\hat{\varphi}_1 = \ln\varphi + y_2\left(\frac{\partial\ln\varphi}{\partial y_1} - \frac{\partial\ln\varphi}{\partial y_2}\right). \tag{5-20}$$

It must be kept in mind in connection with Eq. (5-19) that the partial derivatives are taken with all other mole fractions held constant. Thus in Eq. (5-20) the appropriate partial derivatives are $(\partial\ln\varphi/\partial y_1)_{y_2}$ and $(\partial\ln\varphi/\partial y_2)_{y_1}$. Hence by Eqs. (3-37) and (3-21)

$$\frac{\partial\ln\varphi}{\partial y_1} = \frac{P}{RT}\frac{\partial B}{\partial y_1} = \frac{P}{RT}(B_{11} + y_2 \delta_{12})$$

and

$$\frac{\partial\ln\varphi}{\partial y_2} = \frac{P}{RT}\frac{\partial B}{\partial y_2} = \frac{P}{RT}(B_{22} + y_1 \delta_{12}).$$

Substitution in Eq. (5-20) gives:

$$\ln\hat{\varphi}_1 = \frac{BP}{RT} + \frac{Py_2}{RT}(B_{11} + y_2 \delta_{12} - B_{22} - y_1 \delta_{12})$$

or

$$\ln\hat{\varphi}_1 = \frac{P}{RT}(B + y_2 B_{11} + y_2^2 \delta_{12} - y_2 B_{22} - y_1 y_2 \delta_{12}).$$

7*

Since $y_2 B_{11} = (1 - y_1)B_{11} = B_{11} - y_1 B_{11}$,

$$\ln\hat{\varphi}_1 = \frac{P}{RT}[B + B_{11} - (y_1 B_{11} + y_2 B_{22} + y_1 y_2 \delta_{12}) + y_2^2 \delta_{12}].$$

The term in parentheses equals $B$ according to Eq. (3-21). Thus

$$\ln\hat{\varphi}_1 = \frac{P}{RT}(B_{11} + y_2^2 \delta_{12}). \tag{5-21}$$

Similarly

$$\ln\hat{\varphi}_2 = \frac{P}{RT}(B_{22} + y_1^2 \delta_{12}). \tag{5-22}$$

In general

$$\ln\gamma_i = \ln\hat{\varphi}_i - \ln\varphi_i. \tag{2-70}$$

Thus for a binary system substitution by Eqs. (5-18) and (5-21) gives

$$\ln\gamma_1 = \frac{P}{RT}(B_{11} + y_2 \delta_{12} - B_{11})$$

or

$$\ln\gamma_1 = \frac{P \delta_{12} y_2^2}{RT} \tag{5-23}$$

and similarly

$$\ln\gamma_2 = \frac{P \delta_{12} y_1^2}{RT}. \tag{5-24}$$

Eqs. (5-23) and (5-24) give the activity coefficients of a binary gaseous solution at low pressures.

If Eq. (3-32) for $\ln\varphi$, containing the third virial coefficient as well as the second, is used to develop relations for $\ln\gamma_1$ and $\ln\gamma_2$ valid at higher pressures, very much more complicated expressions result. Even so, they still suffer the disadvantage of being based on an equation of state giving $Z$ as an expansion in $P$ rather than in $1/V$. Thus if one wants to calculate values of $\ln\gamma_i$ at moderate pressures from an equation of state, he may as well start with the true virial expansion. However, this is a pressure-explicit equation, which lends itself much more readily to the use of $T$ and $V$ as primary variables rather than $T$ and $P$. Hence we proceed in a different fashion than in the preceding example.

As a result of Eq. (2-3) we can write *for constant temperature and composition*

$$dA = -P dV.$$

But by the virial equation

$$P = \frac{RT}{V} + \frac{BRT}{V^2} + \frac{CRT}{V^3} + \cdots.$$

Therefore

$$\int_{A^*}^{A} dA = -\int_{V\infty}^{V} \frac{RT}{V} dV - \int_{V\infty}^{V} \frac{BRT}{V^2} dV - \int_{V\infty}^{V} \frac{CRT}{V^3} dV,$$

where integration is at constant temperature and composition and is carried from the zero-pressure state to some finite pressure. This results in the equation

$$A - A^* = -RT\ln V + \frac{BRT}{V} + \frac{CRT}{2V^2} + RT\ln V^\infty. \qquad (5\text{-}25)$$

If in the change of state from zero pressure to a finite pressure the gas had remained ideal, $B$ and $C$ would be zero, and the above integration would give simply

$$A^{\mathrm{id}} - A^* = -RT\ln V^{\mathrm{id}} + RT\ln V^\infty.$$

Subtraction of the results of these two integrations gives

$$A - A^{\mathrm{id}} = -RT\ln\frac{V}{V^{\mathrm{id}}} + \frac{BRT}{V} + \frac{CRT}{2V^2}. \qquad (5\text{-}26)$$

This may also be written

$$(nA) - (nA^{\mathrm{id}}) = -nRT\ln\frac{(nV)}{(nV^{\mathrm{id}})} + \frac{n^2 BRT}{(nV)} + \frac{n^3 CRT}{2(nV)^2}.$$

Differentiation with respect to $n_j$ gives

$$\left[\frac{\partial(nA)}{\partial n_j}\right]_{T,(nV),n_k\neq j} - \left[\frac{\partial(nA^{\mathrm{id}})}{\partial n_j}\right]_{T,(nV^{\mathrm{id}}),n_k\neq j} = -RT\ln\frac{(nV)}{(nV^{\mathrm{id}})}$$
$$+ \frac{RT}{(nV)}\left[2nB + n^2\left(\frac{\partial B}{\partial n_j}\right)\right] + \frac{RT}{2(nV)^2}\left[3n^2 C + n^3\left(\frac{\partial C}{\partial n_j}\right)\right], \qquad (5\text{-}27)$$

where use has been made of the fact that $(\partial n/\partial n_j) = 1$.
As a result of Eq. (2-83) this becomes

$$\mu_j - \mu_j^{\mathrm{id}} = -RT\ln\frac{(nV)}{(nV^{\mathrm{id}})} + \frac{RT}{(nV)}\left[2nB + n^2\left(\frac{\partial B}{\partial n_j}\right)\right]$$
$$+ \frac{RT}{2(nV)^2}\left[3n^2 C + n^3\left(\frac{\partial C}{\partial n_j}\right)\right]. \qquad (5\text{-}28)$$

Since $\overline{G}_j$ is identical with $\mu_j$, Eq. (2-58) can be written

$$d\mu_j = RT\,d\ln\hat{f}_j.$$

If this equation is integrated for the hypothetical change of a solution from the ideal gas state to the real gas state at constant temperature, pressure, and composition, we have

$$\mu_j - \mu_j^{\mathrm{id}} = RT\ln\hat{f}_j - RT\ln(y_j P). \qquad (5\text{-}29)$$

Combination with Eq. (5-28) gives

$$RT\ln\hat{f}_j = -RT\ln\frac{(nV)}{(nV^{\mathrm{id}})} + \frac{nRT}{(nV)}\left[2B + n\left(\frac{\partial B}{\partial n_j}\right)\right]$$
$$+ \frac{n^2 RT}{2(nV)^2}\left[3C + n\left(\frac{\partial C}{\partial n_j}\right)\right] + RT\ln(y_j P). \qquad (5\text{-}30)$$

Since $V^{id} = RT/P$, the first and last terms on the right-hand side of this equation combine to give $-RT \ln(V/y_j RT)$. Therefore for a binary solution

$$\ln \hat{f}_1 = -\ln \frac{V}{y_1 RT} + \frac{1}{V}\left[2B + n\frac{\partial B}{\partial n_1}\right] + \frac{1}{2V^2}\left[3C + n\frac{\partial C}{\partial n_1}\right], \quad (5\text{-}31)$$

$$\ln \hat{f}_2 = -\ln \frac{V}{y_2 RT} + \frac{1}{V}\left[2B + n\frac{\partial B}{\partial n_2}\right] + \frac{1}{2V^2}\left[3C + n\frac{\partial C}{\partial n_2}\right]. \quad (5\text{-}32)$$

For a pure material the above equations reduce to

$$\ln f_j = -\ln \frac{V_j}{RT} + \frac{2B_{jj}}{V_j} + \frac{3C_{jjj}}{2V_j^2}. \quad (5\text{-}33)$$

This leads immediately to

$$\ln \varphi_j = \ln \frac{f_j}{P} = -\ln Z_j + \frac{2B_{jj}}{V_j} + \frac{3C_{jjj}}{2V_j^2} \quad (5\text{-}34)$$

which is the same as Eq. (3-34) developed previously.

Equations (5-31) and (5-32) can also be transformed to give for a binary solution

$$\ln \hat{\varphi}_1 = -\ln Z + \frac{1}{V}\left(2B + n\frac{\partial B}{\partial n_1}\right) + \frac{1}{2V^2}\left(3C + n\frac{\partial C}{\partial n_1}\right), \quad (5\text{-}35)$$

$$\ln \hat{\varphi}_2 = -\ln Z + \frac{1}{V}\left(2B + n\frac{\partial B}{\partial n_2}\right) + \frac{1}{2V^2}\left(3C + n\frac{\partial C}{\partial n_2}\right). \quad (5\text{-}36)$$

Combination of Eqs. (5-35) and (5-36) with Eq. (3-34) shows that they can also be written

$$\ln \hat{\varphi}_1 = \ln \varphi + n\left(\frac{\partial B}{\partial n_1}\right)\left(\frac{1}{V}\right) + \frac{n}{2}\left(\frac{\partial C}{\partial n_1}\right)\left(\frac{1}{V}\right)^2, \quad (5\text{-}37)$$

$$\ln \hat{\varphi}_2 = \ln \varphi + n\left(\frac{\partial B}{\partial n_2}\right)\left(\frac{1}{V}\right) + \frac{n}{2}\left(\frac{\partial C}{\partial n_2}\right)\left(\frac{1}{V}\right)^2. \quad (5\text{-}38)$$

Evaluation of the quantities $n(\partial B/\partial n_1)$, $n(\partial C/\partial n_1)$, etc., can be accomplished through application of Eq. (5-16):

$$n\left(\frac{\partial B}{\partial n_j}\right) = \frac{\partial B}{\partial y_j} - \sum_i \left[y_i\left(\frac{\partial B}{\partial y_i}\right)\right]$$

$$n\left(\frac{\partial C}{\partial n_j}\right) = \frac{\partial C}{\partial y_j} - \sum_i \left[y_i\left(\frac{\partial C}{\partial y_i}\right)\right],$$

where the summation over $i$ includes $j$. These equations depend solely on the fact that $B$ and $C$ are functions of composition. Use of Eq. (5-16) is not intended to imply any direct connection with partial molal properties.

For a binary system we have

$$n\frac{\partial B}{\partial n_1} = \frac{\partial B}{\partial y_1} - y_1\frac{\partial B}{\partial y_1} - y_2\frac{\partial B}{\partial y_2}$$

or

$$n\frac{\partial B}{\partial n_1} = y_2 \left( \frac{\partial B}{\partial y_1} - \frac{\partial B}{\partial y_2} \right). \tag{5-39}$$

Similarly

$$n\frac{\partial B}{\partial n_2} = y_1 \left( \frac{\partial B}{\partial y_2} - \frac{\partial B}{\partial y_1} \right), \tag{5-40}$$

$$n\frac{\partial C}{\partial n_1} = y_2 \left( \frac{\partial C}{\partial y_1} - \frac{\partial C}{\partial y_2} \right), \tag{5-41}$$

$$n\frac{\partial C}{\partial n_2} = y_1 \left( \frac{\partial C}{\partial y_2} - \frac{\partial C}{\partial y_1} \right). \tag{5-42}$$

It must be remembered here that the partial derivatives with respect to mole fraction are taken with all other mole fractions held constant.

The virial coefficients for a binary solution are given as functions of composition by

$$B = y_1 B_{11} + y_2 B_{22} + y_1 y_2 \delta_{12}, \tag{3-21}$$

$$C = y_1 C_{111} + y_2 C_{222} + y_1 y_2 (y_1 \delta_{112} + y_2 \delta_{122}). \tag{3-25}$$

Combining Eqs. (3-21) and (3-25) with Eqs. (5-37) through (5-42) gives finally

$$\ln \hat{\varphi}_1 = \ln \varphi + \frac{2}{V} [(B_{11} - B_{12})y_2 + \delta_{12} y_2^2]$$

$$+ \frac{1}{2V^2} [(C_{111} - C_{222} - \delta_{112})y_2 + 2(2\delta_{112} - \delta_{122})y_2^2$$

$$+ 3(\delta_{122} - \delta_{112})y_2^3], \tag{5-43}$$

$$\ln \hat{\varphi}_2 = \ln \varphi + \frac{2}{V} [(B_{22} - B_{12})y_1 + \delta_{12} y_1^2]$$

$$+ \frac{1}{2V^2} [(C_{222} - C_{111} - \delta_{122})y_1 + 2(2\delta_{122} - \delta_{112})y_1^2$$

$$+ 3(\delta_{112} - \delta_{122})y_1^3]. \tag{5-44}$$

There are a number of other possible forms of these equations. They may, of course, be combined with Eq. (3-34) to eliminate $\ln \varphi$. The following represent one form the resulting equations may take.

$$\ln \hat{\varphi}_1 = -\ln Z + [2B_{12} + 2y_1(B_{11} - B_{12})] \left( \frac{1}{V} \right) \tag{5-45}$$

$$+ \frac{1}{2} [3C_{122} + 6y_1(C_{112} - C_{122}) + 3y_1^2(C_{111} + C_{122} - 2C_{112})] \left( \frac{1}{V} \right)^2,$$

$$\ln \hat{\varphi}_2 = -\ln Z + [2B_{12} + 2y_2(B_{22} - B_{12})] \left( \frac{1}{V} \right) \tag{5-46}$$

$$+ \frac{1}{2} [3C_{112} + 6y_2(C_{122} - C_{112}) + 3y_2^2(C_{222} + C_{112} - 2C_{122})] \left( \frac{1}{V} \right)^2.$$

The activity coefficients are given by Eq. (2-70)

$$\ln\gamma_1 = \ln\hat{\varphi}_1 - \ln\varphi_1$$
$$\ln\gamma_2 = \ln\hat{\varphi}_2 - \ln\varphi_2.$$

However, the values of $\hat{\varphi}_i$ and $\varphi_i$ must be at the same temperature and pressure. The above equations are in terms of volume. Thus if one attempts to combine say Eq. (5-45) with Eq. (5-34) to obtain an expression for $\ln\gamma_1$,

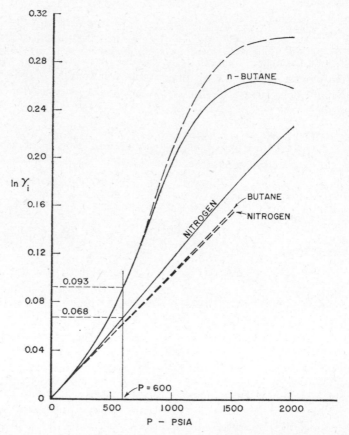

Fig. 5-1. Activity coefficients for nitrogen and n-butane in the binary system containing 49.74% $N_2$ at 370°F

———— From three-term virial equation;   – – – – Experimental values;
------- Eqs. (5-23) and (5-24)

he finds that no simplification can be effected, because the volumes in the two equations are not the same. The best one can do is to compute values of $\ln\hat{\varphi}_i$ and $\ln\varphi_i$ separately and tabulate them for the same temperatures and pressures. The numerical values may then be subtracted.

An example of results calculated through the use of Eqs. (5-34), (5-43), and (5-44) is shown in Fig. 5-1. Values of $\ln \gamma_i$ for both nitrogen and n-butane are plotted as a function of pressure for a mixture containing 49.74% $N_2$ at 370°F. Values of the constants used are given with Fig. 3-3. The virial equation is an entirely adequate representation of the volumetric data for the nitrogen–butane system at 370°C at pressures up to 2000 psia except for mixtures high in butane content. Thus for the nearly equimolal mixture considered here the $\ln \hat{\varphi}_i$ values calculated from the virial equation agree with experimental values. However, the calculated $\ln \gamma_i$ values for butane deviate from the experimental values at pressures above 600 psia because the virial equation does not adequately represent the data for pure butane at higher pressures. The expressions derived for low-pressure applications, Eqs. (5-23) and (5-24), are seen to represent the data very well up to at least 100 psia.

### 5.3. General Equations for Homogeneous Binary Systems.

For a binary system made up of constituents 1 and 2, Eq. (5-9) gives:

$$\overline{M}_1 = M - x_2(\partial M/\partial x_2)$$

or

$$\overline{M}_1 = M + (1 - x_1)(dM/dx_1) \tag{5-47}$$

and

$$\overline{M}_2 = M - x_1(dM/dx_1). \tag{5-48}$$

Use has been made here of the fact that $x_1 + x_2 = 1$. Hence $x_1$ may be regarded as the only independent variable at constant $T$ and $P$, and the partial derivatives may be replaced by total derivatives. Furthermore $dx_1 = -dx_2$. Equations (5-47) and (5-48) lead to the graphical construction shown in Fig. 5-2 for finding $\overline{M}_1$ and $\overline{M}_2$. It is known as the method of tangent intercepts or the Bakhuis–Roozeboom method. The figure is self-explanatory.

Equations analogous to (5-47) and (5-48) can be written for the property changes of mixing and for the excess property changes of mixing:

$$\Delta \overline{M}_1 = \Delta M + (1 - x_1)(d\Delta M/dx_1), \tag{5-49}$$

$$\Delta \overline{M}_2 = \Delta M - x_1(d\Delta M/dx_1), \tag{5-50}$$

and

$$\Delta \overline{M}_1^E = \Delta M^E + (1 - x_1)(d\Delta M^E/dx_1), \tag{5-51}$$

$$\Delta \overline{M}_2^E = \Delta M^E - x_1(d\Delta M^E/dx_1). \tag{5-52}$$

The interrelationships among these various functions are shown in Figs. 5-3, 5-4, and 5-5.

The treatment of experimental data by the classical method of tangent intercepts for the purpose of determining partial molal properties is subject to inherent uncertainties as a result of the necessary graphical operations.

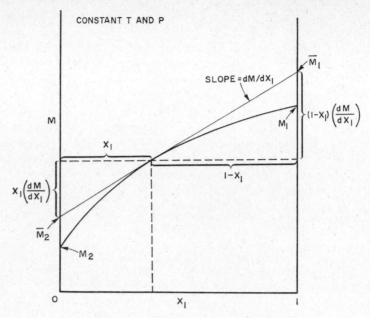

FIG. 5-2. Method of tangent intercepts.

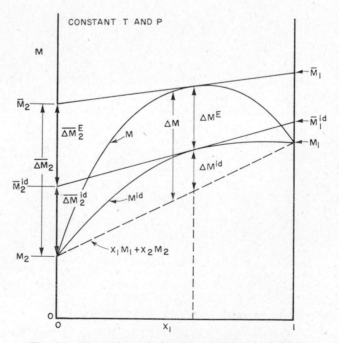

FIG. 5-3. Thermodynamic functions for binary solutions.

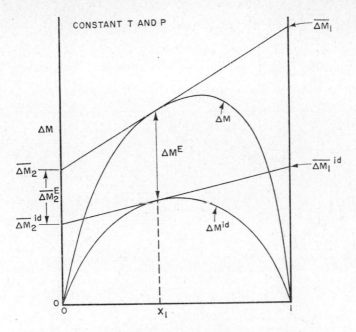

FIG. 5-4. Property changes of mixing for binary solutions.

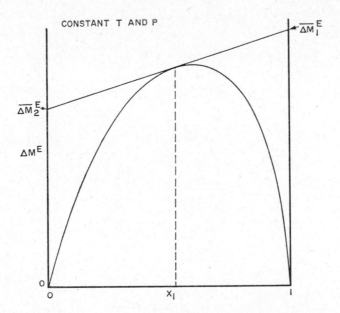

FIG. 5-5. Excess property changes of mixing for binary solutions.

Another method applicable to $\Delta M^E$ values has been proposed by Van Ness and Mrazek†. It makes use of a plot of $\Delta M^E / x_1 x_2$ vs. $x_1$, which in itself is a most sensitive method for the correlation of data. For accurate data it greatly reduces the possible error introduced by the use of graphical techniques. The necessary graphical construction is shown in Fig. 5-6.

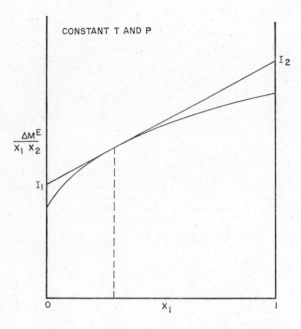

FIG. 5-6. Graphical construction for method of Van Ness and Mrazek.

The partial molal properties $\overline{\Delta M_1^E}$ and $\Delta M_2^E$ are shown to be related to the intercepts $I_1$ and $I_2$ as follows. From the geometry of Fig. 5-6 it is seen that

$$I_1 = \frac{\Delta M^E}{x_1 x_2} - x_1 \frac{d\left(\dfrac{\Delta M^E}{x_1 x_2}\right)}{dx_1}$$

but

$$\frac{d\left(\dfrac{\Delta M^E}{x_1 x_2}\right)}{dx_1} = \frac{\left(\dfrac{d\Delta M^E}{dx_1}\right)}{x_1 x_2} + \left(\frac{\Delta M^E}{x_1 x_2}\right)\left(\frac{x_1 - x_2}{x_1 x_2}\right).$$

† The description of the method of Van Ness and Mrazek which follows was first published and, with permission, is largely taken from the article "Treatment of Thermodynamic Data for Homogeneous Binary Systems", by H. C. Van Ness and R. V. Mrazek, *A.I.Ch.E. Journal*, 5, 209 (1959).

Therefore

$$I_1 = \frac{\Delta M^E}{x_1 x_2} - x_1 \left[ \frac{\left( \dfrac{\mathrm{d}\Delta M^E}{\mathrm{d} x_1} \right)}{x_1 x_2} + \frac{\Delta M^E}{x_1 x_2} \left( \frac{x_1 - x_2}{x_1 x_2} \right) \right].$$

Algebraic manipulation reduces this to

$$I_1 = 2 \left( \frac{\Delta M^E}{x_1 x_2} \right) - \frac{1}{x_2^2} \left[ \Delta M^E + x_2 \left( \frac{\mathrm{d}\Delta M^E}{\mathrm{d} x_1} \right) \right].$$

But Eq. (5-51) shows that

$$\left[ \Delta M^E + x_2 \left( \frac{\mathrm{d}\Delta M^E}{\mathrm{d} x_1} \right) \right] = \overline{\Delta M_1^E}.$$

Therefore

$$\overline{\Delta M_1^E} = x_2^2 \left[ 2 \left( \frac{\Delta M^E}{x_1 x_2} \right) - I_1 \right]. \tag{5-53}$$

Similarly

$$\overline{\Delta M_2^E} = x_1^2 \left[ 2 \left( \frac{\Delta M^E}{x_1 x_2} \right) - I_2 \right]. \tag{5-54}$$

In the limit as $x_1$ approaches zero, $x_2$ approaches unity, and $\Delta M^E/x_1 x_2$ approaches $I_1$. Thus by Eq. (5-53)

$$\lim_{x_1 \to 0} \overline{\Delta M_1^E} = (1)(2 I_1 - I_1) = I_1. \tag{5-55}$$

Similarly

$$\lim_{x_2 \to 0} \overline{\Delta M_2^E} = I_2. \tag{5-56}$$

Thus the intercepts of the curve of $\Delta M^E/x_1 x_2$ with the edges of the diagram represent the limiting values of the partial molal excess properties at infinite dilution.

The same derivation could be presented in terms of $M$ or $\Delta M$ as well as $\Delta M^E$. However, $M/x_1 x_2$ and $\Delta M/x_1 x_2$ (except for the cases where $\Delta M \equiv \Delta M^E$) approach infinity at both $x_1 = 0$ and $x_1 = 1$ and the method fails. This is not true of $\Delta M^E/x_1 x_2$, which remains finite. No practical limitation is imposed on the method as a result, because mixture data can always be easily converted to excess values, provided that the necessary data for the pure constituents are known.

At first thought it might seem that the determination of $\overline{\Delta M_1^E}$ and $\overline{\Delta M_2^E}$ by the method just described would be subject to errors of the same order as the usual method of tangent intercepts, because it too requires the graphical determination of the intercepts of tangents drawn to a curve; however, this is not the case. The difference lies in the fact that the opposite intercepts come into play in the two cases. On the usual plot of $\Delta M^E$ vs. $x_1$ the tangent intercept at $x_1 = 1$ is used to determine $\overline{\Delta M_1^E}$; whereas on the plot of $\Delta M^E/x_1 x_2$ the intercept at $x_1 = 0$ is employed. This is particularly well exemplified in the determination of the limiting values of $\overline{\Delta M_1^E}$ at

$x_1 = 0$ and $\overline{\Delta M_2^E}$ at $x_2 = 0$, that is, the partial properties at infinite dilution. These values are almost impossible to obtain accurately from the usual plot because of the long extrapolations required, but they are simply the intercepts of the curve of $\Delta M^E/x_1 x_2$ vs. $x_1$ at $x_1 = 0$ and at $x_1 = 1$, as indicated by Eqs. (5-55) and (5-56).

The intercepts of the tangents drawn to the $\Delta M^E/x_1 x_2$ curve are of course subject to the normal errors involved in drawing tangents. However, the uncertainty of an intercept increases as the distance of the point of tangency from the intercept increases, and it is clear from Eqs. (5-53) and (5-54) that the greater this distance, the smaller the number by which the intercept is multiplied. Since the multiplying factor $x^2$ decreases as the uncertainty in $I$ increases, the uncertainty in the $\overline{\Delta M_1^E}$ and $\overline{\Delta M_2^E}$ values remains small.

Another advantage of drawing the $\Delta M^E/x_1 x_2$ plot is that it is a very sensitive indication of the precision of the data. If the data are of poor quality, this is usually obvious from the graph; if the data are reasonably good, this plot provides an excellent means of smoothing them. In addition this plot shows at a glance whether sufficient data have been taken to allow the accurate determination of partial properties over the entire composition range.

For highly nonideal systems plots of $\Delta M^E/x_1 x_2$ vs. $x_1$ may exhibit marked curvature, which reduces the precision with which tangents can be drawn and makes the extrapolation of the curve to the edges of the diagram uncertain. It is advantageous in such cases to plot the reciprocal function, $x_1 x_2/\Delta M^E$ vs. $x_1$, as this often results in a much more nearly linear curve. The partial molal quantities are readily determined from this reciprocal plot by:

$$\overline{\Delta M_1^E} = \frac{x_2^2 I_1}{\left(\dfrac{x_1 x_2}{\Delta M^E}\right)^2} \tag{5-57}$$

and

$$\overline{\Delta M_2^E} = \frac{x_1^2 I_2}{\left(\dfrac{x_1 x_2}{\Delta M^E}\right)^2}. \tag{5-58}$$

These equations are derived in a fashion analogous to the derivations of Eqs. (5-53) and (5-54), and all the advantages previously described are retained. Here of course $I_1$ and $I_2$ are the intercepts on a plot of $x_1 x_2/\Delta M^E$ vs. $x_1$.

The use of Eqs. (5-53) and (5-54) is illustrated in Fig. 5-7. Here $(\Delta \ln \varphi)/y_1 y_2$ is plotted vs. $y_1$ for the gaseous system, nitrogen–n-butane at 370°F and 600 psia. Nitrogen is taken as constituent 1. Since the virial equation has already been shown to hold for this system at 370°F and at pressures up to 600 psia, values of $\ln \varphi$ at 600 psia were calculated by Eq. (3-34) for the pure constituents and for the mixtures at each of the five compositions for

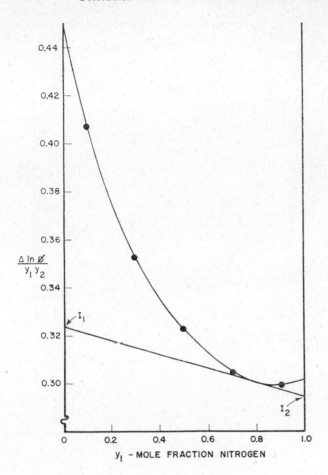

FIG. 5-7. Graphical determination of activity coefficients. Nitrogen–n-butane systems at 370°F and 600 psia.

TABLE 5-1. CALCULATED VALUES FOR FIG. 5-7

| $y_{\text{Nitrogen}}$ | $\ln\varphi$ (Eq. 3-34) | $\Delta \ln\varphi$ | $\dfrac{\Delta \ln\varphi}{y_1\,y_2}$ |
|---|---|---|---|
| 0.0000 | − 0.3176 | 0 | — |
| 0.09468 | − 0.2511 | 0.0349 | 0.4072 |
| 0.2957 | − 0.1457 | 0.0734 | 0.3524 |
| 0.4974 | − 0.0711 | 0.0807 | 0.3228 |
| 0.7016 | − 0.0200 | 0.0638 | 0.3047 |
| 0.9064 | + 0.0099 | 0.0254 | 0.2994 |
| 1.0000 | + 0.0157 | 0 | — |

which Evans and Watson† report data. The virial constants as found from Fig. 3-2 and smoothed in Fig. 3-3 were used. Values of $\Delta \ln\varphi$ were calculated by Eq. (4-32),

$$\Delta \ln\varphi = \ln\varphi - \sum_i (y_i \ln\varphi_i)$$

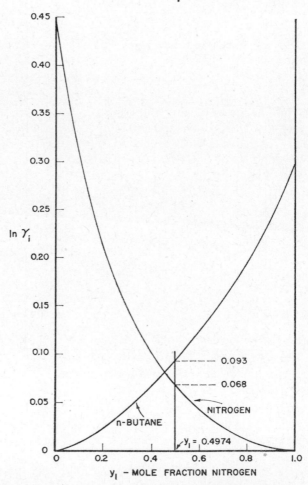

Fig. 5-8. Activity coefficients as a function of composition. Nitrogen–n-butane systeme at 370°F and 600 psia.

and are listed in Table 5-1. It should be noted that the value of $\Delta \ln\varphi$ given for 49.74% nitrogen is 0·0807. This compares very favorably with the result of 0.0808 obtained graphically from Fig. 4-1.

Table 5-1 also lists values of $(\Delta \ln\varphi)/y_1 y_2$ used for the preparation of Fig. 5-7. From this figure values of $\ln\gamma_1$ and $\ln\gamma_2$ can be calculated by

† Op. cit.

Eqs. (5-53) and (5-54), which in this case become

$$\ln\gamma_1 = y_2^2\left[2\left(\frac{\Delta\ln\varphi}{y_1\,y_2}\right) - I_1\right],$$

$$\ln\gamma_2 = y_1^2\left[2\left(\frac{\Delta\ln\varphi}{y_1\,y_2}\right) - I_2\right].$$

The results of these calculations are shown by Fig. 5-8, where $\ln\gamma_1$ and $\ln\gamma_2$ are plotted vs. $y_1$. Values of $\ln\gamma_1$ and $\ln\gamma_2$ at $y_1 = 0.4974$ read from this graph agree exactly with the values read from Fig. 5-1 at 600 psia.

**5.4. Tests for Thermodynamic Consistency.** If $\overline{\Delta M_i}$ or $\overline{\Delta M_i^E}$ data at constant $T$ and $P$ are measured directly (as opposed to measurements of $\Delta M$ or $\Delta M^E$), then the results are subject to a test of thermodynamic consistency provided by the Gibbs–Duhem equation. For excess values this relationship is given by Eq. (4-17):

$$\sum_i \left(x_i\,d\overline{\Delta M_i^E}\right) = 0.$$

For a binary system this becomes

$$x_1\,d\overline{\Delta M_1^E} + x_2\,d\overline{\Delta M_2^E} = 0,$$

which may also be written

$$x_1\left(\frac{d\overline{\Delta M_1^E}}{dx_1}\right) = -x_2\left(\frac{d\overline{\Delta M_2^E}}{dx_1}\right). \tag{5-59}$$

This equation is the basis for what is known as the "slope test." It shows that for thermodynamically consistent data a definite relationship exists between the slopes of the curves of $\overline{\Delta M_1^E}$ and $\overline{\Delta M_2^E}$ vs. $x_1$. Experimental data for these quantities may be tested for agreement with Eq. (5-59). Analogous equations relate $\overline{M_1}$ with $\overline{M_2}$ and $\overline{\Delta M_1}$ with $\overline{\Delta M_2}$. The disadvantage of this test is that the slopes of curves are very difficult to determine accurately, and the uncertainty of the method is often as great as the uncertainty of the data.

One consequence of Eq. (5-59) is that for constant $T$ and $P$

$$\frac{d\overline{\Delta M_1^E}}{dx_1} = 0 \quad\text{at}\quad x_1 = 1$$

and

$$\frac{d\overline{\Delta M_2^E}}{dx_1} = 0 \quad\text{at}\quad x_2 = 1.$$

Thus curves showing $\overline{\Delta M_1^E}$ and $\overline{\Delta M_2^E}$ vs. $x_1$ must become horizontal at $x_1 = 1$ and $x_1 = 0$ respectively, provided only that *all* values of $\Delta \overline{M_1^E}$ and $\overline{\Delta M_2^E}$ remain finite. For nonelectrolyte solutions this requirement

8  CTNES

seems to be satisfied. It should be noted also that $\overline{\Delta M_1^E} = 0$ at $x_1 = 1$ and $\overline{\Delta M_2^E} = 0$ at $x_2 = 1$. This may be seen from Fig. 5-5. Examples of graphs of partial molal properties vs. composition appear in Figs. 5-8 and 5-11.

Since $\ln \gamma_i$'s are partial molal properties, these equations are applicable. Thus at $x_1 = 1$, $\ln \gamma_1 = 0$ and $d \ln \gamma_1 / d x_1 = 0$. Therefore in the vicinity of $x_1 = 1$, $\ln \gamma_1 = 0$. This means that

$$\gamma_1 = \frac{\hat{f}_1}{x_1 f_1} = 1$$

or

$$\hat{f}_1 = x_1 f_1.$$

This is the Lewis and Randall rule, and it becomes valid for any constituent whose mole fraction approaches unity.

In a binary solution when $x_1$ is close to unity, constituent 2 is obviously at high dilution. For this constituent

$$\ln \gamma_2 = \ln \hat{f}_2 - \ln x_2 - \ln f_2.$$

Then

$$\frac{d \ln \gamma_2}{d x_1} = \frac{d \ln \hat{f}_2}{d x_1} + \frac{1}{x_2}$$

and

$$x_2 \frac{d \ln \gamma_2}{d x_1} = x_2 \frac{d \ln \hat{f}_2}{d x_1} + 1.$$

Since the left-hand side of this equation approaches zero as $x_2$ approaches zero, the right-hand side may also be set equal to zero:

$$x_2 \frac{d \ln \hat{f}_2}{d x_1} + 1 = 0$$

or

$$\frac{d \ln \hat{f}_2}{d x_2} = \frac{1}{x_2}$$

or

$$d \ln \hat{f}_2 = d \ln x_2.$$

Integrating

$$\ln \hat{f}_2 = \ln x_2 + \ln k_2$$

or

$$\hat{f}_2 = k_2 x_2.$$

This result may be generalized to the statement that for any constituent of a solution at high dilution

$$\hat{f}_i = k_i x_i,$$

where $k_i$ is a constant. This equation is an extension of Henry's law. Figure 5-9 indicates the regions of applicability of the Lewis and Randall rule and of Henry's law for component 1 of a binary system.

Another test for thermodynamic consistency, known as the "area test", results from writing Eq. (5-59) in the form:

$$x_1\left(-\frac{d\overline{\Delta M_1^E}}{dx_1}\right)dx_1 = (1 - x_1)\left(\frac{d\overline{\Delta M_2^E}}{dx_1}\right)dx_1.$$

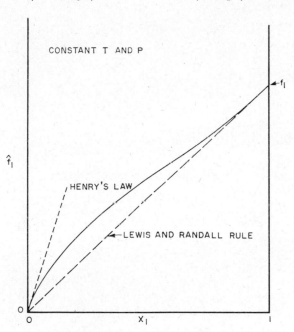

FIG. 5-9. Fugacity as a function of composition.

The two terms of this equation (on the left and right sides) represent the shaded areas shown on Fig. 5-10. Integration from $x_1 = 0$ to $x_1 = 1$ will give the total areas under the two curves, and these must be equal for the area test to be satisfied. This result depends on the fact that the $\overline{\Delta M_1^E}$ and $\overline{\Delta M_2^E}$ curves start at zero at $x_1 = 1$ and at $x_1 = 0$ respectively. The mathematical expression for the area test is

$$\int_0^1 \overline{\Delta M_1^E} \, dx_1 = \int_0^1 \overline{\Delta M_2^E} \, dx_1. \tag{5-60}$$

An analogous equation may be written for $\overline{\Delta M_1}$ and $\overline{\Delta M_2}$ values. Eq. (5-60) may also be written

$$\int_0^1 (\overline{\Delta M_1^E} - \overline{\Delta M_2^E}) \, dx_1 = 0. \tag{5-61}$$

8*

Accordingly the area under the plot of $\left(\overline{\Delta M_1^E} - \overline{\Delta M_2^E}\right)$ vs. $x_1$ from $x_1 = 0$ to $x_1 = 1$ should be zero.

There would seem to be little point in drawing this latter plot in most cases, because the area test can just as easily be made on the former plot (Fig. 5-10) and at the same time examined for at least qualitative agreement with the slope test. It should be noted that the area test will automatically be met when the slope test is satisfied at all values of $x_1$. However the reverse is not true. It is entirely possible to have data which satisfy the

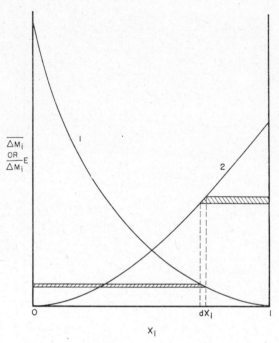

FIG. 5-10. Area test for thermodynamic consistency.

area test but not the slope test, and so it is not generally sufficient merely to adjust the curve of $\left(\overline{\Delta M_1^E} - \overline{\Delta M_2^E}\right)$ vs. $x_1$ to achieve zero area. There is no sure method of adjusting an inconsistent set of independently measured $\overline{\Delta M_1^E}$ and $\overline{\Delta M_2^E}$ values to get correct results. Thus this test suffers from the disadvantage that it does not represent a point-by-point test of the data.

A third method, called the "composition-resolution test" has been proposed by Van Ness.† It represents a general method for the testing of data by the Gibbs–Duhem equation which is straightforward and accurate. Furthermore, it allows a point-by-point evaluation of the data. It is based on the observation that a given curve for the excess property

† H. C. Van Ness, *Chem. Eng. Sci.* **11**, 118 (1959).

change of mixing vs. composition ($x_1$ or $x_2$) can result from an infinite number of sets of experimentally determined values of $\overline{\Delta M_1^E}$ and $\overline{\Delta M_2^E}$, but only one set of values of $\overline{\Delta M_1^E}$ and $\overline{\Delta M_2^E}$ can result from a given curve for the excess property change of mixing. In other words, if the experimental values of $\overline{\Delta M_1^E}$ and $\overline{\Delta M_2^E}$ are combined according to the equation:

$$\Delta M^E = x_1 \overline{\Delta M_1^E} + x_2 \overline{\Delta M_2^E} \qquad (5\text{-}62)$$

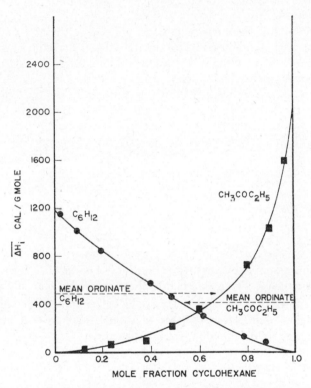

FIG. 5-11. Partial molal heats of mixing. Data of Donald and Ridgway for the cyclohexane–methylethylketone system at 20°C.

and the resulting curve of $\Delta M^E$ vs. $x_1$ is then used (for example, by the method of tangent intercepts) to calculate values of $\overline{\Delta M_1^E}$ and $\overline{\Delta M_2^E}$ the derived set of values should agree with the experimentally measured set. If they do, the data are consistent. If the data are of poor quality, this method can do no more than reject them. But if they are reasonably accurate, the result of this process of testing will be a set of data smoothed in such a way as to be completely consistent.

The "composition" step of this process as represented by Eq. (5-62) presents no difficulty. But the "resolution" step carried out by the classical method of tangent intercepts is usually not sufficiently precise for effective application of the method. The procedures represented by Eqs. (5-53) and (5-54) and by Eqs. (5-57) and (5-58) are entirely adequate, and for this reason the practical application of this test is usually restricted to the excess functions, for which these equations are valid.

If the original data are a set of $\Delta M$ values, the Gibbs–Duhem equation assures thermodynamic consistency for the partial quantities, provided that the calculations are accurate. No objective test for the accuracy of such data is known.

As an example of data which may be tested for thermodynamic consistency, the partial molal heats of mixing for the cyclohexane-methylketone system at 20°C as reported by Donald and Ridgway[†] are available. They are plotted in Fig. 5-11. The curves are drawn to smooth the data and at the same time to meet qualitatively the requirements of the Gibbs–Duhem equation in the regions of infinite dilution. Were the area test of Eq. (5-60) satisfied, the mean ordinates for the two curves would be the same. Since they are not, the data are not consistent and are therefore in error.

The composition-resolution test could also be applied to these data:

$$\Delta H = x_1 \overline{\Delta H_1} + x_2 \overline{\Delta H_2}$$

and

$$\frac{\Delta H}{x_1 x_2} = \frac{\overline{\Delta H_1}}{x_2} + \frac{\overline{\Delta H_2}}{x_1}.$$

Thus by taking smoothed values from Fig. 5-11, a curve of $\Delta H/x_1 x_2$ vs. $x_1$ could be constructed. From this curve, through application of Eqs. (5-53) and (5-54), values of $\overline{\Delta H_1}$ and $\overline{\Delta H_2}$ could be computed for comparison with the original data. However this is a very exacting test, and is not worth attempting unless the area test is satisfied.

[†] M. B. Donald and Kenneth Ridgway, *Chem. Eng. Sci.* **5**, 188 (1956).

# CHAPTER 6

# APPLICATIONS
# TO VAPOR–LIQUID EQUILIBRIUM

**6.1. Criteria of Equilibrium.** We consider here the approach to equilibrium of systems within which composition changes are brought about either by mass transfer between phases or by chemical reaction within a phase, or by both. In order to focus attention on these effects alone, we examine the simplest systems in which they can occur, namely, closed systems in thermal and mechanical equilibrium, both internally and with their surroundings. This means that $P$ and $T$ are uniform throughout any system considered. The state of such a system then depends on the amounts of the phases which constitute it and on their compositions. Such states can be identified, and their thermodynamic properties have definite values provided only that the composition of each phase be essentially uniform throughout the phase, even though chemical and phase equilibrium have not been attained.

However, we know from experiment that the *equilibrium* state reached in a closed system having a particular initial constitution usually depends on only two variables. The formal and complete expression of this observation is known as Duhem's theorem†: For any closed system formed initially from given masses of particular chemical species, regardless of the number of phases and components present and regardless of chemical reactions, the *equilibrium* state is *completely determined* by any two properties of the system, provided only that these two properties are independently variable at the equilibrium state.

When we say *completely determined*, we mean not only that the molal properties of the phases are determined but that the amounts of the phases and thus the *total* properties of the entire system are determined. When we speak of properties of the system, we mean properties attributable to the entire system, i.e., $P$, $T$, total volume, total enthalpy, etc. Thus for purposes of this section it becomes convenient to let the plain symbols, $U$, $H$, $S$, $G$, etc., represent total system properties. Once the general considerations of this section are completed, we will revert to our more usual practice of using these symbols to represent unit properties.

† See Prigogine and Defay as translated by Everett, *Chemical Thermodynamics*, p. 188, Longmans Green, London, 1954.

Duhem's theorem was published in 1899, and apparently largely forgotten. It was entirely unknown to me when in 1955 I published a paper† in which much the same principle was stated. It is easy to think that Duhem's theorem is at odds with the phase rule. This is certainly not true, for the phase rule yields the number of variables required to fix the molal or unit properties of the *phases* making up an *open* system at equilibrium. We are here talking about the complete determination of the equilibrium state of a closed system.

Consider a few simple examples of the application of Duhem's theorem. Let a system be formed by placing a given mass of steam in a piston and cylinder assembly at subatmospheric pressure. We now hold the temperature constant at $100°C$ and adjust the pressure by pushing the piston in. Thus we take $T$ and $P$ as our variables, and fixing these variables establishes the state of the system so long as the saturation pressure is not reached. However, once we reach the saturation pressure the state of the system is no longer determined by $T$ and $P$, for they are no longer *independently variable* for an equilibrium state consisting of liquid and vapor $H_2O$. On the other hand, $T$ and $V$ or $T$ and $S$ or $T$ and $H$ are independently variable, and fixing them does fix the state of the system. Once condensation is complete, $T$ and $P$ again become appropriate variables.

A similar system made up of a vapor mixture of ethanol and water behaves differently. $T$ and $P$ remain independently variable in the two-phase region and are thus suitable variables, with one exception. If the initial composition happens to be the azeotropic composition for the temperature considered, then condensation occurs just as with a pure material, and in this region $T$ and $P$ are not independently variable.

If a system is formed by partially filling a high-pressure vessel with liquid ammonia at say $25°C$ and then pressuring to a high pressure with a gaseous mixture of hydrogen and nitrogen, two different situations are possible. Once the vessel is closed, the volume of the system is fixed. If then the vessel is placed in a constant-temperature bath, two system properties will be fixed, and the system will adjust itself to one of two definite states depending on whether or not chemical reaction takes place. At $25°C$ it is very unlikely that the reaction

$$3H_2 + N_2 \rightleftharpoons 2NH_3$$

will proceed at a detectable rate. In this event an unstable equilibrium state will be reached that is not in any way influenced by the chemical reaction. Hydrogen and nitrogen will saturate the liquid phase, and ammonia will evaporate until the two phases are at mechanical, thermal and phase equilibrium. The final state will be different if the walls of the vessel catalyze the chemical reaction. At $25°C$ the equilibrium is far to the right, and the

† H. C. Van Ness, *Chem. Eng. Sci.* **4**, 279 (1955).

system at equilibrium will now contain more ammonia and less hydrogen and nitrogen than formerly. Both states are fixed for given values of $T$ and $V$, but in the former it must be noted that the components are treated as non-reacting. Even though chemical reaction is theoretically possible, it does not in fact take place.

The properties of closed systems which are *not* at equilibrium depend on more than two variables. These additional variables are usually chosen to be compositions, and the number required depends on the complexity of the system.

Our object now is to develop equations for the property changes which occur in closed systems as they proceed from initial non-equilibrium states toward a final equilibrium state. We have already specified that $T$ and $P$ are to be uniform throughout any system. In addition we restrict consideration to systems on which the only force is that of fluid pressure. Then any work effect is given by

$$\mathrm{d}W = P\,\mathrm{d}V.$$

The first law for a closed system is expressed by

$$\mathrm{d}U = \mathrm{d}Q - \mathrm{d}W.$$

Substitution for $\mathrm{d}W$ yields

$$\mathrm{d}U = \mathrm{d}Q - P\,\mathrm{d}V. \tag{6-1}$$

The entropy change of our closed system may be considered to consist of two parts—the part resulting from heat transfer to the system and given by $\mathrm{d}Q/T$, and the part resulting from irreversibilities within the system, accounted for here by irreversible mass transfer or chemical reaction, which we will designate $\mathrm{d}S_{\mathrm{irr}}$. The total entropy change of the system is therefore

$$\mathrm{d}S = \frac{\mathrm{d}Q}{T} + \mathrm{d}S_{\mathrm{irr}}$$

and

$$\mathrm{d}Q = T\,\mathrm{d}S - T\,\mathrm{d}S_{\mathrm{irr}}. \tag{6-2}$$

Substitution in Eq. (6-1) gives

$$\mathrm{d}U = T\,\mathrm{d}S - P\,\mathrm{d}V - T\,\mathrm{d}S_{\mathrm{irr}}. \tag{6-3}$$

This equation describes the irreversible processes we are considering as they actually occur. It may be compared with the general relation which describes reversible processes for which $\mathrm{d}S_{\mathrm{irr}} = 0$:

$$\mathrm{d}U = T\,\mathrm{d}S - P\,\mathrm{d}V.$$

Of course, when integrated, this latter equation connects any two *equilibrium* states of the system regardless of how the change actually occurred—reversibly or irreversibly; but as a differential equation it can only describe *reversible* processes as they actually occur. This is the reason for the requirement that the two states between which its integral form is applied be equilibrium states and hence *possible* of connection by a reversible process.

We are not in general able to determine values of $d S_{irr}$. However, a perfectly general requirement as a result of the second law is that $d S_{irr}$ must be positive, approaching zero in the limit as the process approaches reversibility. Thus

$$d S_{irr} \geqq 0. \tag{6-4}$$

The best we can do with Eq. (6-3) then is to insert this inequality, and write:

$$d U \leqq T d S - P d V. \tag{6-5}$$

If a process occurs at constant entropy and volume, then Eq. (6-5) becomes:

$$d U_{S,V} \leqq 0. \tag{6-6}$$

What this means is that in any change toward equilibrium of a closed system constrained to constant entropy and volume, the total internal energy of the system must decrease. No change whatsoever in the opposite direction (away from equilibrium) is possible. It is not sufficient that $\varDelta U_{S,V} < 0$ for a finite change of state. *Every increment* of the change must result in a decrease in the internal energy of the system. Hence the equilibrium state, if reached along a path of constant $S$ and $V$, must be one of minimum total internal energy. It follows that any closed system not initially in phase or chemical equilibrium and constrained to changes at constant $S$ and $V$ will adjust itself to a state of minimum total internal energy in so far as it is able and must always tend in this direction.

If the equilibrium state at a given $S$ and $V$ is one of minimum internal energy with respect to all possible changes, then at equilibrium

$$d U_{S,V} = 0. \tag{6-7}$$

This is a perfectly general criterion of equilibrium, but it is by no means the only possible one.

By definition
$$G = U + P V - T S.$$
Thus
$$d G = d U + P d V + V d P - T d S - S d T.$$

Substitution for $d U$ by Eq. (6-3) gives

$$d G = V d P - S d T - T d S_{irr}.$$

The same remarks apply to this equation as to Eq. (6-3). Also, since

$$d S_{irr} \geqq 0,$$
$$d G \leqq V d P - S d T$$
and
$$d G_{T,P} \leqq 0. \tag{6-8}$$

Equation (6-8) is entirely analogous to Eq. (6-6). It shows that a closed system not initially in phase or chemical equilibrium and constrained to changes at constant $T$ and $P$ will always change toward a state representing a minimum value of the Gibbs function, which state is the equilibrium state for that $T$ and $P$. Hence the equation

$$dG_{T,P} = 0 \tag{6-9}$$

is another criterion of equilibrium, and is in fact the one universally used in chemical thermodynamics, because $T$ and $P$ are the variables not only most commonly measured, but also most easily controlled.

Consider the simple example of a closed system containing gaseous ammonia, hydrogen, and nitrogen, approaching chemical equilibrium according to the reaction:

$$3H_2 + N_2 \rightleftharpoons 2NH_3.$$

Let the initial system be formed of 3 moles of hydrogen and 1 mole of nitrogen or alternatively of the stoichiometric equivalent of 2 moles of ammonia. If we let $X$ represent the moles of ammonia present at any instant, the system will contain at that instant

$$X \text{ moles of } NH_3,$$

$$3 - (3/2) X \text{ moles of } H_2,$$

$$1 - (1/2) X \text{ moles of } N_2.$$

Based upon the stoichiometric relation only, the moles of ammonia present in the system can vary from $X = 0$ to $X = 2$. For this system $X$ can clearly be taken as the variable characterizing composition. As a result of Eq. (6-8), we can represent the general shape of a plot of $G$ vs. $X$ for this system as shown in Fig. 6-1.

For each $T$ and $P$ there will be a definite equilibrium composition for all stoichometrically equivalent closed systems, and this composition is calculable through application of the criterion that $dG_{T,P} = 0$ at this composition. The arrows on the curve indicate the *only* direction in which processes at constant $T$ and $P$ can proceed. It should be recalled that we are discussing *irreversible* processes. No process is possible at constant $T$ and $P$ which would proceed from one point on the curve to a higher one. This is merely a special form of the second law, which is the most general expression of the restriction on the direction in which a process may proceed.

The criterion of equilibrium that $dG_{T,P} = 0$ at the equilibrium state for a closed system on which the only force is fluid pressure may at first thought appear to be very limited in its application, for only rarely does the engineer encounter a closed system, let alone one that actually approaches an equilibrium state at constant $T$ and $P$. How is it that we can actually apply this criterion for the calculation of equilibrium states reached in *any* fashion, whether $T$ and $P$ are constant or not, and in *any* fluid system, whether closed or open and on which any force can operate? The reason is that once an equilibrium state is reached, no further changes occur and the system exists in this state at a particular $T$ and $P$. How this state was actually attained is completely immaterial, and for purposes of calculation one may as well consider the path followed in getting there to have been one of constant $T$ and $P$ in a closed system.

Other criteria of equilibrium are also possible and are found by analogous methods to be

$$\mathrm{d}H_{S,P} = 0 \quad \text{and} \quad \mathrm{d}A_{T,V} = 0.$$

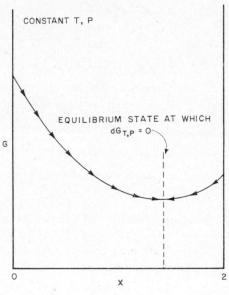

CONSTANT T, P

EQUILIBRIUM STATE AT WHICH
$dG_{T,P} = 0$

G

O

X

2

Fig. 6-1.

Since Duhem's theorem requires the two variables considered to establish the state of a closed system to be independently variable at the equilibrium state, it might be thought that when the several criteria of equilibrium are applied, the variables considered must be independent. That is, for $\mathrm{d}U_{S,V} = 0$ to apply, $S$ and $V$ should be independently variable, and for $\mathrm{d}G_{T,P} = 0$ to apply, $T$ and $P$ should be independently variable, etc. This is not true, for the pair of variables used in each criterion are special. It was shown in Chapter 2 (p. 12) that $U = u(S, V)$, $G = g(T, P)$, etc., for closed systems in equilibrium states *without exception*. Thus $T$ and $P$ determine $G$ even though $T$ and $P$ are not independently variable and $S$ and $V$ determine $U$ even though $S$ and $V$ are not independently variable. However, this is no violation of Duhem's theorem, for while $G$ is always a function of its special variables $T$ and $P$ in closed systems at equilibrium, the other thermo-dynamic properties are not, unless $T$ and $P$ are independently variable.

Thus when $T$ and $P$ are not independent, fixing them determines $G$ only and not the remaining thermodynamic properties, and hence does not completely determine the state of the system. The same may be said for the other functions and their special variables.

The four criteria for equilibrium are equivalent, and any one could be applied to any problem. However, convenience usually dictates the choice of the Gibbs function criterion, for in engineering practice we invariably establish or know the temperature and pressure at which our systems are to reach equilibrium.

As applied to phase equilibrium this criterion requires that the transfer of $dn_i$ moles of component $i$ from phase $(')$ to phase $('')$ must occur at equilibrium in such a way that $dG_{T,P} = 0$.

In general for this transfer

$$dG_{T,P} = (\overline{G}_i'' - \overline{G}_i')\, dn_i.$$

If $dG_{T,P}$ is to be zero, then $\overline{G}_i'' = \overline{G}_i'$, and this equality becomes a condition or criterion of phase equilibrium. This is also written

$$\mu_i'' = \mu_i',$$

where $\mu_i$ is called the chemical potential of component $i$ in a particular phase.

Thus our criteria for equilibrium between simple phases are that:

   (a) The temperature be uniform throughout the system,
   (b) The pressure be uniform throughout the system,
   (c) The chemical potential for each constituent be uniform throughout the system.

For a completely rigorous proof of the necessity and sufficiency of these criteria reference may be made to the original works of J. Willard Gibbs.†

For chemical equilibrium within a phase a differential amount of reaction occurring at equilibrium must result in a differential Gibbs function change equal to zero, $dG_{T,P} = 0$. In general, the Gibbs function change of a phase at constant $T$ and $P$ is given by (see Eq. 2-47):

$$dG_{T,P} = \overline{G}_1\, dn_1 + \overline{G}_2\, dn_2 + \overline{G}_3\, dn_3 + \cdots$$

or

$$dG_{T,P} = \mu_1\, dn_1 + \mu_2\, dn_2 + \mu_3\, dn_3 + \cdots.$$

Since at equilibrium this must be zero

$$\sum_i (\mu_i\, dn_i) = 0.$$

For a chemical reaction the $dn_i$'s are proportional to the stoichiometric numbers, $\nu_i$.

Thus

$$\sum_i (\mu_i\, \nu_i) = 0$$

† Gibbs, *Collected Works*, Yale University Press, New Haven, 1928.

and this is taken as the criterion of equilibrium for a chemical reaction at a given $T$ and $P$. It should be noted that the $\nu_i$'s for the products are taken as positive and for the reactants, negative. For example, consider the reaction:

$$a\,A + b\,B \rightleftharpoons l\,L + m\,M.$$

The criterion of equilibrium requires

$$l\,\mu_L + m\,\mu_M - a\,\mu_A - b\,\mu_B = 0.$$

**6.2. Vapor–Liquid Equilibrium—The General Problem.** We have already indicated the criteria of phase equilibria for fluid sytems. The problem to be considered here is the general one of identifying equilibrium states from thermodynamic calculations through application of these criteria to systems made up of a liquid and a vapor phase in intimate contact.

Included in the definition of the fugacity of a constituent in solution is Eq. (2-68):

$$d\bar{G}_i = R\,T\,d\ln\hat{f}_i \qquad \text{(const. } T\text{)}.$$

For a vapor phase, integration of this equation at constant $T$ and $P$ from an initial state of pure vapor $i$ to a final state of $i$ as a constituent in a vapor solution gives:

$$\bar{G}_i^V - G_i^V = R\,T\ln(\hat{f}_i^V/f_i^V).$$

Similarly for a liquid phase we get a completely analogous equation:

$$\bar{G}_i^L = G_i^L = R\,T\ln(\hat{f}_i^L/f_i^L).$$

If the liquid solution of which $i$ is a constituent is in equilibrium with the vapor phase of which $i$ is a constituent, the two preceding equations may be subtracted to give:

$$\bar{G}_i^V - \bar{G}_i^L - (G_i^V - G_i^L) = R\,T\ln\frac{\hat{f}_i^V f_i^L}{\hat{f}_i^L f_i^V}.$$

But among our criteria for phase equilibrium is the requirement that $\bar{G}_i^V = \bar{G}_i^L$. Thus the above equation becomes

$$G_i^V - G_i^L = -R\,T\ln\frac{\hat{f}_i^V f_i^L}{\hat{f}_i^L f_i^V}. \qquad (6\text{-}10)$$

Now $G_i^V - G_i^L$ can also be obtained by integration at constant $T$ and $P$ of Eq. (2-64), $d\,G_i = R\,T\,d\ln f_i$. This gives immediately

$$G_i^V - G_i^L = -R\,T\ln(f_i^L/f_i^V). \qquad (6\text{-}11)$$

Comparison of Eqs. (6-10) and (6-11) shows that

$$\hat{f}_i^V = \hat{f}_i^L. \qquad (6\text{-}12)$$

Since Eq. (6-12) results as a direct consequence of the requirement for phase equilibrium that $\overline{G}_i^V = \overline{G}_i^L$, it too is a criterion of phase equilibrium, and is in fact the one commonly used.

The usual phase-equilibrium problem is to calculate the composition of a vapor phase in equilibrium with a liquid phase of given composition or vice versa. Compositions may be introduced into the equation by the use of the fugacity coefficient of a constituent in solution, which by definition is $\hat{\varphi}_i = \hat{f}_i/x_i P$, or $\hat{f}_i = x_i \hat{\varphi}_i P$. Thus

$$\hat{f}_i^V = y_i \hat{\varphi}_i^V P = \hat{f}_i^L = x_i \hat{\varphi}_i^L P,$$

where we have used $y_i$ for vapor mole fractions and $x_i$ for liquid mole fractions. Hence

$$y_i \hat{\varphi}_i^V = x_i \hat{\varphi}_i^L. \tag{6-13}$$

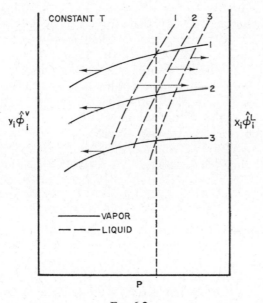

FIG. 6-2.

The rigorous application of this equation requires the calculation by methods discussed earlier of $\hat{\varphi}_i$ values for both liquid and vapor phases as a function of temperature, pressure, and composition.

If one knows, for example, the composition and the temperature of a vapor phase in eqilibrium with a liquid phase, then $\hat{\varphi}_i^V$ values can be calculated as a function of pressure for each constituent. For a ternary system the results might appear as shown by the solid lines in Fig. 6-2. The question now is whether there is a liquid solution which at the same temperature gives curves of $x_i \hat{\varphi}_i^L$ that, constituent for constituent, all intersect the vapor curves at the same pressure, as is indicated in Fig. 6-2. If such a liquid solution exists, it must have the equilibrium composition and the common pressure of intersection of the curves must be the equilibrium pressure. Multiple trial and error calculations are obviously required for this procedure. The difficulty is that each $\hat{\varphi}_i^L$ is a function of liquid composition, and liquid composition is what is sought. Thus this rigorous thermodynamic calculation is of interest only if an accurate equation of state is known—one for which the constants for mixtures bear a known relation to those for the pure constituents and one which is valid throughout the vapor, two-phase, and liquid regions.

This rigorous general method is at present of very limited utility. However, it has been used successfully to develop a correlation valid for the light hydrocarbons. The volumetric properties for the pure light hydrocarbons ($C_1$ through $C_7$) were represented by the Benedict, Webb, Rubin equation of state, and the equilibrium ratios ($y_i/x_i$) resulting from calculation were published in 1950 by the M. W. Kellogg Co. in the form of 324 charts† for 12 light hydrocarbons at pressures up to 3600 psia. Equilibrium ratios (called $K$ values) are actually given directly up to only 1000 psia in a set of 192 charts. The variables used are temperature, pressure, and the molal average boiling points of the liquid and vapor phases. This latter variable is employed as a relatively simple (but approximate) method of taking into account the effect of composition on the equilibrium ratios. Such extensive correlations are not available for other systems, and the only recourse is to experimental data or to methods based on assumptions which often have little relation to physical reality. Calculational procedures which make use of the assumption of ideal solutions, for example, can lead to gross errors, and should be used with the greatest caution.

### 6.3. Vapor–Liquid Equilibrium at Low Pressures.

The most common pressure for chemical processing is atmospheric or thereabouts, and it is therefore not surprising that particular attention has been given the subject of vapor–liquid equilibrium at low pressures—up to several atmospheres. Under these conditions certain quite reliable assumptions can be made about the behavior of the vapor phase which allow development of an accurate equation for the calculation of liquid-phase activity coefficients from phase–equilibrium data. Since the activity coefficient is related to composition and is a precisely defined thermodynamic function, its calculation and correlation is desirable.

By definition,

$$\gamma_i = \frac{\hat{f}_i}{x_i f_i}$$

† See Benedict, Webb, and Rubin, *Chemical Engineering Progress*, **47**, 419, 449, 571, 609 (1951) and **48**, 207 (1952).

or

$$\hat{f}_i^L = \gamma_i^L x_i f_i^L \quad \text{and} \quad \hat{f}_i^V = \gamma_i^V y_i f_i^V.$$

As a result of the criteria of equilibrium

$$\gamma_i^L x_i f_i^L = \gamma_i^V y_i f_i^V$$

or

$$\gamma_i^L = \frac{y_i}{x_i} \frac{f_i^V}{f_i^L} \gamma_i^V = \frac{y_i}{x_i} \frac{f_i^V/P}{f_i^L/P} \gamma_i^V$$

or

$$\ln \gamma_i^L = \ln \frac{y_i}{x_i} + \ln \frac{\varphi_i^V}{\varphi_i^L} + \ln \gamma_i^V. \tag{6-14}$$

Since we are dealing with low pressures, we can take the simplest form of the virial equation of state to represent with sufficient accuracy the volumetric behavior of the vapor phase. It is in fact this assumption which limits the pressure to which our subsequent equations apply. With this understanding, $\ln \varphi_i^V$ is given by Eq. (3-37):

$$\ln \varphi_i^V = \frac{B_{ii} P}{RT}.$$

The liquid-phase $\ln \varphi_i^L$ must be calculated in two parts. At temperature $T$ and at the vapor pressure of pure $i$, the fugacity coefficient for the liquid phase is equal to the fugacity coefficient of the vapor phase and is therefore given by the same equation:

$$\ln \varphi_i' = \frac{B_{ii} P_i'}{RT},$$

where the (') indicates values at the vapor pressure. Now the change in $\ln \varphi_i^L$ in going from the vapor pressure $P_i'$ to the solution pressure $P$ is given by integration of Eq. (3-1):

$$\ln \varphi_i^L - \ln \varphi_i' = \int_{P_i'}^{P} \frac{-\alpha_i}{RT} dP = \frac{1}{RT} \int_{P_i'}^{P} \left( V_i^L - \frac{RT}{P} \right) dP$$

or

$$\ln \varphi_i^L = \frac{B_{ii} P_i'}{RT} + \frac{1}{RT} \int_{P_i'}^{P} V_i^L dP - \ln \frac{P}{P_i'}.$$

Since the volumes of liquids are insensitive to small changes in pressure, $V_i^L$ may be taken as constant in the integral, giving

$$\ln \varphi_i^L = \frac{B_{ii} P_i'}{RT} + \frac{V_i^L}{RT} (P - P_i') - \ln \frac{P}{P_i'}.$$

Combining the equations for $\ln\varphi_i^V$ and $\ln\varphi_i^L$, we have

$$\ln\frac{\varphi_i^V}{\varphi_i^L} = \ln\varphi_i^V - \ln\varphi_i^L = \frac{B_{ii}}{RT}(P - P_i') - \frac{V_i^L}{RT}(P - P_i') + \ln\frac{P}{P_i'}$$

or

$$\ln\frac{\varphi_i^V}{\varphi_i^L} = \frac{(B_{ii} - V_i^L)(P - P_i')}{RT} + \ln\frac{P}{P_i'}. \tag{6-15}$$

Substitution of Eq. (6-15) in Eq. (6-14) gives

$$\ln\gamma_i^L = \ln\frac{y_i P}{x_i P_i'} + \frac{(B_{ii} - V_i^L)(P - P_i')}{RT} + \ln\gamma_i^V. \tag{6-16}$$

If the vapor phase is assumed to be an ideal solution (but not an ideal gas), then $\gamma_i^V = 1$ and the last term of Eq. (6-16) is zero. This introduces an additional approximation which is frequently not justified. For binary solutions we have already shown in Eqs. (5-23) and (5-24) that $\ln\gamma_i^V$ is readily calculated from virial coefficients. Thus for a binary solution at low pressures:

$$\left.\begin{aligned}\ln\gamma_1^L &= \ln\frac{y_1 P}{x_1 P_1'} + \frac{(B_{11} - V_1^L)(P - P_1')}{RT} + \frac{P\,\delta_{12}\,y_2^2}{RT}, \\ \ln\gamma_2^L &= \ln\frac{y_2 P}{x_2 P_2'} + \frac{(B_{22} - V_2^L)(P - P_2')}{RT} + \frac{P\,\delta_{12}\,y_1^2}{RT}.\end{aligned}\right\} \tag{6-17}$$

These equations allow the calculation of liquid-phase activity coefficients for binary solutions at low pressures from vapor–liquid equilibrium data and a minimum of volumetric information. If the vapor is an ideal gas, the last two terms become insignificant, and we get the commonly used expression

$$\gamma_i^L = \frac{y_i P}{x_i P_i'}.$$

It may also be written

$$y_i P = \gamma_i^L x_i P_i',$$

where $y_i P$ is partial pressure. In this form $\gamma_i^L$ appears as a correction factor to Raoult's law. If $\gamma_i^L = 1$ as for an ideal solution,

$$y_i P = x_i P'$$

which is Raoult's law.

Although Raoult's law represents the behavior of a very limited class of solutions, it does provide something of a standard with which to compare the characteristics of any solution. Thus one speaks of positive and negative deviations from Raoult's law. A liquid solution which at a given temperature exerts a vapor pressure greater than would be predicted by Raoult's law is said to exhibit a positive deviation. This almost invariably requires activity coefficients greater than unity.

If positive deviations become sufficiently large, the vapor pressure of the solution will exhibit a maximum with respect to composition at constant temperature, and the solution will form a minimum-boiling (maximum pressure) azeotrope. The limit of this behavior is the solution which separates into two liquid phases over a range of compositions. The constant-boiling system which results is known as a heterogeneous azeotrope. The pressure-composition curves for binary solutions exhibiting positive deviations from Raoult's law are illustrated in Fig. 6-3. In each diagram the dashed lines represent Raoult's law. Since the activity coefficient approaches unity

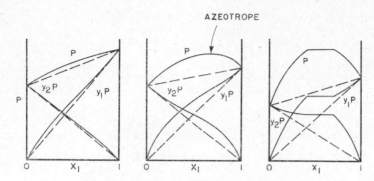

FIG. 6-3. Constant-$T$. $P$–$x$ diagrams. Positive deviations from Raoult's law.

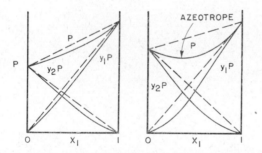

FIG. 6-4. Constant-$T$. $P$–$x$ diagrams. Negative deviations from Raoult's law.

with zero slope ($y_i$ vs. $x_i$) for any constituent whose mole fraction approaches unity, the partial pressure curve becomes tangent to the line representing Raoult's law as that constituent approaches purity.

Negative deviations from Raoult's law are characterized by activity coefficients less than unity. If these deviations are sufficiently large, such solutions form maximum-boiling (minimum pressure) azeotropes. However, this sort of deviation never leads to separation into two phases containing the original chemical species. Rather, the limiting effect is chemical reaction and compound formation. The types of diagram encountered are indicated in Fig. 6-4. Again the dashed lines represent Raoult's law.

9*

It is clear that deviations from Raoult's law are necessary for the occurrence of azeotropes. However, the magnitude of the deviations required for azeotrope formation depends on the system considered. Thus if the vapor pressures of the two constituents forming a binary system are almost the same, only slight deviations result in a maximum or minimum in the solution vapor pressure. Where the pure-constituent vapor pressures are quite different, large deviations are required.

Deviations from Raoult's law naturally have their origin in the molecular structures of the solutions considered. Although much remains to be learned about this subject, present knowledge does provide a good qualitative insight into observed solution behavior. An excellent elementary treatment is given by Prigogine and Defay.†

The activity coefficients of the constituents of liquid solutions at low pressure are functions of liquid composition and temperature. The effect of pressure is so small as to be negligible. Nevertheless, the accurate calculation of activity coefficients from phase-equilibrium data requires the complete determination of equilibrium states. From Eqs. (6-17) we see that the vapor composition $(y_1, y_2)$ in equilibrium with a liquid of composition $(x_1, x_2)$ must be known for a particular $T$ and $P$. The pressure enters directly in the primary term on the right-hand side of the equation. The major influence of temperature is in its effect on the vapor pressures of the pure constituents, $P_1'$ and $P_2'$. In addition, $B_{11}$, $B_{22}$, and $\delta_{12}$ are functions of temperature. The determination of values for these virial coefficients is the most difficult and uncertain part of the calculation represented by Eqs. (6-17). Experimental data are seldom available from which to calculate them, and theoretical and empirical methods are in the formative stages of evolution toward reliable and workable correlations. That a start has been made is clear from several recent papers.††

**6.4. Representation of Activity Coefficients for Binary Liquids.** The solution property directly related to activity coefficients is the excess Gibbs function of mixing. For a binary solution, Eq. (4-16) gives:

$$\Delta G^E / R T = x_1 \ln\gamma_1 + x_2 \ln\gamma_2. \tag{6-18}$$

Thus this quantity is calculable from vapor–liquid equilibrium data. The other exact equation which relates the activity coefficients to $\Delta G^E / R T$ is

---

† I. Prigogine and R. Defay, as translated by D. H. Everett, *Chemical Thermodynamics*, Chapt. XXV, Longmans Green, London, 1954. A more advanced treatment is given by I. Prigogine, *The Molecular Theory of Solutions*, North Holland, Amsterdam, 1957.
†† Cline, Black, *Ind. Eng. Chem.*, **50**, 391 (1958).
  J. M. Prausnitz, *A.I.Ch.E. Journal*, **5**, 3 (1959).
  J. M. Prausnitz, and R. N. Keeler, *A.I.Ch.E. Journal*, **7**, 399 (1961).
  J. M. Prausnitz, and A. L. Myers, *A.I.Ch.E. Journal*, **9**, 5 (1963).

Eq. (4-24), which for a binary system becomes:

$$d\left(\frac{\Delta G^E}{RT}\right) = \frac{\Delta V}{RT}\,dP - \frac{\Delta H}{RT^2}\,dT + (\ln\gamma_1 - \ln\gamma_2)\,dx_1. \qquad (6\text{-}19)$$

We will apply this equation to liquid phases in equilibrium with their vapors, first at constant temperature, and second at constant pressure. It is not, of course, *necessary* to impose these restrictions, but in practice vapor–liquid equilibrium data are always taken either at constant temperature or pressure.

For constant temperature Eq. (6-19) may be written:

$$\frac{d(\Delta G^E/RT)}{dx_1} = \ln\gamma_1 - \ln\gamma_2 + \frac{\Delta V}{RT}\left(\frac{dP}{dx_1}\right). \qquad (6\text{-}20)$$

For constant pressure Eq. (6-19) becomes:

$$\frac{d(\Delta G^E/RT)}{dx_1} = \ln\gamma_1 - \ln\gamma_2 - \frac{\Delta H}{RT^2}\left(\frac{dT}{dx_1}\right). \qquad (6\text{-}21)$$

Equations (6-20) and (6-21) are of identical form, and may both be represented by the equation:

$$\frac{d(\Delta G^E/RT)}{dx_1} = \ln\gamma_1 - \ln\gamma_2 + \varepsilon, \qquad (6\text{-}22)$$

where

$$\varepsilon = \frac{\Delta V}{RT}\left(\frac{dP}{dx_1}\right) \quad \text{for constant-}T\text{ data}$$

and

$$\varepsilon = -\frac{\Delta H}{RT^2}\left(\frac{dT}{dx_1}\right) \quad \text{for constant-}P\text{ data.}$$

Total derivatives may be used in these equations because for binary systems in vapor–liquid equilibrium, constrained to constant temperature or pressure, there is but a single independent variable, here taken as $x_1$. The derivatives $dP/dx_1$ and $dT/dx_1$ are of course the slopes of the pressure-composition and temperature-composition curves for equilibrium at constant temperature and at constant pressure respectively.

Equations (6-18) and (6-22) may be combined to give:

$$\ln\gamma_1 + x_2\,\varepsilon = \frac{\Delta G^E}{RT} + x_2\,\frac{d(\Delta G^E/RT)}{dx_1} \qquad (6\text{-}23)$$

and

$$\ln\gamma_2 - x_1\,\varepsilon = \frac{\Delta G^E}{RT} - x_1\,\frac{d(\Delta G^E/RT)}{dx_1}. \qquad (6\text{-}24)$$

These are expressions for the activity coefficients of the constituents of binary liquid solutions in equilibrium with their vapors at constant temperature or pressure. In either case $\Delta G^E/RT$ is a function of $x_1$. Experience shows that the function most conveniently related to $x_1$ is not $\Delta G^E/RT$

itself, but $\Delta G^E / x_1 x_2 R T$. If this quantity is expressed as a power series in $x_1$, we have

$$\frac{\Delta G^E}{x_1 x_2 R T} = a + b x_1 + c x_1 + \ldots$$

Actually, it turns out that an equivalent and more convenient power series is the following:

$$\frac{\Delta G^E}{x_1 x_2 R T} = B + C(2x_1 - 1) + D(2x_1 - 1)^2 + \ldots \qquad (6\text{-}25)$$

It should be noted that $2x_1 - 1 = x_1 - x_2 = 1 - 2x_2$. The variable $(2x_1 - 1)$ thus takes values of $-1$ to $+1$.

The analytical expression represented by Eq. (6-25) may be combined with Eqs. (6-23) and (6-24) to yield directly:

$$\begin{aligned} \ln\gamma_1 + x_2\,\varepsilon = (x_2)^2\,[B &- C(4x_2 - 3) + D(2x_2 - 1)(6x_2 - 5) \\ &- E(2x_2 - 1)^2(8x_2 - 7) + \ldots], \end{aligned} \qquad (6\text{-}26)$$

$$\begin{aligned} \ln\gamma_2 - x_1\,\varepsilon = (x_1)^2\,[B &+ C(4x_1 - 3) + D(2x_1 - 1)(6x_1 - 5) \\ &+ E(2x_1 - 1)^2(8x_1 - 7) + \ldots]. \end{aligned} \qquad (6\text{-}27)$$

These two equations may be combined to give

$$\begin{aligned} \ln\frac{\gamma_1}{\gamma_2} + \varepsilon = {}& - B(x_1 - x_2) + C(6x_1 x_2 - 1) + D(x_1 - x_2)(8x_1 x_2 - 1) \\ & + E(x_1 - x_2)^2(10x_1 x_2 - 1) + \ldots \end{aligned} \qquad (6\text{-}28)$$

Note from Eq. (6-22) that

$$\ln\frac{\gamma_1}{\gamma_2} + \varepsilon = \frac{\mathrm{d}(\Delta G^E / R T)}{\mathrm{d}x_1}.$$

Hence Eq. (6-28) is an expression for the derivative of $\Delta G^E / R T$ with respect to $x_1$.

We now consider certain special cases.

1. If $B = C = D = E = \cdots = 0$, then by Eq. (6-25) $\Delta G^E / R T$ also $= 0$. For this to be true with any generality, the solution must be ideal, and $\varepsilon = 0$. In this event $\gamma_1 = \gamma_2 = 1$. Solutions formed of very similar constituents such as isomers or adjacent members of homologous series are frequently ideal for all practical purposes.

2. When $B \neq 0$, but $C = D = E = \cdots = 0$, then

$$\ln\gamma_1 + x_2\,\varepsilon = B\,x_2^2,$$
$$\ln\gamma_2 - x_1\,\varepsilon = B\,x_1^2.$$

This type of equation was first proposed by A. W. Porter†. They hold for systems which are not too dissimilar, which have nearly the same molecular

† Porter, *Trans. Faraday Soc.* 16, 336 (1921).

volumes, and which exhibit no specific interactions like hydrogen bonding. An example is the toluene–heptane system. The plot of $\Delta G^E/x_1 x_2 RT$ vs. $x_1$ for such a system is a horizontal line.

3. When $B \neq 0$, $C \neq 0$, but $D = E = \cdots = 0$, then

$$\ln\gamma_1 + x_2 \varepsilon = (x_2)^2 [B - C(4x_2 - 3)],$$

$$\ln\gamma_2 - x_1 \varepsilon = (x_1)^2 [B + C(4x_1 - 3)].$$

These equations are of the common 2-constant Margules type. They are usually written in the equivalent form:

$$\ln\gamma_1 + x_2 \varepsilon = (x_2)^2 [\alpha + 2x_1(\beta - \alpha)]$$

$$\ln\gamma_2 - x_1 \varepsilon = (x_1)^2 [\beta + 2x_2(\alpha - \beta)].$$

Many examples are given in the literature of systems for which the data may be fit by these equations. The plot of $\Delta G^E/x_1 x_2 RT$ for such a system gives a straight but not horizontal line.

4. For systems which are more complex than those described above, the $\Delta G^E/x_1 x_2 RT$ vs. $x_1$ plot is a curved line, and more complicated equations are required to represent the data. In such cases it is often advantageous to try an equation of different form, as described below.

An alternative to the representation of $\Delta G^E/x_1 x_2 RT$ as a power series in $x_1$ or equivalently in $(2x_1 - 1)$ is the expression of the reciprocal function $x_1 x_2 RT/\Delta G^E$ as a power series:

$$\frac{x_1 x_2}{\Delta G^E/RT} = B + C(2x_1 - 1) + D(2x_1 - 1)^2 + \ldots \qquad (6\text{-}29)$$

Combination of Eq. (6-29) with Eqs. (6-23) and (6-24) gives

$$\ln\gamma_1 + x_2 \varepsilon =$$

$$\frac{(x_2)^2 [B - C - D(2x_2 - 1)(2x_2 - 3) + E(2x_2 - 1)^2(4x_2 - 5) - \ldots]}{[B - C(2x_2 - 1) + D(2x_2 - 1)^2 - E(2x_2 - 1)^3 + \ldots]^2},$$

$$(6\text{-}30)$$

$$\ln\gamma_2 - x_1 \varepsilon =$$

$$\frac{(x_1)^2 [B + C - D(2x_1 - 1)(2x_1 - 3) - E(2x_1 - 1)^2(4x_1 - 5) - \ldots]}{[B + C(2x_1 - 1) + D(2x_1 - 1)^2 + E(2x_1 - 1)^3 + \ldots]^2}.$$

$$(6\text{-}31)$$

Again a few special cases are of particular interest. The situation for which $B = C = D = E = \cdots = 0$ is not realistic, for this would require $\Delta G^E$ to be infinite. The following are of practical interest:

1. $B \neq 0$, $C = D = E = \cdots = 0$. In this case the Porter equations result. These have been discussed, and need not be considered again.

2. $B \neq 0$, $C \neq 0$, $D = E = \cdots = 0$. This case yields the famous van Laar equations, and requires a linear relation of

$$\frac{x_1 x_2}{\Delta G^E / RT} \quad \text{to } x_1.$$

Here

$$\ln \gamma_1 + x_2 \varepsilon = \frac{x_2^2 (B - C)}{[B - C(2x_2 - 1)]^2},$$

$$\ln \gamma_2 - x_1 \varepsilon = \frac{x_1^2 (B + C)}{(B + C(2x_1 - 1))^2}.$$

These equations are commonly written in a more convenient but equivalent form:

$$\ln \gamma_1 + x_2 \varepsilon = \frac{\alpha}{\left[1 + \dfrac{\alpha}{\beta} \left( \dfrac{x_1}{x_2} \right)\right]^2}$$

$$\ln \gamma_2 - x_1 \varepsilon = \frac{\beta}{\left[1 + \dfrac{\beta}{\alpha} \left( \dfrac{x_2}{x_1} \right)\right]^2}.$$

The van Laar equations have perhaps been the most useful of all empirical equations proposed for representing activity coefficients derived from vapor–liquid equilibrium data. They are a bit more cumbersome than the Margules equations, but often fit data more closely for complex systems.

3. When the plot of $\dfrac{x_1 x_2}{\Delta G^E / RT}$ is a curved line representation by equations of the form considered here becomes less attractive because of their increased complexity. An alternative, of course, is to resort to equations of yet another form.

A summary of the requirements for the representation of data by the analytical forms discussed is given in Fig. 6-5.

It must be remembered in connection with this discussion that it is vapor–liquid equilibrium data that are under consideration. Since such data are invariably taken at constant temperature (with pressure varying) or at constant pressure (with temperature varying), equations which depend on constancy of temperature *and* pressure are not in general valid. This is the origin of the terms containing $\varepsilon$ in the foregoing equations. Were temperature and pressure both constant, $\varepsilon$ would be zero and our equations would express no more than the relationships between partial molal properties and the solution property. But the fact remains that vapor–liquid equilibrium data for binary systems cannot be taken with *both* temperature and pressure held constant. Hence our equations must reflect the temperature or pressure dependence of the experimental observations.

With constant-pressure data, for which temperature varies, it may be advantageous to deal with the function $\Delta G^E / x_1 x_2$ rather than with

$\Delta G^E / x_1 x_2 RT$. In this event we apply Eq. (4-25) to a binary liquid:

$$d(\Delta G^E) = \Delta V \, dP - \Delta S^E \, dT + R T(\ln \gamma_1 - \ln \gamma_2) \, dx_1$$

or

$$\frac{d(\Delta G^E)}{dx_1} = R T(\ln \gamma_1 - \ln \gamma_2) + \varepsilon', \qquad (6\text{-}32)$$

where

$$\varepsilon' = -\Delta S^E \left( \frac{dT}{dx_1} \right) \quad \text{for constant-}P \text{ data}.$$

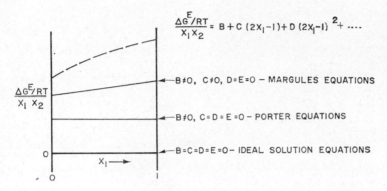

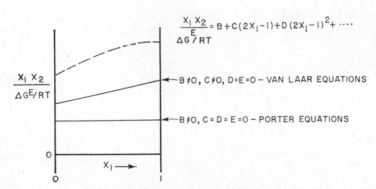

FIG. 6-5. Analytical relations.

Equation (6-18) may be written

$$\Delta G^E = x_1 R T \ln \gamma_1 + x_2 R T \ln \gamma_2. \qquad (6\text{-}33)$$

Equations (6-32) and (6-33) combine for constant-pressure data to give

$$R T \ln \gamma_1 + x_2 \varepsilon' = \Delta G^E + x_2 \left( \frac{d\Delta G^E}{dx_1} \right), \qquad (6\text{-}34)$$

$$R T \ln \gamma_2 - x_1 \varepsilon' = \Delta G^E - x_1 \left( \frac{d\Delta G^E}{dx_1} \right). \qquad (6\text{-}35)$$

If we assume that $\Delta G^E/x_1 x_2$ can be represented by a power series in $x_1$, then we can write

$$\frac{\Delta G^E}{x_1 x_2} = B + C(2x_1 - 1) + D(2x_1 - 1)^2 + \cdots$$

As a result

$$R T \ln\gamma_1 + x_2\,\varepsilon' = (x_2)^2 [B - C(4x_2 - 3)$$
$$+ D(2x_2 - 1)(6x_2 - 5) - \ldots],$$
$$R T \ln\gamma_2 - x_1\,\varepsilon' = (x_1)^2 [B + C(4x_1 - 3)$$
$$+ D(2x_1 - 1)(6x_1 - 5) + \ldots].$$

Again we examine certain special cases:

1. $B = C = D = E = \cdots = 0$. Since $\Delta G^E = 0$, $\varepsilon' = 0$, and we have again an ideal solution, for which $\gamma_1 = \gamma_2 = 1$.

2. If $B \neq 0$, $C = D = E = \cdots = 0$, then

$$R T \ln\gamma_1 + x_2\,\varepsilon' = B x_2^2, \qquad R T \ln\gamma_2 - x_1\,\varepsilon' = B x_1^2.$$

If, in addition, $B$ is independent of $T$, then $\Delta G^E = x_1 x_2 B$, and is also independent of temperature. Since $\partial\Delta G^E/\partial T = -\Delta S^E$, the excess entropy change of mixing is then zero, and $\varepsilon' = 0$. Hence

$$R T \ln\gamma_1 = B x_2^2, \qquad R T \ln\gamma_2 = B x_1^2.$$

Systems which conform to these equations are called "regular". Since $\Delta G^E = \Delta H - T\Delta S^E$, then for regular solutions $\Delta G^E = \Delta H$, and $\Delta H$ is also independent of temperature.

3. If $B \neq 0$, $C \neq 0$, $D = E = \cdots = 0$, then equations of the Margules type result:

$$R T \ln\gamma_1 + x_2\,\varepsilon' = (x_2)^2 [B - C(4x_2 - 3)]$$
$$R T \ln\gamma_2 - x_1\,\varepsilon' = (x_1)^2 [B + C(4x_1 - 3)].$$

If we consider the reciprocal function

$$\frac{x_1 x_2}{\Delta G^E} = B + C(2x_1 - 1) + D(2x_1 - 1)^2 + \cdots$$

then the case where $B \neq 0$, $C \neq 0$, $D = E = \cdots = 0$ is of interest. One gets equations of the van Laar type. Expressed in the usual form, they are

$$R T \ln\gamma_1 + x_2\,\varepsilon' = \frac{\alpha}{\left[1 + \dfrac{\alpha}{\beta}\left(\dfrac{x_1}{x_2}\right)\right]^2},$$

$$R T \ln\gamma_2 - x_1\,\varepsilon' = \frac{\beta}{\left[1 + \dfrac{\beta}{\alpha}\left(\dfrac{x_2}{x_1}\right)\right]^2}.$$

The question of whether it is better to try to represent $\ln\gamma_i$ or $R T \ln\gamma_i$ for constant-pressure data by analytical expressions has been discussed for years. All evidence indicates that this question has no general answer. It depends entirely on the system studied.

The equations considered above have been in use for many years, except that the $\varepsilon$ and $\varepsilon'$ terms have invariably been omitted. We have preferred here to develop completely rigorous equations, with the thought that if simplifications are subsequently made, it will be clear what kind of approximations are introduced.

The omission of the $\varepsilon$ terms can usually be justified for constant-temperature data on the basis that the volume change of mixing $\Delta V$ for liquids is almost always very small. Hence $\varepsilon = (\Delta V/R T)(\mathrm{d}P/\mathrm{d}x_1)$ is negligible. Unfortunately, constant-temperature data are not too common, as the usual practice among engineers is to take data at constant pressure. For constant-pressure data, $\varepsilon = -(\Delta H/R T^2)(\mathrm{d}T/\mathrm{d}x_1)$ may well be significant, and is certainly not negligible for highly non-ideal systems. On the other hand the heat-of-mixing data necessary for the evaluation of this term are rarely known, particularly at the temperatures where vapor–liquid equilibrium data are of practical interest. Furthermore no general method for estimating $\Delta H$ for non-ideal solutions is known. This undoubtedly accounts for the fact that the $\varepsilon$ term has in practice always been omitted from correlations of activity coefficient data. Heat-of-mixing data are now being accumulated, and as they become known they should certainly be used in the exact equations presented here. Even with the necessary data the question remains as to how the $\varepsilon$ term should be treated. Unfortunately this term is not easily represented by a simple analytical expression, let alone one of general validity. It appears necessary therefore to treat it graphically or numerically.

**6.5. Tests for Thermodynamic Consistency.** Activity coefficients derived from binary vapor–liquid equilibrium data are subject to the three tests for thermodynamic consistency discussed in Section 5.4. These tests can be applied equally well to $P$-$x$-$y$ data at constant temperature or to $T$-$x$-$y$ data at constant pressure. However, because such data are taken at constant temperature or constant pressure but not both, the tests as described in Section 5.4 are not directly applicable to activity coefficients derived from such data. The proper tests appear as a consequence of Eqs. (6-22), (6-23), and (6-24).

Equation (6-22) may be written

$$\left(\ln \frac{\gamma_1}{\gamma_2} + \varepsilon\right) \mathrm{d}x_1 = \mathrm{d}(\Delta G^E/R T).$$

Integration from $x_1 = 0$ to $x_1 = 1$ gives

$$\int_0^1 \ln \frac{\gamma_1}{\gamma_2} \mathrm{d}x_1 = -\int_0^1 \varepsilon \, \mathrm{d}x_1. \tag{6-36}$$

This result depends on the fact that $\Delta G^E/RT$ is zero both at $x_1 = 0$ and at $x_1 = 1$. Equation (6-36) means that the areas under $\ln\gamma_1$ and $\ln\gamma_2$ vs. $x_1$ curves are not in general equal and that the difference is given by $\int_0^1 \varepsilon \, dx_1$.

For the case of constant-temperature data where $\varepsilon$ is generally negligible, the area test requires the areas under the $\ln\gamma_1$ and $\ln\gamma_2$ vs. $x_1$ curves to be equal. An alternative plot is $\ln(\gamma_1/\gamma_2)$ vs. $x_1$.

A similar area test is obtained from Eq. (6-32) for constant-pressure data

$$\int_0^1 RT \ln \frac{\gamma_1}{\gamma_2} \, dx_1 = -\int_0^1 \varepsilon' \, dx_1. \tag{6-37}$$

It should be noted that $\varepsilon'$ is related to $\Delta S^E$ and is not in general zero.

The appropriate slope test is obtained by differentiating Eqs. (6-23) and (6-24) with respect to $x_1$. Comparison of the results shows

$$x_1 \left[ \frac{d(\ln\gamma_1 + x_2\,\varepsilon)}{dx_1} \right] = -x_2 \left[ \frac{d(\ln\gamma_2 - x_1\,\varepsilon)}{dx_1} \right]. \tag{6-38}$$

Equation (6-38) easily reduces to

$$x_1 \left( \frac{d\ln\gamma_1}{dx_1} \right) = -x_2 \left( \frac{d\ln\gamma_2}{dx_1} \right) + \varepsilon.$$

Since $\varepsilon$ becomes zero at both $x_1 = 0$ and $x_1 = 1$, this equation shows that curves of $\ln\gamma_1$ and $\ln\gamma_2$ vs. $x_1$ either for constant temperature or constant pressure become tangent to the horizontal at their respective origins. The only requirement is that $\ln\gamma_1$ and $\ln\gamma_2$ never become infinite; this is substantiated by experimental data. Similar equations are obtained from Eqs. (6-34) and (6-35). The slope test is not a convenient one, and is included here only for the sake of completeness.

The composition-resolution test makes use of Eq. (6-18) for the calculation of $\Delta G^E/RT$ from the experimentally determined activity coefficients. If then $\Delta G^E/RT$ is plotted vs. $x_1$ for either constant-temperature or constant-pressure data, the resulting curve may appear as in Fig. 6-6. The intercepts of the tangents drawn to this curve are not partial molal properties (i.e., $\ln\gamma_1$ and $\ln\gamma_2$), because $T$ and $P$ are not both constant. However, the intercepts are seen from inspection of the diagram to represent

$$\frac{\Delta G^E}{RT} + x_2 \left[ \frac{d(\Delta G^E/RT)}{dx_1} \right]$$

and

$$\frac{\Delta G^E}{RT} - x_1 \left[ \frac{d(\Delta G^E/RT)}{dx_1} \right].$$

Reference to Eqs. (6-23) and (6-24) shows that these quantities and thus the tangent intercepts are equal to $\ln\gamma_1 + x_2\,\varepsilon$ and $\ln\gamma_2 - x_1\varepsilon$. Thus the "resolution" of the $\Delta G^E/RT$ curve gives values for $\ln\gamma_1 + x_2\,\varepsilon$ and $\ln\gamma_2 - x_1\,\varepsilon$. If values for $\varepsilon$ are known or are known to be negligible, then the $\ln\gamma_1$ and $\ln\gamma_2$ values may be calculated for comparison with the values calculated directly from the experimental data.

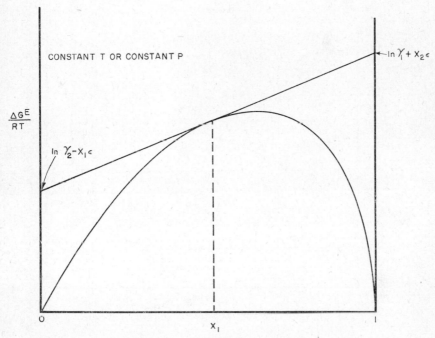

FIG. 6-6. Classical method of tangent intercepts applied to constant-$T$ or constant-$P$ data.

It was shown in Section 5.3 that a far superior method for the determination of tangent intercepts would result from use of the function $\Delta G^E/x_1 x_2 RT$ rather than $\Delta G^E/RT$ itself. The necessary construction is shown in Fig. 6-7. The tangent intercepts on this plot, $I_1$ and $I_2$, are related to the required quantities by

$$\ln\gamma_1 + x_2\,\varepsilon = (x_2)^2\left(2\frac{\Delta G^E}{x_1 x_2 RT} - I_1\right)$$

and

$$\ln\gamma_2 - x_1\,\varepsilon = (x_1)^2\left(2\frac{\Delta G^E}{x_1 x_2 RT} - I_2\right).$$

Thus the $\ln\gamma_1$ and $\ln\gamma_2$ values are given by

$$\frac{\ln\gamma_1}{x_2} = x_2\left(2\frac{\Delta G^E}{x_1 x_2 RT} - I_1\right) - \varepsilon$$

and

$$\frac{\ln\gamma_2}{x_1} = x_1\left(2\frac{\Delta G^E}{x_1\,x_2\,R\,T} - I_2\right) + \varepsilon.$$

It should be noted that

$$\frac{\Delta G^E}{x_1\,x_2\,R\,T} = \frac{\ln\gamma_1}{x_2} + \frac{\ln\gamma_2}{x_1}.$$

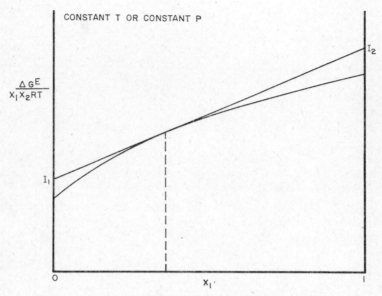

CONSTANT T OR CONSTANT P

FIG. 6-7. Method of Van Ness and Mrazek.

Thus comparison is most conveniently made between experimental and derived values of $(\ln\gamma_1)/x_2$ and $(\ln\gamma_2)/x_1$. Reference to Section 5.3 will also indicate that it is sometimes convenient to deal with the reciprocal function $x_1\,x_2\,R\,T/\Delta G^E$. If the "composition-resolution" test shows the data to be essentially consistent, it will also provide a method of smoothing them so that the resulting curves are thermodynamically consistent. Completely analogous procedures are of course possible for constant-pressure data where it is desired to use the function $\Delta G^E$ itself rather than $\Delta G^E/R\,T$. It should be mentioned that this test is very sensitive and hence is useful only for very excellent data.

**6.6. Influence of Temperature on Activity Coefficients.** From Eq. (4-24)

$$\frac{\partial(\Delta G^E/R\,T)}{\partial T} = \frac{-\Delta H}{R\,T^2}.$$

This equation is often called the Gibbs–Helmholtz equation. In addition, it follows from the basic definitions of the quantities involved that

$$\partial(\Delta H)/\partial T = \Delta C_p.$$

Now the heat capacities of liquids (including solutions) are usually essentially linear with temperature. Thus for a particular composition

$$\Delta C_p = a + bT$$

and

$$d(\Delta H) = (a + bT)\,dT.$$

Integration gives

$$\Delta H = aT + bT^2/2 + c. \tag{6-39}$$

Substitution into the Gibbs–Helmholtz equation gives

$$d\left(\frac{\Delta G^E}{RT}\right) = -\left(\frac{a}{RT} + \frac{b}{2R} + \frac{c}{RT^2}\right)dT.$$

Integration yields

$$\frac{\Delta G^E}{RT} = \frac{-a\ln T}{R} - \frac{bT}{2R} + \frac{c}{RT} + \frac{I}{R}, \tag{6-40}$$

where $I$ is a constant.

This is the general equation relating $\Delta G^E$ to temperature provided the heat capacities of liquids are linear in $T$. Strictly, it applies to solutions of constant composition and pressure. However, pressure has such a small influence on liquid properties we need not in practice concern ourselves with pressure changes, so long as they are moderate and so long as the critical point is not approached.

We may also write

$$\Delta G^E = -aT\ln T - bT^2/2 + c + IT.$$

Since

$$\Delta S^E = -\partial(\Delta G^E)/\partial T$$

we have

$$\Delta S^E = a\ln T + bT + (a - I).$$

If $\Delta C_p$ is constant, $\Delta C_p = a$ and $b = 0$.
Then

$$\Delta H = aT + c$$

and is linear in $T$. Also

$$\Delta S^E = a\ln T + (a - I)$$

and is linear in $\ln T$. Finally

$$\frac{\Delta G^E}{RT} = \frac{-a\ln T}{R} + \frac{c}{RT} + \frac{I}{R}.$$

As a second special case, consider $\Delta C_p = 0$. Then $a = b = 0$. As a result, $\Delta H = c$ and is independent of $T$. Furthermore $\Delta S^E = -I$ and is also constant, independent of $T$. It is in general true that if $\Delta H^E$ is independent of $T$, then $\Delta S^E$ is also, and vice versa. Finally, $\Delta G^E = c + IT$ and is linear in $T$. If *in addition* it should be found that $\Delta S^E = 0$, then $I = 0$, and $\Delta G^E = \Delta H = c$. This is the behavior which characterizes "regular" solutions.

If heat-of-mixing data are determined over a range of temperatures, it is clear from Eq. (6-39) that the constants $a$, $b$, and $c$ could be determined for given solutions. These constants appear in Eq. (6-40) as well. All that remains in Eq. (6-40) is a single undetermined constant, and this may be found from vapor–liquid equilibrium data at a single temperature. Then one could calculate $\Delta G^E/RT$ at any temperature within the range for which the constants were determined. It should be noted that $a$, $b$, $c$, and $I$ are functions of composition. From $\Delta G^E/RT$ values so calculated the $\ln\gamma_1$ and $\ln\gamma_2$ values for a given temperature can be determined through application of Eqs. (6-23) and (6-24). For constant temperature $\varepsilon$ may be considered negligible. Once $\ln\gamma_1$ and $\ln\gamma_2$ values are known as a function of $x_1$, Equations (6-17) can be solved for the equilibrium pressures and vapor compositions. Rearrangement of Eqs. (6-17) gives:

$$\ln y_1 = \ln \frac{\gamma_1 x_1 P_1'}{P} - \frac{(B_{11} - V_1^L)(P - P_1')}{RT} - \frac{P\delta_{12}y_2^2}{RT},$$

$$\ln y_2 = \ln \frac{\gamma_2 x_2 P_2'}{P} - \frac{(B_{22} - V_2^L)(P - P_1')}{RT} - \frac{P\delta_{12}y_1^2}{RT}.$$

In addition to these equations $y_1 + y_2 = 1$. Solution is by trial.

The point of this discussion is that if vapor–liquid equilibrium data are known for one condition, either constant temperature or constant pressure, then heat-of-mixing data may be used to extend them to other conditions, provided the pressure is kept low. Direct calculation of constant-pressure data by the method described is more difficult; however one can repeat the constant-temperature calculations at close enough temperature intervals to allow constant-pressure loci to be described.

The reverse of the above procedure is also possible. If vapor–liquid equilibrium data are taken over a range of temperatures, sets of the constants $a$, $b$, $c$, and $I$ can be determined. From these, $\Delta H$ and $\Delta S^E$ values can be calculated as a function of temperature. However, data of very high quality are required because of the inherent loss of accuracy resulting from the differentiation necessary to this procedure.

### 6.7. Calculation of Vapor–Liquid Equilibria from Vapor Pressure Data.

Considerable effort has been expended over a period of many years on the direct measurements of pressures, temperatures, and compositions of equilibrated vapor and liquid phases. The fact that such data can be tested for thermodynamic consistency indicates an overdetermination of the equilibrium states. In other words, it is not necessary to make so many experimental measurements. Since vapor composition is the most difficult quantity to measure, methods have been developed for finding the compositions of the vapor phase at equilibrium by calculation from the properties of the liquid phase. All one need do by way of experiment is to measure vapor pressures as a function of temperature over binary liquid solutions of known composition. The calculational methods are based on equations which depend on some form of the Gibbs–Duhem relation as written for the Gibbs function of the liquid phase. Although this procedure greatly simplifies the experimental task, it does shift a considerable burden to the theoretical equations which make the calculation of equilibrium data possible.

There are two general methods for the computation of vapor-phase compositions from vapor-pressure data. The one which has received greatest attention† may be termed *indirect*, because it employs the Gibbs–Duhem equation as an auxiliary to produce expressions for the liquid-phase activity coefficients. Vapor-phase compositions are then calculated from the activity coefficients. Usually, some analytic expression is assumed to give the dependence of the excess Gibbs function on liquid composition. The activity coefficient equations are then deduced from it. A trial procedure is employed to determine the coefficients in these equations so that the equilibrium and material balance requirements are met. The simplifying assumptions usually required are least restrictive in the case of constant temperature, and all the articles cited refer to this case. However, in theory the method can be made exact and general, and a recent paper by Tao†† presents a numerical method which is capable of completely rigorous application. Nevertheless, in practice approximations are usually necessary, and a general disadvantage of the method is that these approximations enter in such an indirect fashion that it is difficult to determine their effect.

The other calculational method, which is the subject of this section, allows the *direct* calculation of vapor compositions from vapor-pressure data. This direct relationship connecting the variables is called the general coexistence equation, because it is an equation which must be satisfied when phases coexist at equilibrium. It is a first order differential equation which is suitable for numerical solution, most conveniently accomplished with the aid of a digital computer. One starts with a general form of the Gibbs–Duhem equation. The common forms of this equation, valid only at constant temperature and pressure, are of course inadequate for the treatment of data taken with varying temperature or pressure. A convenient form of the general equation, valid at variable temperature and pressure, is Eq. (2-75).

This equation, relating pressure, temperature, and fugacities for any liquid or vapor phase, whether in equilibrium with another phase or not, is the starting point for the derivation of the general coexistence equation. For a binary system it becomes:

$$\frac{V}{RT} dP + \frac{(H^{id} - H)}{RT^2} dT = x_1 d \ln \hat{f}_1 + x_2 d \ln \hat{f}_2. \qquad (6\text{-}41)$$

† J. A. Barker, *Austral. J. Chem.*, **6**, 207 (1953).
  S. D. Christian, *J. Phys. Chem.*, **64**, 764 (1960).
  H. W. Prengle and G. F. Palm, *Ind. Eng. Chem.*, **49**, 1769 (1957).
†† L. C. Tao, *Ind. Eng. Chem.*, **53**, 307 (1961).

If Equation (6-41) is written first for the vapor phase and then for the liquid phase, the two resulting equations are easily combined, because the conditions for equilibrium require the pressure, temperature, and fugacities respectively to be identical in the two phases. Thus subtraction of the two equations gives:

$$\frac{V^V - V^L}{RT} dP - \frac{(H^V - H^L) - (y_1 - x_1)(H_1^{id} - H_2^{id})}{RT^2} dT$$

$$= (y_1 - x_1) d\ln\frac{\hat{f}_1}{\hat{f}_2}. \tag{6-42}$$

Use has been made here of the fact that $y_2 - x_2 = -(y_1 - x_1)$. Equation (6-42) will remain valid if $(y_1 - x_1)d\ln(y_2 f_2^V/y_1 f_1^V)$ is both added and subtracted on the right-hand side:

$$\frac{V^V - V^L}{RT} dP - \frac{(H^V - H^L) - (y_1 - x_1)(H_1^{id} - H_2^{id})}{RT^2} dT$$

$$= (y_1 - x_1) d\ln\frac{\hat{f}_1/y_1 f_1^V}{\hat{f}_2/y_2 f_2^V} - (y_1 - x_1) d\ln\frac{y_2 f_2^V}{y_1 f_1^V}.$$

Substitution of the activity coefficient $\gamma_i^V$ for $\hat{f}_i/y_i f_i^V$ and rearrangement give:

$$\frac{V^V - V^L}{RT} dP - \frac{(H^V - H^L) - (y_1 - x_1)(H_1^{id} - H_2^{id})}{RT^2} dT$$

$$+ (y_1 - x_1) d\ln\frac{f_2^V}{f_1^V} = (y_1 - x_1) d\ln\frac{\gamma_1^V}{\gamma_2^V} + \frac{y_1 - x_1}{y_1(1 - y_1)} dy_1. \tag{6-43}$$

But for a pure material, by Eq. (2-77):

$$d\ln f_i = \frac{V_i}{RT} dP + \frac{H_i^{id} - H_i}{RT^2} dT.$$

Hence

$$d\ln\frac{f_2^V}{f_1^V} = \frac{V_2^V - V_1^V}{RT} dP + \frac{(H_2^{id} - H_1^{id}) - (H_2^V - H_1^V)}{RT^2} dT.$$

Substitution of this last equation into Equation (6-43) gives:

$$\frac{V^V - V^L + (y_1 - x_1)(V_2^V - V_1^V)}{RT} dP$$

$$- \frac{(H^V - H^L) + (y_1 - x_1)(H_2^V - H_1^V)}{RT^2} dT$$

$$= (y_1 - x_1) d\ln(\gamma_1^V/\gamma_2^V) + \frac{y_1 - x_1}{y_1(1 - y_1)} dy_1$$

If the factors in the left-hand terms are multiplied out [again using the identity, $-(y_1 - x_1) = y_2 - x_2$] the resulting terms, $V^V - y_1 V_1^V - y_2 V_2^V$

and $H^V - y_1 H_1^V - y_2 H_2^V$, may be replaced by the volume change and heat of mixing in the vapor, $\Delta V^V$ and $\Delta H^V$, respectively. The completely rigorous general coexistence equation resulting is then:

$$\psi \, \mathrm{d}P + \Omega \, \mathrm{d}T = (y_1 - x_1) \, \mathrm{d} \ln \frac{\gamma_1^V}{\gamma_2^V} + \frac{y_1 - x_1}{y_1(1 - y_1)} \, \mathrm{d}y_1, \qquad (6\text{-}44)$$

where

$$\psi = \frac{\Delta V^V + x_1 \, V_1^V + x_2 \, V_2^V - V^L}{RT},$$

$$\Omega = \frac{-(\Delta H^V + x_1 \, H_1^V + x_2 \, H_2^V - H^L)}{RT^2}.$$

General integration of this equation for variable temperature and pressure is neither practical nor necessary. Data are invariably taken either at constant temperature or at constant pressure. Thus there are two cases to be considered:

(a) Integration with pressure–liquid composition (P-x) data taken at constant temperature, and

(b) Integration with temperature–liquid composition (T-x) data taken at constant pressure.

*Constant temperature.* In this case the $\Omega \, \mathrm{d}T$ term drops out, and Eq. (6-44) becomes:

$$\psi \, \mathrm{d}P = (y_1 - x_1) \, \mathrm{d} \ln \frac{\gamma_1^V}{\gamma_2^V} + \frac{y_1 - x_1}{y_1(1 - y_1)} \, \mathrm{d}y_1. \qquad (6\text{-}45)$$

Clearly, information in addition to a P-x relationship is required for rigorous integration of Eq. (6-45). Specifically, $\psi$ and the activity coefficients of the components in the vapor phase must be evaluated. To do this exactly requires very extensive P-V-T data for both the pure components and their mixtures over the entire composition range. Such data are invariably unavailable, and in their absence suitable approximations must be made. This is probably most conveniently done for low pressures by means of the virial equation of state truncated to the second term. The necessary equations for the vapor-phase activity coefficients are Eqs. (5-23) and (5-24). Their direct combination gives as a very close approximation at low pressure:

$$\ln \frac{\gamma_1^V}{\gamma_2^V} = \frac{\delta_{12} \, P}{RT} (1 - 2y_1). \qquad (6\text{-}46)$$

Since $\delta_{12}$ is a function of temperature only, $\delta_{12}/RT$ is constant at constant temperature. It follows that

$$\mathrm{d} \ln \frac{\gamma_1^V}{\gamma_2^V} = \frac{\delta_{12}}{RT} [-2P \, \mathrm{d}y_1 + (1 - 2y_1) \, \mathrm{d}P].$$

Equation (6-45) then becomes

$$\psi \, dP = (y_1 - x_1) \frac{\delta_{12}}{RT} [(1 - 2y_1) \, dP - 2P \, dy_1] + \frac{y_1 - x_1}{y_1(1 - y_1)} \, dy_1.$$

Rearrangement gives:

$$\frac{dy_1}{dP} = \frac{\psi - (1 - 2y_1)(y_1 - x_1)(\delta_{12}/RT)}{\dfrac{y_1 - x_1}{y_1(1 - y_1)} - (y_1 - x_1)(2P\delta_{12}/RT)}. \tag{6-47}$$

Numerical integration of this equation is not difficult with the aid of a digital computer. Of course, a practical means for evaluating $\psi$ must be at hand. If $P$-$V$-$T$ data for both the pure components and the mixtures are known, $\psi$ can be evaluated exactly. If not, approximations are necessary. In terms of second virial coefficients $\psi$ is given for low pressures to a very close approximation by:

$$\psi = \frac{y_1 y_2 \delta_{12} - V^L + x_1 B_{11} + x_2 B_{22}}{RT} + \frac{1}{P}. \tag{6-48}$$

The reduction of $\Delta V^V$ to $y_1 y_2 \delta_{12}$ results from Eq. (4-35).

Second virial coefficients for the pure components may be known from experimental work or they may be estimated from empirical equations† or by generalized correlations††. For values of $\delta_{12}$ one must have in addition the interaction coefficient $B_{12}$. For this, experimental data are rarely available. However, the work of Prausnitz †† indicates methods of estimation. Since virial coefficients are independent of pressure, conscious extrapolation to fictitious states is avoided. Values of $V^L$, the molal volume of the liquid phase, are usually easily determined experimentally. Estimates of sufficient accuracy are also easy to make. It should be noted that in Eq. (6-48) the first term on the right-hand side, complicated as it may appear, is actually small compared with $1/P$, at least at low pressures (up to several atmospheres). Hence, the estimates of $\delta_{12}$, $V^L$, $B_{11}$, and $B_{22}$ need not be of high accuracy in order to obtain an excellent approximation to the $P$-$y$ curve by integration of Eq. (6-47).

If one assumes the vapor phase to be an ideal solution, $\delta_{12}$ is zero, and Eq. (6-48) becomes

$$\psi = \frac{x_1 B_{11} + x_2 B_{22} - V^L}{RT} + \frac{1}{P}. \tag{6-49}$$

If one assumes the vapor phase to be an ideal gas and in addition assumes the liquid volume to be negligible, then the first term on the right of Eq. (6-48)

---

† Cline Black, *Ind. Eng. Chem.*, **50**, 391 (1958).
†† J. M. Prausnitz, *A.I.Ch.E. Journal*, **5**, 3 (1959).

is zero, and Eq. (6-47) reduces to its simplest form:

$$\frac{dy_1}{d \ln P} = \frac{y_1 (1 - y_1)}{y_1 - x_1}.$$

(6-50)

This equation has been known for many years. What has not been known is the inherent error introduced by the assumptions on which it is predicated.

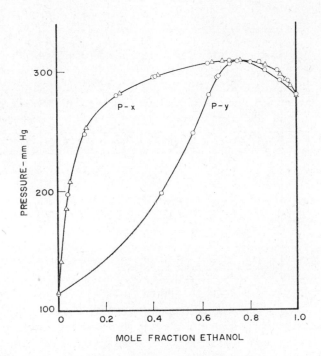

FIG. 6-8. Vapor–liquid equilibrium data for ethanol–toluene at 55°C.

Triangles = P-x data of Ljunglin
Circles   = data of Kretschmer and Wiebe

The P-y curve is calculated by Eq. (6-47).

For an illustration of this method we may make use of the data of Ljunglin† for the ethanol–toluene system. Figure 6-8 shows Ljunglin's vapor-pressure data at 55°C as triangles on the P-x curve. The curve is drawn so as to best correlate the data points. The P-y curve has been calculated from the P-x curve by numerical integration of Eq. (6-47). The required

† J. J. Ljunglin, Ph. D. Thesis, Rensselaer Polytechnic Institute, 1961. See also, J. J. Ljunglin and H. C. Van Ness, *Chem. Eng. Science*, **17**, 531 (1962).

auxiliary data are as follows. Let ethanol be constituent 1, and toluene, constituent 2.

$$B_{11} = -1440 \text{ cc/g mole}$$
$$B_{22} = -1400 \text{ cc/g mole}$$
$$\delta_{12} = 1370 \text{ cc/g mole}$$
$$V_1^L = 61 \text{ cc/g mole} \left.\right\} \text{ combined linearly for } V^L.$$
$$V_2^L = 110 \text{ cc/g mole}$$

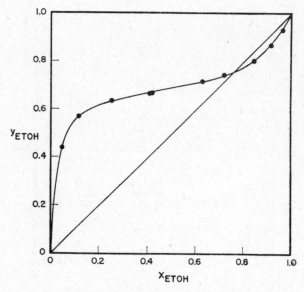

FIG. 6-9. $y$-$x$ diagram for ethanol–toluene at 55°C. The curve is based on the data of Ljunglin. The circles are from Kretschmer and Wiebe.

The second virial coefficients were calculated by the method of Black†, and $\delta_{12}$ was determined by the method of Prausnitz.††

The circles shown in Fig. 6-8 are the data of Kretschmer and Wiebe§ at 55°C, and are included for comparison. Figure 6-9 shows the same results on a $y$-$x$ diagram. The solid line on this graph represents the calculated $y$ values, and the circles are the experimental data of Kretschmer and Wiebe.

The errors introduced by making simplifying assumptions are shown by Fig. 6-10. Curve B shows the difference between values of $y$ calculated by Eq. (6-47) with $\psi$ given by Eq. (6-49) and by the same equations with $S_{12}$ taken as zero. In other words it shows the error introduced by the assumption that the vapor is an ideal solution. Similarly, curve A shows the

† Op. cit.
†† Op. cit.
§ C. B. Kretschmer, and R. Wiebe, *J. Amer. Chem. Soc.*, **71**, 1793 (1949).

difference between values of $y$ as calculated by Eq. (6-47) with the complete expression for $\psi$ and by Eq. (6-50). That is, it shows the error introduced by the assumption that the vapor is an ideal gas and the minor assumption that the liquid volume is negligible. The striking result of these calculations is that on average the assumption of ideal gases leads to slightly smaller errors than the assumption of ideal solution in the vapor. In either case

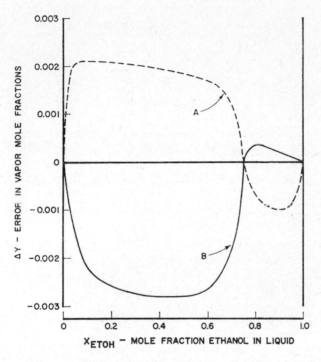

Fig. 6-10. Errors in vapor composition caused by simplifying assumptions. Ethanol–toluene at 55°C. Data of Ljunglin.

Curve A: Error introduced by assuming vapor to be an ideal gas and by neglecting liquid volume.
Curve B: Error introduced by assuming vapor to be an ideal solution.

the errors are quite small even for this highly non-ideal system. However, the major non-idealities appear in the liquid phase, and no assumptions need ever be made for this phase. At higher pressures the vapor phase non-idealities would be more important.

*Constant pressure.* In this case Eq. (6-44) becomes

$$\varOmega \, \mathrm{d}T = (y_1 - x_1) \, \mathrm{d} \ln \frac{\gamma_1^V}{\gamma_2^V} + \frac{y_1 - x_1}{y_1(1 - y_1)} \mathrm{d}y_1. \tag{6-51}$$

In addition to having $T$-$x$ data, one must be able to evaluate both $\Omega$ and the vapor activity coefficients. The basic equation for $\Omega$,

$$\Omega = \frac{-(\Delta H^V + x_1 H_1^V + x_2 H_2^V - H^L)}{R T^2},$$

includes terms that are not easily evaluated. Actually, the quantity in parentheses is a very close approximation to the integral heat of vaporization at the equilibrium temperature of the liquid phase. Values for this quantity are rarely known. Another very accurate estimate is given by the expression, $x_1 L_1 + x_2 L_2 - \Delta H^L$. Hence

$$\Omega = \frac{\Delta H^L - x_1 L_1 - x_2 L_2}{R T^2}, \tag{6-52}$$

where $L_1$ and $L_2$ are the molal heats of vaporization of the pure materials at the equilibrium temperature.

This equation does not result from a complete abandonment of rigor, but comes about merely by dropping terms that are entirely negligible at low pressures compared with the latent heats. Even the liquid heat of mixing $\Delta H^L$ is seldom more than a few per cent of the latent heat terms. Clearly, accurate values for the pure-component latent heats must be known.

Treatment of the $\ln(\gamma_1^V/\gamma_2^V)$ term is not so simple in the case of variable temperature, because $\delta_{12}$ is a function of temperature. It is convenient to rewrite Eq. (6-51) as follows:

$$\Omega \frac{dT}{dy_1} = (y_1 - x_1)\frac{d\ln(\gamma_1^V/\gamma_2^V)}{dy_1} + \frac{y_1 - x_1}{y_1(1 - y_1)}. \tag{6-53}$$

There are three simple methods of treating the first term on the right which allow integration to be carried out readily.

First, the vapor phase can be assumed an ideal solution, and the term drops out. The resulting equation,

$$\Omega \frac{dT}{dy_1} = \frac{y_1 - x_1}{y_1(1 - y_1)} \tag{6-54}$$

is of a form that has appeared in literature for many years. However, there has been no agreement on what should be substituted for $\Omega$.

Second, the derivative,

$$\frac{d\ln(\gamma_1^V/\gamma_2^V)}{dy_1},$$

can be assumed constant over the entire composition range. Since the term is small at low pressures, this should prove an adequate means of treatment in most cases. What it amounts to is an assumption that a plot of $\ln(\gamma_1^V/\gamma_2^V)$ vs. $y_1$ is linear. The end values of such a plot (and hence the slope) can be determined from Eq. (6-46) applied for $y_1 = 0$ and $y_1 = 1$.

Third, Eq. (6-53) can be integrated by either of the methods suggested above. This will give a tentative $T$-$y$ relation which allows a plot of $\ln(\gamma_1^V/\gamma_2^V)$ vs. $y_1$ to be constructed. This curve may be represented analytically and differentiated to give an expression for $d\ln(\gamma_1^V/\gamma_2^V)/dy_1$ in terms of $y_1$. Substitution into Eq. (6-53) allows a second integration. If the $T$-$y$ relation is changed significantly, the procedure can be repeated.

Unless the latent heats of the $\Omega$ term are precisely known, all this may not be worthwhile. Any appreciable uncertainty in the latent heats will certainly overshadow the small effect of non-ideal solution in the vapor.

If constant-pressure data are sought and it proves difficult to provide a satisfactory treatment for the activity coefficients or to obtain adequate data for $\Omega$, it is always possible to repeat the constant-temperature calculations at close enough temperature intervals to allow a constant-pressure locus to be described. This may well be the best method of calculating constant-pressure data. Equation (6-47) then becomes the only one requiring integration. It gives constant-temperature results directly, and for constant-pressure data a computer program can easily be written to carry the integration to the given pressure at a series of temperatures.

A principal advantage of the calculational approach to binary vapor–liquid equilibrium is that vapor-pressure data which may be obtained in a short time with simple equipment and technique represent a potentially large amount of equilibrium data.

The coexistence equations also represent another means of testing the thermodynamic consistency of experimentally determined $P$-$x$-$y$ or $T$-$x$-$y$ data. Since the vapor composition can be calculated from either $T$-$x$ or $P$-$x$ data, the values so calculated can be compared with experimental vapor compositions. Agreement, of course, indicates consistency; disagreement, inconsistency.

Where the solution investigated forms an azeotrope the slopes of the $P$-$x$ and $T$-$x$ curves become zero at the azeotropic composition, and calculations cannot be carried through such a point. One must then work from both ends of the curve toward the azeotrope. The azeotropic composition itself is probably best determined from a $y$-$x$ plot after calculations have been carried to within a reasonable distance of the azeotrope. This is especially true if the $P$-$x$ or $T$-$x$ curve is quite flat near the azeotrope.

A number of special applications of the foregoing equations are of interest. First consider azeotropes, for which $x_1 = y_1$. Equation (6-45) for constant temperature then reduces to $dP = 0$. This is true whether differential pressure variations are considered with respect to vapor composition or with respect to liquid composition. Hence for the azeotropic point

$$(dP/dy_1)_T = (dP/dx_1)_T = 0.$$

Similarly for constant pressure, Eq. (6-51) reduces to $dT = 0$.

Hence

$$(dT/dy_1)_P = (dT/dx_1)_P = 0.$$

We now consider the relation between $T$ and $P$ for the series of azeotropic compositions which result over a range of these variables. For $y_1 = x_1$, Eq. (6-44) reduces to

$$dP/dT = -\Omega/\psi.$$

For $\Omega$ we may use the expression given by Eq. (6-52). The simplest procedure for $\psi$ is to note that it is identical with $(V^V - V^L)/RT$. For low pressures $V^L$ is negligible compared with $V^V$, and may be neglected. Hence

$$\psi = V^V/RT = Z/P,$$

where $Z$ is the compressibility factor for the azeotropic mixture as a vapor. Substitution for $\Omega$ and $\psi$ gives

$$\frac{dP}{dT} = \frac{x_1 L_1 + x_2 L_2 - \Delta H^L}{(RT^2)(Z/P)}$$

or

$$-\frac{d\ln P}{d(1/T)} = \frac{x_1 L_1 + x_2 L_2 - \Delta H^L}{ZR}.$$

Thus the slope of a plot of $\ln P$ vs. $1/T$ for azeotropic states is given by this equation. Experimental results indicate that this line is often nearly straight. There is no theoretical reason why this should be so. When it is, it results from a fortuitous variation of the terms in the above equation in such a way that their combination is essentially constant.

The limiting values which certain quantities approach at infinite dilution are of interest. First consider the liquid activity coefficients as given by Eqs. (6-17). For component 1:

$$\ln\gamma_1^L = \ln\frac{y_1 P}{x_1 P_1'} + \frac{(B_{11} - V_1^L)(P - P_1')}{RT} + \frac{P\,\delta_{12}\,y_2^2}{RT}.$$

In the limit as $x_1 \to 0$, $y_1 \to 0$, $y_2 \to 1$, and $P \to P_2'$. Thus

$$\lim_{x_1\to 0} \ln\gamma_1^L = \lim_{x_1\to 0} \ln\frac{y_1}{x_1} + \ln\frac{P_2'}{P_1'} + \frac{(B_{11} - V_1^L)(P_2' - P_1')}{RT} + \frac{P_2'\,\delta_{12}}{RT}.$$

But

$$\lim_{x_1\to 0} \ln\frac{y_1}{x_1} = \ln \lim_{x_1\to x} \frac{y_1}{x_1} = \ln\left(\frac{dy_1}{dx_1}\right)_{x_1=0}.$$

Therefore

$$\lim_{x_1\to 0} \ln\gamma_1^L = \ln\left(\frac{dy_1}{dx_1}\right)_{x_1=0} + \ln\frac{P_2'}{P_1'} + \frac{(B_{11} - V_1^L)(P_2' - P_1')}{RT} + \frac{P_2'\,\delta_{12}}{RT}.$$

Since the last two terms are small at low pressures, we have approximately

$$(\gamma_1^L)_{x_1=0} = \frac{P_2'}{P_1'}\left(\frac{dy_1}{dx_1}\right)_{x_1=0}.$$

Analogous equations result for component 2. These equations show how limiting values of the activity coefficients in dilute solutions are related to the limiting slopes of a $y$-$x$ curve for vapor–liquid equilibrium. They are valid for either constant-pressure or constant-temperature data.

Limiting values of $dy_1/dP$ and $dy_1/dT$ are useful as starting values for the numerical integrations of Eqs. (6-47) and (6-53). Consider Eq. (6-47) first, the constant-temperature case. The quantity we want is $\lim_{x_1 \to 0}(dy_1/dP)_T$.

When $x_1 \to 0$, $y_1 \to 0$, $x_2 \to 1$, and $y_2 \to 1$. Furthermore, from the basic definition of $\psi$ (following Eq. 6-44)

$$\psi \to \frac{V_2^V - V_2^L}{RT}.$$

Therefore Eq. (6-47) becomes

$$\lim_{x_1 \to 0}(dy_1/dP)_T = \left(\frac{V_2^V - V_2^L}{RT}\right)\lim_{x_1 \to 0}\left(\frac{y_1}{y_1 - x_1}\right),$$

$$\lim_{x_1 \to 0}\left(\frac{y_1}{y_1 - x_1}\right) = \lim_{x_1 \to 0}\frac{(dy_1/dx_1)_T}{(dy_1/dx_1)_T - 1} = \lim_{x_1 \to 0}\frac{(dy_1/dP)_T}{(dy_1/dP)_T - (dx_1/dP)_T}.$$

Combination of these two equations gives:

$$\lim_{x_1 \to 0}(dy_1/dP)_T - \lim_{x_1 \to 0}(dx_1/dP)_T = (V_2^V - V_2^L)/RT.$$

This equation relates the initial slopes of the constant-temperature $P$-$x$ and $P$-$y$ curves. The equation can also be transformed to give:

$$\lim_{x_1 \to 0}(dy_1/dx_1)_T = 1 + \left(\frac{V_2^V - V_2^L}{RT}\right)\lim_{x_1 \to 0}(dP/dx_1)_T.$$

At the other limit as $x_1 \to 1$ and $y_1 \to 1$, we obtain similar equations:

$$\lim_{x_1 \to 1}(dy_1/dP)_T - \lim_{x_1 \to 1}(dx_1/dP)_T = -(V_1^V - V_1^L)/RT$$

and

$$\lim_{x_1 \to 1}(dy_1/dx_1)_T = 1 - \left(\frac{V_1^V - V_1^L}{RT}\right)\lim_{x_1 \to 1}(dP/dx_1)_T.$$

It should be noted that $V_i^V - V_i^L$ is merely the volume change of vaporization of pure $i$ at the saturation pressure.

Completely analogous treatment of Eq. (6-53) for the constant-pressure case gives similar equations:

$$\lim_{x_1 \to 0}(dy_1/dT)_P - \lim_{x_1 \to 0}(dx_1/dT)_P = -L_2/RT^2$$

$$\lim_{x_1 \to 0}(dy_1/dx_1)_P = 1 - (L_2/RT^2)\lim_{x_1 \to 0}(dT/dx_1)_P,$$

$$\lim_{x_1 \to 1}(dy_1/dT)_P - \lim_{x_1 \to 1}(dx_1/dT)_P = L_1/RT^2,$$

$$\lim_{x_1 \to 1}(dy_1/dx_1)_P = 1 + (L_1/RT^2)\lim_{x_1 \to 1}(dT/dx_1)_P.$$

An interesting result is obtained from the second of the above equations if it is assumed that the $y_1$ vs. $x_1$ curve is essentially a straight line from $x_1 = 0$ to small values of $x_1$. Then in this region $(dy_1/dx_1)_P = C$, a constant. Now if we take this equation to be valid not just at $x_1 = 0$ but also for small values of $x_1$, then it may be written:

$$\frac{\varDelta T}{\varDelta x_1} = \frac{(1 - C)(R T_2^2)}{L_2} \quad \text{(constant } P\text{).}$$

Since $\varDelta T = T - T_2$ and $\varDelta x_1 = x_1 - 0$

$$T - T_2 = \frac{(1 - C)(R T_2^2)}{L_2} x_1,$$

where $T_2$ is the boiling point of pure component 2 at the prevailing pressure. This equation gives the boiling point change (either an increase or a decrease) resulting from the addition of small amounts of a volatile solute to a volatile solvent.

If a non-volatile solute is added to a volatile solvent, $(dy_1/dx_1)_P = C = 0$, and the above equation becomes

$$T - T_2 = \frac{R T_2^2}{L_2} x_1.$$

This is the equation for the boiling-point elevation in a dilute solution of a nonvolatile solute.

**6.8. Experimental Measurements.** If we start with the requirement that vapor–liquid equilibrium data be made available for a given binary system over the range of temperatures and pressures of practical interest, then the question to be answered is: What experimental measurements should be made and how should they be made? A better way of phrasing the question would be to ask: How can we obtain the maximum return in useful data from a minimum investment in experimental effort? An unequivocal answer to this latter question is not yet possible for binary systems in general, but it is one that should be carefully considered by anyone faced with the problem for a particular system.

One might measure directly the necessary $P$-$x$-$y$ data at a series of temperatures or the required $T$-$x$-$y$ data at a series of pressures. In either event two general methods are available. The most obvious procedure is to equilibrate the phases in a closed bomb by vigorous shaking or stirring. The apparatus is immersed in a constant-temperature bath, the equilibrium pressure is measured, and the phases are sampled for analysis. Although this method appears to be of primitive simplicity, it is rarely used at low pressures. The primary difficulty is that the vapor phase must be sampled so extensively to obtain a sufficient sample for analysis that the equilibrium state is altered. This problem arises because analysis of a sample in the vapor state has always proved difficult, hence vapor samples have always been condensed for analysis, and this requires the withdrawal of a considerable amount of vapor. An additional disadvantage is that each datum point requires a separate experiment.

Because of the disadvantages of the "static" method just described, virtually all experimenters of recent years have made use of the equilibrium still in which a "dynamic" equilibrium is established between liquid and vapor phases. In this equipment the phases are recirculated into and out of contact with each other. As the vapor phase leaves the equilibrium chamber it is condensed and flows to a reservoir where it is stored as a liquid. The liquid phase is similarly stored, and sampling of the phases is from these reservoirs. The two streams then flow to a mixing chamber, after which the solution formed is partially vaporized to create two phases again. The possibility of storing material of the vapor composition, but as a liquid, is the primary reason for the popularity of the circulatory still. In spite of this, the taking of data with stills is not without its own difficulties. In particular, the question always arises as to whether in a dynamic system true equilibrium is reached and whether the recorded values of temperature and pressure are actually the equilibrium values. Analysis of the phases is of course necessary, and this operation together with the necessary calibrations of the instrument used take considerable time. Nevertheless, many systems have been investigated with this technique, and the equilibrium still must be considered a practical and versatile device for taking vapor–liquid equilibrium data.†

Another avenue of approach, long known to be possible but relatively little used, is that of finding the compositions of one of the equilibrium phases from properties of the other by calculation. This makes unnecessary the measurement of vapor-phase compositions and makes the static method of equilibration of phases attractive. The failure of this method to gain wide acceptance in the past is likely due to a lack of rigor in the derivation and application of the equations which have formerly been used. This has made most difficult any measure of the uncertainty of results. With the development of the exact coexistence equation described in the preceding section, this calculational method becomes most attractive, and affords a path to a more routine determination of binary vapor–liquid equilibria than is possible through purely experimental approaches. Experimental effort is greatly reduced in that no chemical analyses are required. Vapor compositions are calculated, and the liquid phase is made up so as to have a known composition. Vapor pressures are easily obtained over a range of temperatures and are easily correlated. This permits the calculation of equilibrium compositions at an unlimited number of temperatures

---

† For a description of many of the stills that have been used successfully see: E. Hála, J. Pick, V. Fried and O. Vilím, *Vapor–Liquid Equilibrium*, Pergamon Press, London 1958.

and pressures. A possible disadvantage of this method is that it makes use of the Gibbs–Duhem equation for the calculation of results, and therefore the data cannot be tested for thermodynamic consistency by means of this equation. On the other hand the method assures the consistency of the calculated results. An experimental problem is that the liquids used to prepare samples for vapor-pressure determinations in a static system must be thoroughly degassed, i.e., purged of all dissolved gases. Otherwise the measured vapor pressures will be too high.

Yet another method which relies partially on thermodynamic analysis combines vapor–liquid equilibrium measurements at one condition of temperature or pressure with heat-of-mixing data for the liquid phase. This method was indicated in Section 6.6. If vapor–liquid equilibrium data are already available at one condition, say 760 mm Hg as determined by an equilibrium still, then extension to other conditions may perhaps be most easily made by measuring heats of mixing.† The analytical methods suggested in Section 6.6 are usually entirely appropriate; however, the necessary calculations can also be made graphically or numerically by the proper application of the basic equations.

† For a simple and accurate method applicable to endothermic systems see: R. V. Mrazek, and H. C. van Ness, *A.I.Ch.E. Journal*, **7**, 190 (1961).

CHAPTER 7

# EPILOGUE

THE primary purpose of this monograph has been to introduce the various functions found useful in the treatment of thermodynamic data for solutions and to develop the mathematical equations interrelating these functions and connecting them with experimentally measurable quantities. The general nature of these equations suggests their application to a wide variety of phenomena observed for fluid systems. However, a detailed treatment of their application has been given only for vapor–liquid equilibria at low pressures. The object has been to provide the *basis* for detailed treatment of particular applications, and the material on vapor–liquid equilibria at low pressures serves merely as an example. The reason for employing this particular example is that it has been rather completely worked out. This is in distinct contrast to many other possible applications, about which relatively much less is known. It will also be noted that although the general equations we have developed are applicable to multicomponent systems, our illustrations of their use have been restricted to binary systems. The expectation is, of course, that once one is able to treat binary systems with facility, the extension to multicomponent systems will come quite naturally.

In closing this monograph it seems reasonable to discuss briefly certain aspects of solution behavior for which the methods of thermodynamic analysis are by no means fully developed. Classical thermodynamics is not a closed book. One is not even certain that the most suitable functions for the treatment of all applications have been discovered or invented. For those whose knowledge of the subject includes an appreciation of its deficiencies, classical thermodynamics retains the fascination of a growing science. Further, its combination with the considerations of molecular physics and statistical mechanics offers real opportunity for progress in the understanding of the properties of materials. Such understanding is, of course, requisite to the formulation of methods for the prediction of physical properties.

**7.1. Partially Miscible Binary Liquids.** It was mentioned in the preceding chapter that systems which exhibit large positive deviations from Raoult's law tend toward separation into two liquid phases, whereas those exhibiting negative deviations do not show miscibility gaps. Thus systems which separate into two liquid phases are made up of constituents for which the activity coefficients are appreciably greater than unity. Thus by Eq. (4-16), $\Delta G^E$ is positive for such systems. This is not a thermodynamic requirement, but experience shows it generally to be true.

Any mixing process carried out at constant temperature and pressure is obviously irreversible. It was shown in Section 6.1 that any system of constant mass not initially at equilibrium and constrained to changes at constant $T$ and $P$ will always adjust itself toward a state representing a minimum value of the Gibbs function. Hence if pure constituent 1 is mixed with pure constituent 2 at constant $T$ and $P$, the Gibbs function for the solution formed must be less than the sum of the Gibbs functions of the pure constituents. Thus

$$G < x_1 G_1 + x_2 G_2,$$
$$G - x_1 G_1 - x_2 G_2 < 0$$

or

$$\Delta G < 0.$$

Hence for mixing processes at constant $T$ and $P$, $\Delta G$ must always be negative whether the system is completely miscible or not. For systems that form two liquid phases an additional consideration is involved. If by forming two phases the system can achieve a lower value of the Gibbs function than would be the case were a single phase to form, then the system will split into two phases, for this represents the minimum Gibbs function value of which the system is capable, and hence is the equilibrium state. Since $\Delta G$ must be negative in any event, it is clear that $\Delta G$ for the case of formation of two phases must be *more* negative than would be the case were a single phase formed upon mixing.

Two examples of this behavior are shown by the lowest curves ($\Delta G/RT$ vs. $x_1$) of Fig. 7-1. The solid curves plus the center portions shown dotted represent $\Delta G/RT$ for the binary system based on the assumption of complete miscibility. It will be shown presently for a system which separates into two phases that $\Delta G/RT$ for the composition range of incomplete miscibility is given by a straight line connecting the points representing the solutions which form the two separate phases. Such a line must lie below the curve which would result for complete miscibility.

In addition we have the requirement of phase equilibrium between the two coexisting liquid phases. At a given temperature and pressure for a binary system, these two phases are of fixed composition, and variations in the total composition of the two-phase system come about as a result of changes in the relative amounts of the two phases. So throughout the region of partial miscibility the same two phases are in equilibrium. This equilibrium requires that

$$\hat{f}_1' = \hat{f}_1''$$

and

$$\hat{f}_2' = \hat{f}_2'',$$

where (') indicates the first phase and ('') designates the second. We may also write, since $f_1$ and $f_2$ represent the fugacities of the pure components as liquids at the $T$ and $P$ of the solution,

$$\hat{f}_1'/f_1 = \hat{f}_1''/f_1 \quad \text{and} \quad \hat{f}_2'/f_2 = \hat{f}_2''/f_2.$$

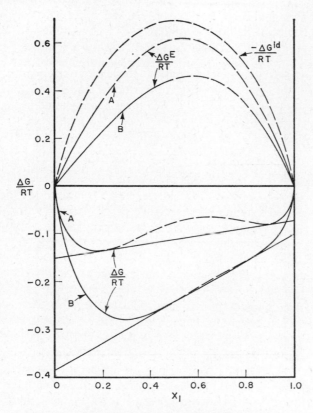

Fig. 7-1. Gibbs function curves for liquid systems, illustrating separation into two phases. Constant $T$ and $P$.

These quantities are activities; hence

$$\hat{a}_1' = \hat{a}_1'' \quad \text{and} \quad \hat{a}_2' = \hat{a}_2''.$$

It is obviously also true that

$$\ln \hat{a}_1' = \ln \hat{a}_1''$$

and

$$\ln \hat{a}_2' = \ln \hat{a}_2''.$$

From Table 4-1 we see that

$$\overline{\Delta G_i}/RT = \ln \hat{a}_i.$$

Thus $\ln\hat{a}_i$ is related to $\Delta G/RT$ as a partial molal property. Therefore the intercepts of tangents drawn to a plot of $\Delta G/RT$ vs. $x_1$ for a binary system give $\ln\hat{a}_1$ and $\ln\hat{a}_2$. For the two-phase region the activities must be identical in the separate phases, so we need not refer separately to $\hat{a}'_1$ and $\hat{a}''_1$, etc. Specifically

$$\ln\hat{a}'_1 = \ln\hat{a}''_1 = \ln\hat{a}_1 = \overline{\Delta G_1}/RT$$

and

$$\ln\hat{a}'_2 = \ln\hat{a}''_2 = \ln\hat{a}_2 = \overline{\Delta G_2}/RT.$$

Moreover, the activities remain constant throughout the region of partial miscibility, for the same phases exist at constant $T$ and $P$. It follows that the tangent intercepts of a plot of $\Delta G/RT$ must be constant throughout this

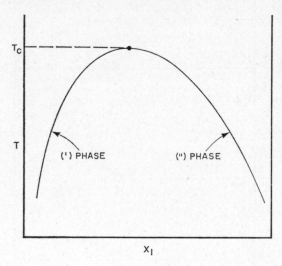

FIG. 7-2. Solubility curve, illustrating the upper critical solution temperature.

region. Clearly, a straight-line relation between $\Delta G/RT$ and $x_1$ in this region satisfies the requirement. Furthermore, as illustrated in Fig. 7-1, this straight line must be tangent to the curves at either end of the diagram that represent the regions of miscibility. The reason is, of course, that the limiting compositions for the miscible regions are also the compositions of the phases that coexist in the region of partial miscibility, and therefore the tangent drawn at the limiting compositions of the miscible regions must have the same intercepts as the straight line representing the region of partial miscibility.

All this may be summarized as follows. If the $\Delta G/RT$ vs. $x_1$ curve for a binary liquid that would result upon the assumption of complete solubility is such that an external straight line can be drawn so as to be tangent to the curve at two points, then the two points of tangency represent the limits of complete miscibility and the straight line connecting the two points represents the $\Delta G/RT$ vs. $x_1$ relation in this region of partial miscibility.

The compositions at which a binary system becomes incompletely miscible depend on the temperature. Pressure is also a variable, but not an important one so long as the liquid–vapor critical region is not approached. Thus one often finds reference to solubility curves, i.e., plots of temperature vs. the compositions representing the limits of complete solubility, without any specification as to pressure. Such a curve is illustrated in Fig. 7-2, and normally represents data at about atmospheric pressure or at the vapor pressures of the solutions considered.

A temperature is often found above which the system is completely miscible at all compositions. Such a temperature is known as an upper critical solution temperature or an upper consolute temperature. Solutions also exist which exhibit lower critical solution temperatures, and examples are known where both upper and lower critical solution temperatures are found. The conditions for the existence of upper and lower critical solution temperatures are discussed by Rowlinson.†

The mathematical conditions for establishing the solubility curve are obvious from the geometry of Fig. 7-1. The two compositions representing the limits of complete miscibility are designated by $x_1'$ and $x_1''$. Clearly

$$\frac{\mathrm{d}(\Delta G/RT)}{\mathrm{d}x_1}\bigg|_{x_1'} = \frac{\mathrm{d}(\Delta G/RT)}{\mathrm{d}x_1}\bigg|_{x_1''} \tag{7-1}$$

and

$$\frac{\Delta G}{RT}\bigg|_{x_1'} - \frac{\Delta G}{RT}\bigg|_{x_1''} = \frac{\mathrm{d}(\Delta G/RT)}{\mathrm{d}x_1}(x_1' - x_1''). \tag{7-2}$$

These equations fail at the critical solution temperature, and an additional condition must be employed. The dotted curves on the $\Delta G/RT$ vs. $x_1$ plots of Fig. 7-1 represent unstable conditions of a single-phase system. Such curves clearly must contain two points of inflection. As the miscibility gap narrows and the critical solution temperature is approached, these two points approach each other and finally merge at the critical solution temperature. At such a point of merger of inflection points, both the second and third derivatives are zero. Thus at the critical solution point

$$\frac{\mathrm{d}^2(\Delta G/RT_c)}{\mathrm{d}x_1^2} = \frac{\mathrm{d}^3(\Delta G/RT_c)}{\mathrm{d}x_1^3} = 0, \tag{7-3}$$

$\Delta G/RT$ is, of course, given by

$$\frac{\Delta G}{RT} = \frac{\Delta G^{\mathrm{id}}}{RT} + \frac{\Delta G^{E}}{RT}.$$

† J. S. Rowlinson, *Liquids and Liquid Mixtures*, Butterworths, 1959.

11*

Thus by Eq. (4-6) for a binary system

$$\frac{\Delta G}{RT} = x_1 \ln x_1 + x_2 \ln x_2 + \frac{\Delta G^E}{RT}.$$

If we now assume that $\Delta G^E$ can be represented by a particular form of equation, then solubility data may be used for the evaluation of constants in the equation. Thus if

$$\Delta G^E = x_1 x_2 [B + C(2x_1 - 1)],$$

then

$$\frac{\Delta G}{RT} = x_1 \ln x_1 + x_2 \ln x_2 + x_1 x_2 \left[ \frac{B}{RT} + \frac{C}{RT}(2x_1 - 1) \right]. \quad (7\text{-}4)$$

Equations (7-1), (7-2), and (7-4) may be combined to eliminate $\Delta G/RT$. The final result, after considerable algebraic reduction, is a pair of equations giving $B$ and $C$ for a particular temperature as functions of $x_1'$ and $x_1''$ for that temperature:

$$\ln \frac{x_1'(1 - x_1'')}{(1 - x_1')x_1''} = \left\{ -\frac{2B}{RT} + \frac{6C}{RT}[1 - (x_1'' + x_1')] \right\} (x_1'' - x_1'), \quad (7\text{-}5)$$

$$\ln \frac{1 - x_1'}{1 - x_1''} = \left\{ \frac{B}{RT}(x_1'' + x_1') + \frac{C}{RT}[(x_1'' - x_1')^2 + 3(x_1'' + x_1')^2 \right.$$

$$\left. -3(x_1'' + x_1')] \right\} (x_1'' - x_1'). \quad (7\text{-}6)$$

These equations may be solved simultaneously for $B/RT$ and $C/RT$ once values of $x_1'$ and $x_1''$ have been determined from experimental data. The values of the constants so determined may then be used in Eq. (7-4) to construct the complete $\Delta G/RT$ vs. $x_1$ curve for the temperature in question. Examples are given in Fig. 7-1.

For the curves labeled A, it was first assumed that a particular solution exhibited a miscibility gap between $x_1' = 0.2$ and $x_1'' = 0.9$. The constants $B/RT$ and $C/RT$ were then found by Eqs. (7-5) and (7-6). Finally, values of $\Delta G/RT$ were calculated by Eq. (7-4). Similarly for the curves labeled B, a miscibility gap was assumed between $x_1' = 0.5$ and $x_1'' = 0.8$. Figure 7-1 shows in addition to $\Delta G/RT$, its components, $\Delta G^E/RT$ and the negative of $\Delta G^{id}/RT$. It is instructive to note that while $\Delta G^{id}/RT$ vs. $x_1$ is completely symmetrical and $\Delta G^E/RT$ vs. $x_1$ is of simple form, the sum

$$\frac{\Delta G}{RT} = \frac{\Delta G^{id}}{RT} + \frac{\Delta G^E}{RT}$$

gives complex curves. Thus a complicated relation between $\Delta G^E/RT$ and composition is not a requirement for solutions which exhibit miscibility gaps.

Once the $\Delta G^E/RT$ curve has been established, the activity coefficients for the liquid phases can be calculated, and the vapor–liquid equilibrium relationship can be established, at least approximately. The accuracy of calculations such as these is dependent upon the validity of the assumption that $\Delta G^E$ can be represented as a function of composition by an equation of the form employed. This severely limits the utility of the method just illustrated. However, it does indicate how in principle one may make use of solubility data in the calculation of thermodynamic properties for solutions. More accurate methods, both analytical and numerical, have been devised by Klaus† for determining activity coefficients from solubility data. These require, in addition, heat-of-mixing data so that the effect of temperature may be taken into account.

If one has data for the critical solution point, he must use the relations of Eq. (7-3). As an illustration we again assume

$$\Delta G^E = x_1 x_2 [B + C(2x_1 - 1)].$$

Then combination of Eq. (7-4) with Eq. (7-3) gives

$$\frac{B}{RT_c} = \frac{1}{2x_1 x_2}\left[1 - \frac{(x_1 - x_2)^2}{2x_1 x_2}\right] \tag{7-7}$$

and

$$\frac{C}{RT_c} = \frac{(x_1 - x_2)}{12(x_1 x_2)^2}. \tag{7-8}$$

These equations allow $B/RT_c$ and $C/RT_c$ to be determined for the critical solution temperature isotherm. Thus if the critical solution point is found to exist at $x_1 = x_2 = 0.5$, then $C/RT_c = 0$ and $B/RT_c = 2$. Conversely, if $C$ (and therefore $C/RT_c$) is known to be zero, then the consolute point must occur at $x_1 = x_2 = 0.5$. Attention has been called several times in earlier chapters to a special kind of solution called *regular*. For such a solution $C$ is zero and $B$ is independent of temperature. Thus for such a solution $B = 2RT_c$ at all temperatures, and Eq. (7-6) reduces to

$$\ln\frac{1 - x_1'}{1 - x_1''} = \frac{2T_c}{T}(x_1'' + x_1')(x_1'' - x_1').$$

If in this equation one exchanges $x_1'$ for $x_1''$ and vice versa, the equation is unaltered. Since $x_1'$ is a function of $x_1''$ (as shown by the solubility curve) the necessary and sufficient condition for this to be true is that

$$x_1'' = 1 - x_1' \quad \text{and} \quad x_1' = 1 - x_1''$$

or that

$$x_1'' + x_1' = 1.$$

† R. L. Klaus, Ph.D. Thesis, Rensselaer Polytechnic Institute, 1963.

Thus the solubility curve represented by the above equation is symmetrical about $x_1 = 0.5$, and the entire curve can be represented by the equation

$$\ln \frac{1 - x_1}{x_1} = \frac{2T_c}{T} (1 - 2x_1)$$

or

$$T = \frac{2T_c(2x_1 - 1)}{\ln \left( \dfrac{x_1}{1 - x_1} \right)} .$$

This is a well-known result, and is in fact the only case for which an explicit equation has been predicted for the solubility curve.

### 7.2. High-Pressure Phase Equilibria.

This is a large and complex subject about which considerable empirical information is available. Thermodynamic analysis, however, is usually conspicuous by its absence. High-pressure equlilibria considerations are often complicated by azeotropy and especially by critical phenomena. The behavior of binary systems which are completely miscible in the liquid–vapor critical region is relatively familiar, though perhaps surprisingly different from that of single-component systems. Binary systems that exhibit miscibility gaps in the liquid–vapor critical region show the most extraordinary behavior. It is rarely described and is therefore totally unfamiliar to all but a handful of research workers in the field. Detailed qualitative consideration is given by Rowlinson† to the complete range of observed phase-equilibrium behavior.

The general problem of vapor–liquid equilibrium was discussed in Section 6.2. The rigorous method of solution presented there through the use of fugacity coefficients is entirely appropriate in principle to high-pressure equilibria. However, the method is impractical except for special cases, and will remain so until a satisfactory equation of state is developed for liquid solutions. Thus in Section 6.3, where the less complex problem of vapor–liquid equilibria at low pressures was treated in detail, the activity coefficient rather than the fugacity coefficient was used in the treatment of both phases. The advantage of the activity coefficient is that it relates the fugacity of a constituent in solution to the fugacity of the same constituent in another state (the standard state) for which fugacity values may be more readily determined. The use of activity coefficients is certainly not inherently limited to low pressures. The particular procedures employed in Section 6.3 were, however, based on the assumption of low pressures. Thus it was possible to neglect the direct effect of pressure on liquid properties and to employ the truncated virial equation for the vapor phase. Relaxation of the restriction to low pressures is not so easy. In the first place the simplest form of the virial equation will no longer suffice to

† J. S. Rowlinson, op. cit.

describe the properties of the vapor phase. Even the use of the virial expansion in densities truncated to the third term may not be adequate. Even if it is, third virial coefficients for solutions are rarely known, and methods of estimation are at best crude. One must also have data on the volumetric properties of liquids in order to take into account correctly the effect of pressure on liquid-phase properties. Thus volumetric data, either directly measured or as given by an adequate equation of state, must be available for both the vapor and liquid phases in addition to phase-equilibrium data themselves if one is to reduce the equilibrium data to thermodynamic variables.

An even more serious problem arises with the activity coefficients themselves. By definition, $\gamma_i = \hat{f}_i / x_i f_i^0$. It is by no means clear how the standard state represented by $f_i^0$ should be chosen. In Chapter 6 we took the standard state for constituent $i$ to be pure $i$ at the temperature and pressure of the solution and in the same physical state. For both the liquid phase and the vapor phase this will normally require the standard state for one or the other of the constituents to be fictitious or hypothetical. The more volatile constituent will exist only as a vapor at the solution temperature and pressure, and the less volatile, only as a liquid. For azeotropic systems both constituents may exist only as vapors or only as liquids. In any event fictitious states must be employed, and properties in such states can be obtained only by extrapolation. At low pressures, the extrapolation is short. Moreover, by use of the simplest expression of the virial equation the extrapolation is automatic and always done in a consistent fashion. At high pressures it is rarely possible to fulfill these conditions, and the standard state becomes ill-defined. Even more serious is the situation that arises when the solution temperature is above the critical temperature of one of the constituents. One then must hypothesize a liquid state for that constituent in a region where the pure liquid cannot exist no matter what the pressure.

For the vapor phase the problem of standard states can be avoided by use of fugacity coefficients rather than activity coefficients. Thus

$$\hat{f}_i^V = \hat{\varphi}_i^V y_i P.$$

For the liquid phase we will leave the question of standard states unsettled for the moment, and write

$$\hat{f}_i^L = \gamma_i^L x_i f_i^0.$$

Since $\hat{f}_i^V = \hat{f}_i^L$ for phase equilibrium, the above equations combine to give:

$$\gamma_i = \frac{\hat{\varphi}_i y_i P}{x_i f_i^0}, \tag{7-9}$$

where the superscripts $L$ and $V$ have been dropped. We need merely remember that activity coefficients and standard states are being used for the liquid phase and that fugacity coefficients are used only for the vapor phase.

Considerable attention has been given in earlier chapters to the calculation of $\hat{\varphi}_i$ values. If we assume $\hat{\varphi}_i$ calculable, then all that is needed in Eq. (7-9) in addition to an experimentally determined $y_i$-$x_i$-$P$ state at a given temperature is a value of $f_i^0$. As has been pointed out before, the choice of a standard state for a constituent is arbitrary within the restrictions that it must always be at the solution temperature and that it must be a state of fixed composition.

The standard state most commonly used by engineers has been that of the pure liquid at the solution $T$ and $P$. For this choice

$$\lim_{x_i \to 1} \gamma_i = 1.$$

This limiting value results because the state of constituent $i$ in solution becomes the standard state as $x_i$ approaches unity. This choice of standard state has a number of important advantages. The most obvious is that activity coefficients so based relate a solution property to a pure-component property. Thus only data for pure materials are needed to evaluate the standard-state properties. Since one would like to relate solution properties in so far as possible to those of the pure components, this choice of standard state is a natural one. Furthermore, this standard state is the same for a given material regardless of the constitution of the solution of which it forms a part. Finally, the general thermodynamic equations relating activity coefficients to other properties find their simplest expression and their most direct relation to experimentally observable quantities when this particular standard state is employed. Compare, for example, Eq. (4-20) with Eq. (4-21).

When this standard state is physically attainable, the desirability of its use seems clear. However, where this state is necessarily fictitious or hypothetical, practical difficulties intercede, as already mentioned, and may largely or completely balance the theoretical advantages of its use. Thus use of hypo-thetical standard states in high-pressure solution equilibria can be made completely acceptable only through the development of a universally applicable method that will give completely consistent results for the extra-polation of pure liquid properties. One effort in this direction has been described by Prausnitz.†

An alternative standard state for liquids can be defined by making reference to solution behavior as infinite dilution is approached by the constituent being considered. At high dilution Henry's law (in terms of fugacity) is applicable:

$$\hat{f}_i = k_i x_i,$$

† J. M. Prausnitz, *A.I.Ch.E. Journal*, **6**, 78 (1960).

where $k_i$ is a constant given by

$$k_i = \lim_{x_i \to 0} (\hat{f}_i / x_i).$$

We may arbitrarily set

$$f_i^0 = k_i = \lim_{x_i \to 0} (\hat{f}_i / x_i).$$

Physically, $f_i^0$ is the fugacity constituent $i$ would have at $x_i = 1$ if Henry's law were actually valid over the entire concentration range. Clearly, this standard state is not a real one, but it is explicitly defined. It is clear from the definition of $\gamma_i$ that for this standard state

$$\lim_{x_i \to 0} \gamma_i = 1.$$

The pressure must also be specified for this standard state, and there are a number of possible choices. An extensive discussion of this standard state in high-pressure equilibria calculations has been given by Prausnitz.[†] Use of this standard state presents its own complications and disadvantages. Not the least of these is the fact that the standard state value for a given constituent depends on solution properties, and data for the solution must be available in the region of high dilution. For applications to ternary and higher order systems the manner in which infinite dilution is approached is arbitrary and must be specified.

Yet another possible standard state is that of the pure constituent at the solution $T$ and $P$ but always in its *real* physical state. This choice does not seem to have been given serious consideration. Yet it appears to retain all of the advantages attendant to the use of pure constituents as standard states without introducing the complications which inevitably arise through the use of non-attainable physical states, whether unambiguously defined or not. It may seem odd to consider using a gas as the standard state to which to refer the properties of a component of a liquid solution. However, the most difficult problems arise with hypothetical standard states in the region where critical phenomena are encountered. In this region the dissimilarities between phases is not marked, and the use of real states does not appear particularly incongruous. Were this standard state adopted, Eq. (7-9) would become:

$$\gamma_i^L = \frac{\hat{\varphi}_i^V y_i P}{x_i f_i^{\text{real}}} = \left( \frac{\hat{\varphi}_i^V}{\varphi_i^{\text{real}}} \right) \left( \frac{y_i}{x_i} \right).$$

Clearly, if $\hat{\varphi}_i^V$ can be evaluated, so can $\varphi_i^{\text{real}}$ by exactly the same methods. Note that

$$\lim_{x_i \to 1} \gamma_i^L = 1.$$

[†] J. M. Prausnitz, *Chem. Eng. Sci.*, in press.

The possibility of employing this convention was pointed out earlier in connection with Eq. (4-21).

These considerations of phase equilibria are not limited to vapor–liquid equilibria. They apply as well to the solubility of gases in liquids and of liquids in gases. Again Prausnitz† has provided interesting discussions of these topics.

One may well inquire why an effort should be made to reduce phase-equilibrium data to thermodynamic variables. The reason is that only in such terms are the data subject to meaningful correlation, to extension and generalization, to interpretation, and to tests for consistency. These variables provide the link between the observable properties of materials and the molecular interactions which are responsible for them. Any real understanding of macroscopic behavior must ultimately be based on the principles of molecular physics, and only the thermodynamic variables are interpretable on this scale.

† In addition to the papers already cited, see: J. M. Prausnitz, *A.I.Ch.E. Journal,* **5,** 161 (1959); J. M. Prausnitz, *A.I.Ch.E. Journal,* **4,** 269 (1958).

# INDEX

Activity, 32
  in partially miscible systems, 153, 154
Activity coefficient, 31
  and activity, 32
  analytical representation, 124–131
    Margules equations, 127–130
    Porter equations, 126–130
    van Laar equations, 128–130
  and fugacity coefficient, 33, 75
  and the Gibbs–Duhem equation, 78–80
  and the Gibbs function, 75, 124–126
  logarithm of, as partial property, 75, 102–105
  from solubility data, 157
  and the standard state, 31, 32, 78, 79, 160–162
  temperature influence on, 134–136
  from vapor–liquid equilibrium, 120–122
    limiting values, 146, 147
  from the virial equation, 92, 96, 97
Azeotropes, 112, 123, 145, 146, 158

Benedict, M., 59, 120
Bird, R. B., 47
Black, Cline, 124, 140, 142
Boiling point change in dilute solutions, 148

Chemical equilibrium, 112–118
Chemical potential, 34, 38, 39, 93
  total differential of, 35
Clapeyron equation, 43
Coexistence equation, 137–139
Compressibility factor, 26, 27
  generalized correlation of, 62, 66
  properties calculated from, 81, 82
Corresponding states, principle of, 63–68
Criteria of equilibrium, 111–118
Critical phenomena, 158
Critical solution temperature, 155, 157
Curtiss, C. F., 47

Defay, R., 111, 124
Donald, M. B., 110
Duhem's theorem, 111–113, 116

Energy, concept of, 4
  conservation of (*see* First law of thermodynamics) internal, 4–8, 25
  as criterion of equilibrium, 114
Enthalpy, 11, 25
  change on mixing (*see* Property changes of mixing)
Enthalpy deviation, 36
  calculation of, 41, 58, 59
  generalized correlation of, 64
Entropy, 7–9, 26
  change on mixing (*see* Property changes of mixing)
Entropy deviation, 41
  calculation of, 41, 59
Equation of state, 18, 45–61
  Benedict–Webb–Rubin, 59
  ideal gas, 18
  Redlich and Kwong, 60
  virial, 45–59
    activity coefficients calculated from, 92, 96, 97
    fugacities calculated from, 93, 94
    fugacity coefficients calculated from, 54–57, 91, 92, 94, 95
    property changes of mixing calculated from, 83, 84
  virial, in pressure, 51
Equilibrium, criteria of, 111–118
  internal and external, 6
  and reversibility, 6, 113, 114
  (*See also* Chemical equilibrium; Phase equilibrium; Vapor–liquid equilibrium; Liquid–liquid equilibrium)
Evans, R. B., III, 48
Exact differential, 13
Excess Gibbs function of mixing, 75
  for partially miscible systems, 155–157
  total differential of, 79, 80
  and vapor–liquid equilibrium, 124–131
  from the virial equation, 83
Excess properties (*see* Property changes of mixing)

163